# Vibrant Watercolor Birds

24 Effortless Projects of Showstopping Avian Species

Madhu S
Creator of Femvisionary

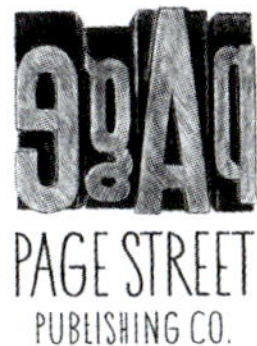

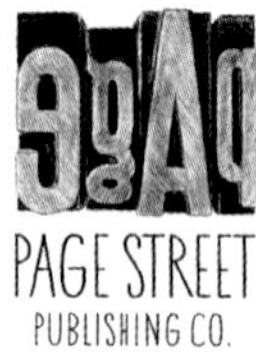



First published in 2022 by
Page Street Publishing Co.
27 Congress Street, Suite 1511
Salem, MA 01970
www.pagestreetpublishing.com



Distributed by Macmillan, sales in Canada by The Canadian Manda Group.

26 25 24 23 22 1 2 3 4 5

ISBN-13: 978-1-64567-653-9
ISBN-10: 1-64567-653-6

Library of Congress Control Number: 2022935160

Cover and book design by Julia Tyler for Page Street Publishing Co.
Photography by Madhu S

Printed and bound in the United States

Page Street Publishing protects our planet by donating to nonprofits like The Trustees, which focuses on local land conservation.

To the inner child in all of us—
remember to play with creativity, dance
with colors and live with passion.

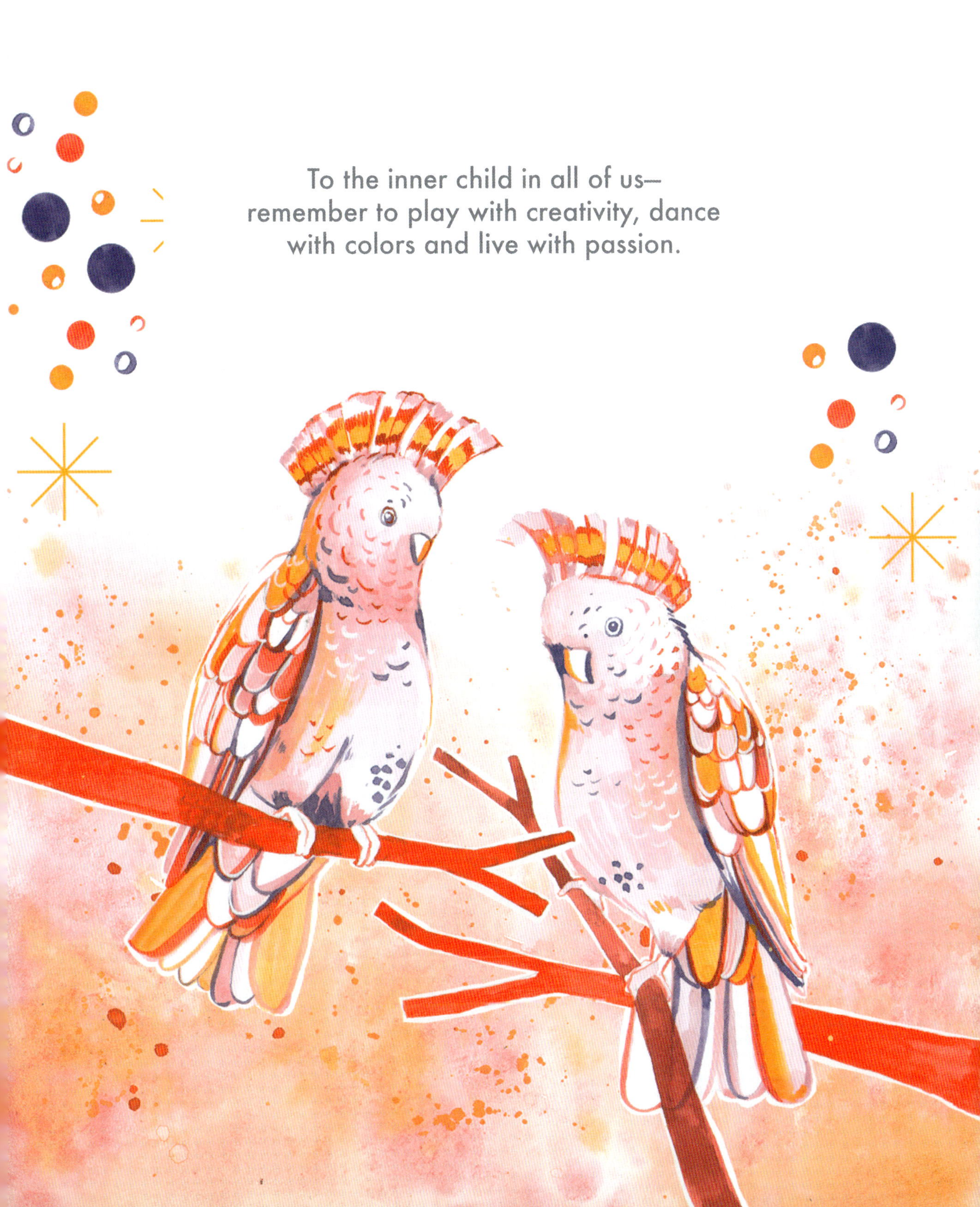

# Contents

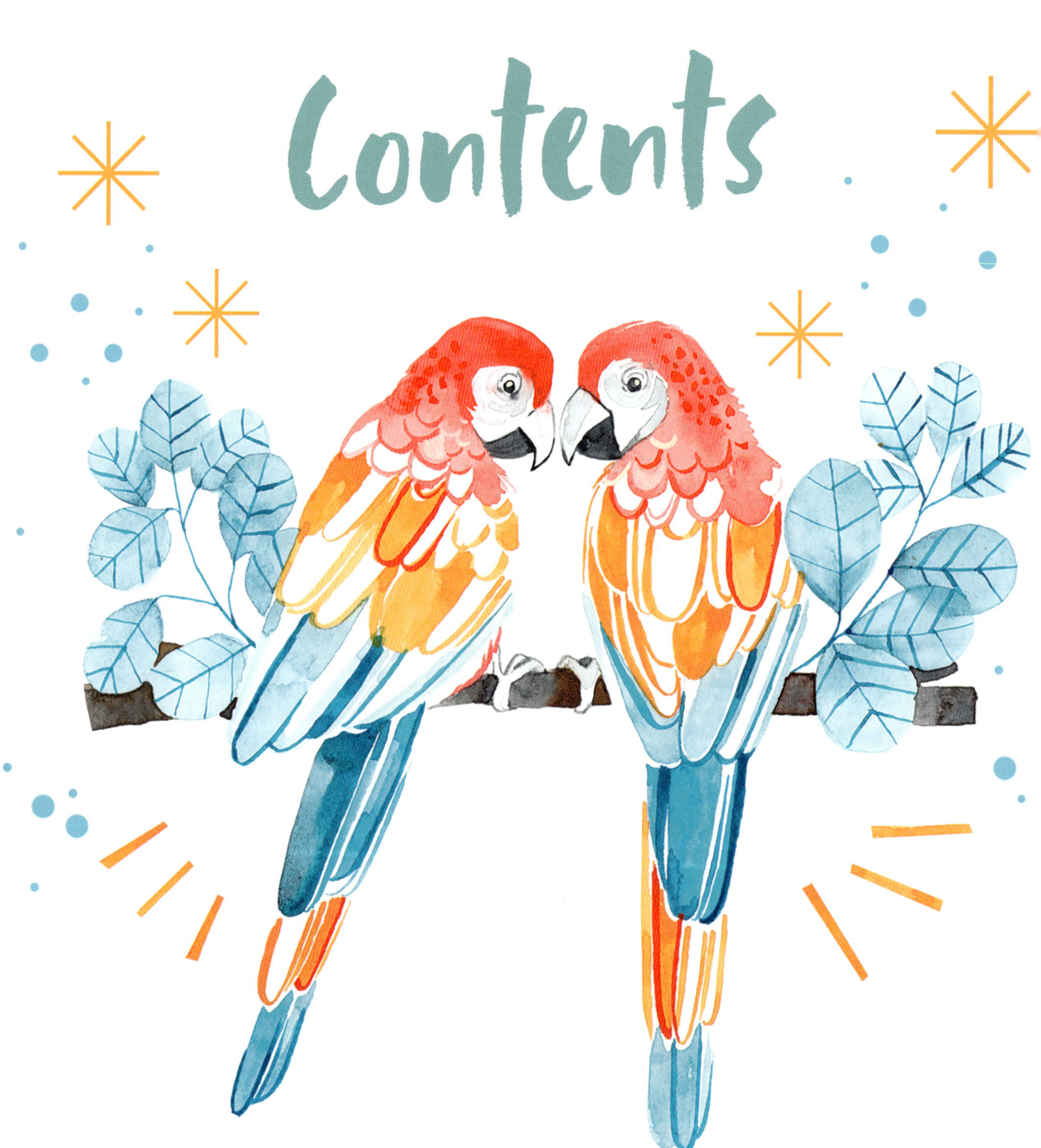

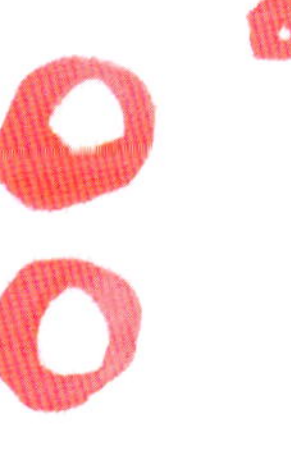

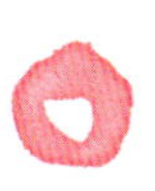

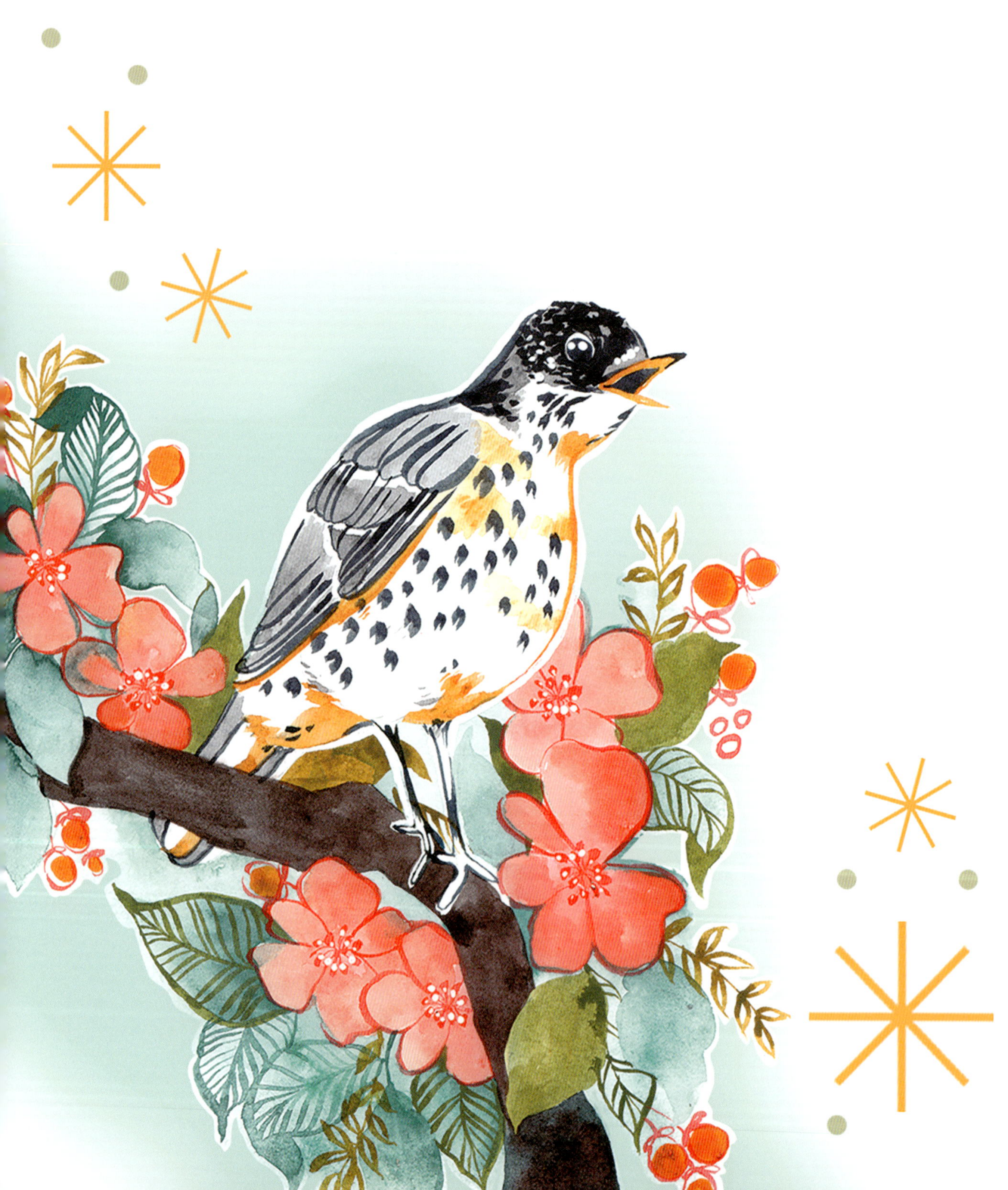

# Introduction

This is the perfect book to get started on your journey into watercolors! Watercolors have a very special place in my heart. Years ago, I first started playing around with them; I still remember the moment when I painted a simple leaf with watercolors like it was yesterday—the way the water moved on the paper and the lovely effect it created. I knew I was in love with the medium. Since then, even though I have used other mediums, I always go back to watercolors.

I have been painting for over ten years now and have passionately taught around 8,000 art students worldwide. Through my teaching journey, I have realized what is important to any beginner. I truly believe that ninety percent of the subject is motivation. When you choose a subject you are excited about, it makes the process of painting so much more fun. Hence, I chose the topic of birds. Think sparrows, flamingoes, parrots, hummingbirds, eagles and so much more. Excited already?

Well, there are many lessons we are going to learn in this book, such as painting feathers, adding textures, balancing colors and choosing backgrounds to appropriately suit the final composition. Additionally, I will be sharing my tips and tricks so that you get the best possible results.

I know you are going to love this book. Let's dive into the world of watercolor birds!

# How to Use This Book

Before you get started, I suggest going over the introductory chapters at the beginning of this book. This information will be very useful for you as we move on to our tutorials. I especially recommend spending more time on the chapter background elements. These basic exercises are very important and will be used in the upcoming chapters to paint compositions.

There are four main categories of birds in this book: garden birds, tropical birds, aquatic birds and mountain birds. In each category, we will be painting six different birds. You can start with any category that excites you.

The projects move from beginner level to intermediate level in every category of birds. This is indicated by a feather symbol from one to three—one feather indicates a beginner level with fewer steps, while three feathers represent an intermediate level with more steps. Keep in mind that intermediate doesn't automatically mean difficult—it just means that the painting involves more steps and can take longer. There are also Pro-Tips peppered throughout this book, with helpful suggestions on everything from materials to painting techniques.

Every small step is progress. By using lovely bright colors, you can pretty much be guaranteed an amazing painting. Thus, another tip I would give you is to use the colors mentioned in the tutorial.

Watercolors are all about skill, so keep practicing each tutorial to become even more comfortable and proficient. Keep in mind that as you continue painting every new project, you will find that it becomes easier and easier. So, enjoy that process. Happy painting!

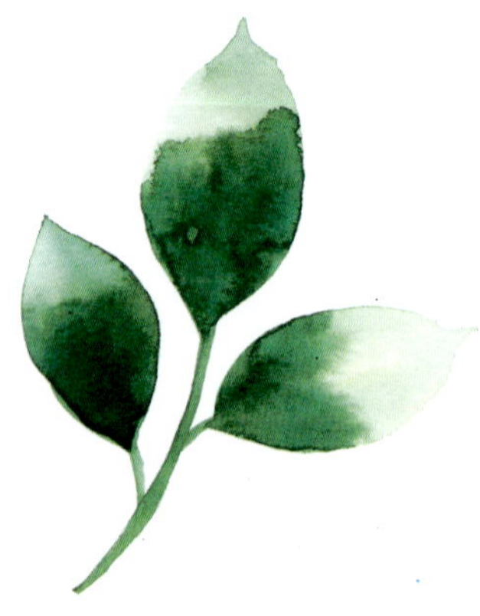

# Materials

Buying watercolor supplies can be very confusing. However, I believe in simplifying the process. I usually tell my students to invest in just five basic supplies: watercolor paper, a good quality watercolor paint set, a size 4 round brush, a size 000 mop brush, a size 0 script liner brush and white acrylic paint. Once you have the basic materials to practice watercolors, you can easily add other items of your choosing, such as custom paints, various brushes or any other tools that you enjoy using as you fall in love with the medium.

Now let's talk more about these supplies.

## Watercolor Paper

I still remember standing in front of a rack of watercolor loose sheets and pads ten years ago, wondering what to purchase. This used to be a very complex process, since after buying the sheet you would need to stretch it. The information available about this process was limited and confusing.

However, now there are many user-friendly prestretched watercolor papers and pads available. To further understand which papers to use, let us discuss the types of watercolor sheets.

The three types of paper available in the market are hot press, rough and cold press paper. I don't want to go into too much detail about each paper, so I am just going to focus on what you need to know to make your decision on what to buy.

**Hot press paper** is pressed down with hot steam during the manufacturing process and hence the paper is plain with no texture. This type of paper is great for detailed artwork.

Next, there is **rough paper** which is extremely grainy in texture. This paper is made by using cold steam during the manufacturing process. Due to the grainy tooth of the paper, it can hold a lot of water. Therefore, it is perfect for landscapes and large-scale paintings, but it cannot be used for detailed paintings.

Finally, we have **cold press paper**, which is what I recommend using for the projects in this book. This type of paper is made using gentle warm steam. Hence, it maintains a slightly grainy texture. Since it is not too grainy, it is great for detailed paintings. Because it also has a slight texture, it can hold more paint than hot press paper. Since this paper can be used for a large variety of paintings, it is perfect for the projects within this book.

Now the weight of the paper directly reflects how much water can be used on the paper before it buckles or rips. To give you a little bit of context, let me compare the weight of some other papers that are available in the market. Normal inkjet paper that we use for everyday office printing is only 60gsm (28lb), and if you ever spilled water on it, you would immediately see the paper tear or bend. There are also 100gsm (47lb) papers, which can be seen mainly in high quality notebooks. However, if you try to paint with watercolors on your notebook paper, you will notice it bend or buckle. Thus, for watercolors we need a heavier paper: I generally suggest using paper above 200gsm (95lb).

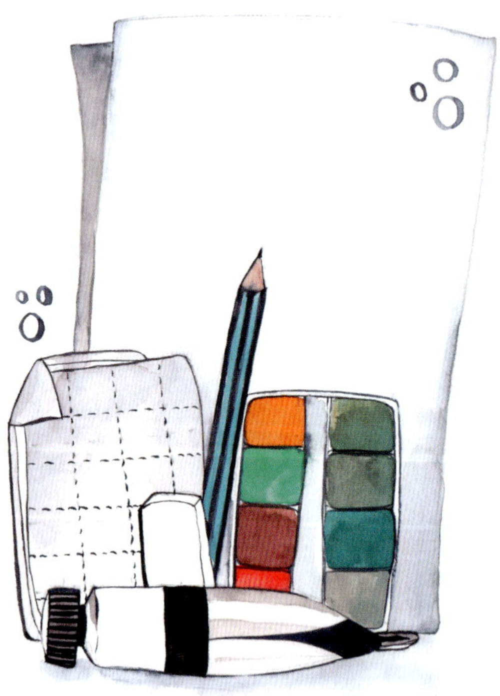

Among brands already available in the market, I suggest some of the more price-friendly brands so that you can practice your skills. I generally use Fabriano or Canson cold press 250gsm (117lb) loose papers.

## Watercolor Paints

Choosing paints is a very important part of the process. Investing in good-quality paints can drastically improve your art. Let's talk about the different factors involved in choosing the right paints/pigments.

### Grades

There are different grades of paints available. If you turn over a paint tube, you can see the letters A, B or C. The letters indicate the quality of the pigments. A-grade pigment is of the highest quality and is an artist-grade paint. Meanwhile, B-grade pigments are student-grade paints, and C-grade pigments are the lowest grade paints.

I suggest starting with a mid-level quality in the range of B, since you will be able to get the best use out of your paints at a reasonable price point and capture the essence of watercolors.

### Pans or Tubes

Another question that pops up is what is more convenient to use—paint pans (trays in which paint can be filled) or paint tubes. I love using paint pans because I find it easier to pick up the paint. Generally, when you take your paint from a tube, there can be wastage. To make the best use of the paint, pans are more user-friendly.

Another benefit of using paint pans is that you can carry them easily from place to place and they are much easier to store. Generally as a rule, I keep my watercolor paint tubes and pans away from sunlight and water to avoid any damage. Always keep your paint pans in a box to avoid them drying out.

Another benefit of paint pans is that they can be arranged according to your preference. I like to keep all my reds together and all my blues together so that I can easily pick any pigment I want.

Finally, it can be hard to figure out what the actual pigment is in watercolors, since multiple colors may look the same but swatch differently. Thus, while using paint pans, I prepare a swatch card as you will see in the below image. A swatch card is simply a dab of the paint on paper that shows the exact color of the paint. You can label the swatch card or even add brand details to further organize your collection.

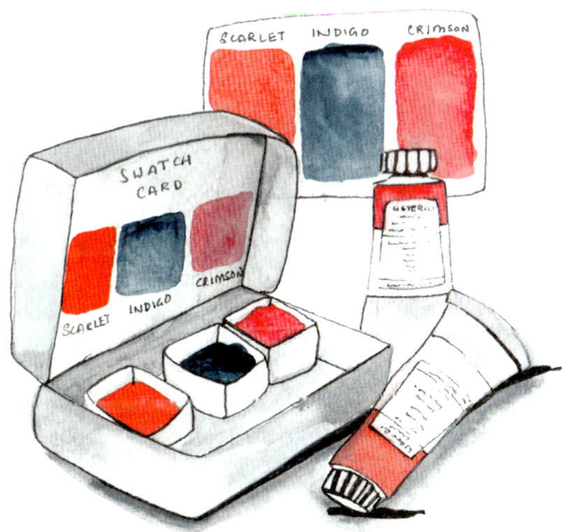


**Pro-Tip:** Since all brands may not have paint pans, I also tend to buy paint tubes and then transfer them to empty pans.

## Choosing Colors

There are many ways to choose which paint colors to buy. For this book, I have suggested some of my favorite pigments below. I use these colors often.

The main colors we will be using within the book are:

- Indigo Blue
- Ultramarine Blue
- Turquoise Blue
- Ultramarine Violet
- Scarlet Red
- Crimson Red
- Bright Orange
- Burnt Sienna
- Burnt Umber
- Chrome Yellow
- Ivory Black
- Hunter's Green
- Viridian Green
- White

It is okay if you are not able to find all the colors, because in the chapter All About Watercolor Paints on page 15, we will be talking more about mixing your own colors. That way, even if you do not have the exact color, you can create your own. Watercolor is all about playing with colors, so don't be afraid to mix and match.

If you would like to buy individual tubes, you can purchase brands such as Winsor & Newton Cotman series, White Nights (formerly known as St. Petersburg Watercolours) or Mijello Mission. An even easier way is to buy paint pan sets. Art Philosophy® is my favorite brand since they have themed sets.

> **Pro-Tip:** By simply purchasing the Watercolor Confections® Odyssey and Currents sets from Art Philosophy, you will have all the colors I mentioned previously.

## Watercolor Brushes

Brushes are the next important aspect of the painting. I can't tell you how many times bad or low-grade brushes have ruined my painting. Low-grade brushes can lose their shape and shed bristles, which can be frustrating. Therefore, getting a good quality brush is very important. In a moment, I'll talk about all the brushes we'll be using in this book.

There are a lot of great brands for watercolor brushes. I love using the Silver Brush 3000S Black Velvet® round brushes in sizes 4 or 6. I also like the Winsor & Newton Cotman series and the Art Essentials watercolor brushes.

### Common Shapes of Bristles

A size 4 round brush is a favorite among watercolor artists. It can hold a good amount of water and can be used for painting leaves, details and more shapes. Size 0 round brushes are very small, while size 12 is better for larger paintings since it is bigger in size.

A size 000 mop brush is great for larger areas. We will be using this brush for painting backgrounds. It is useful to have a mop brush in hand since it can be used to cover larger portions quickly. Even though the size of the brush is only 000, it is very big because of the shape of the bristles. Sizes 0 and 1 are even bigger and are better suited for larger painting areas.

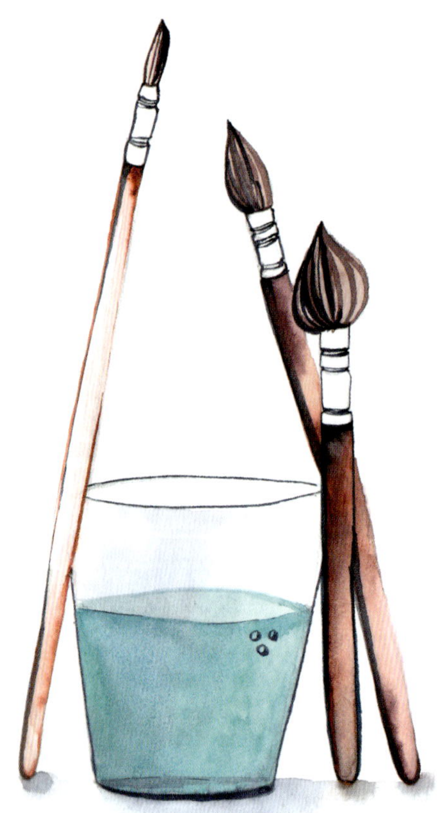

A size 000 script liner brush is my favorite for smaller details. I love using it for outlines, eye details and spot clusters. These come in different sizes, so you can also purchase size 1. However, as the size goes higher, the brush becomes longer and wider. This can become hard to control, so I prefer using a size 000 or size 1.

## White Acrylic Paint

We will be using lovely white acrylic paint in these projects. This is mainly for the eyes and also for some more textured details. Acrylic paint is water resistant and opaque, which is the opposite of watercolor paints. As you paint, you will notice that with watercolor, the layers stack on each other, starting from a lighter wash to a dark wash. When acrylic white paint is added to this dark wash, it gives an interesting overall look to the composition.

## Color Mixing Palette

Another tool we will be using is a color mixing palette. These are easily available in any stationery shop. Alternatively, you can use a glass or ceramic plate to mix your colors.

This is essential if you are using watercolor paint tubes, since you will need to squeeze very little paint onto the palette and then add water to use the paint. If you are using paint pans, you will receive a paint palette along with the kit (generally the top cover of the box).

Since watercolors are water soluble, you can easily wash the palette under running water or with a wet cloth.

## Pencil and Eraser

For these projects, we will need a standard pencil for the base drawing and an eraser to remove any harsh marks. You can also use a kneadable eraser to erase pencil marks. Compared to normal erasers that come as blocks and erase the pencil marks completely, kneadable erasers can be shaped. You can then use these erasers to erase small areas easily. They also tend to erase the pencil marks lightly, leaving a pencil mark impression on the paper. Thus, we are left with a light pencil drawing of the base over which we can easily paint with watercolors.

## Water Cups and Tissue Paper

When using watercolors, having a cup of water on hand is a must. You might have to keep two cups if you don't want to get up multiple times to refresh the water. However, I do enjoy getting up and walking to exercise my legs. You will also need tissue paper, paper towels or a cloth to dab the excess water from the brush.

> **Pro-Tip:** Always use a damp brush while painting. Dry brushes will not fully bring out the translucency of watercolors, while a dripping wet brush will make your paints very watered down. So, when you dip your brush in water, before using the paint, dab your brush on a dry tissue. That way, you ensure you are using a properly damp brush.

## Hair Dryer

Waiting for layers to dry before moving on to the next step can take a long time. To speed up the process of painting with watercolor, a bonus tip that I wish I had known a lot sooner is to keep a hair dryer handy. This way, you can dry your painting after every layer and continue.

While using a hair dryer, keep the setting on warm, at the lowest speed. That way, you do not move around the water on your paper too much. I generally start about 10 inches (25.4 cm) from the paper with quick zig-zag motions. As I see the painting dry further, I move closer to about 5 inches (12.7 cm) and continue the zig-zag motions around areas that are still wet. Finally I move even closer to about 3 inches (7.6 cm) and focus on the final smaller areas that are still wet.

Things to keep in mind while using a dryer:

- Tape down your paper, so that it doesn't fly around when you are trying to dry it.
- Avoid using extremely high heat until you are comfortable because you may end up moving the water on the paper too much, leaving fuzzy impressions.
- Craft dryers available in the market provide high heat that is very concentrated in one area. This could end up moving the water on the paper as well, and may lead to the paper bending. It's best to avoid using this tool until you are comfortable with a lower heat hair dryer.

# All About Watercolor Paints

One of the best aspects of watercolors is that you can mix your own colors. Don't have green? Well not to worry, because you can mix blue and yellow to get a lovely shade of green. To further understand this, creating a color wheel is the perfect way to explore color mixing. Crimson red, chrome yellow and ultramarine blue are primary colors. Using just these three colors, you can mix any color apart from white and black.

Combining two of the primary colors in equal portions gives you a secondary color. Equal parts of red and yellow make orange. Equal parts of blue and yellow make green and, finally, equal parts of red and blue make purple.

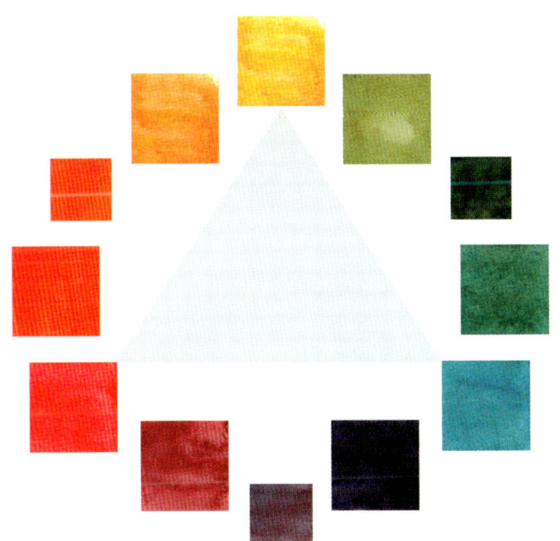

primary, secondary and tertiary colors

Now, when more of one primary color is mixed with less of another primary color, we get tertiary colors. For example, more yellow and a dash of blue will yield a light green. Similarly, mixing more blue and a dash of yellow will make a blue-green.

## Activating Your Watercolor Paints

Before we start experimenting with watercolors, it is important that you activate your watercolors. This is a critical step, so pay attention. When you buy watercolor pans or tubes, the paint is respectively dry or on the thicker, drier side. Thus, the paint needs to be activated before it can be used. You can simply add some drops of water to the paint to activate it. As the water is absorbed into the paint, you will notice that it is much easier to use.

If you are using a paint pan, simply add drops of water to the paints you will be using to activate them. If you are using paint tubes, simply squeeze a little paint onto a palette and add a drop of water to it. Be sure to squeeze only a drop of paint from the tube, since that is more than enough.

Once activated, you can use a damp brush and swish it on your activated paint to load the brush and start your painting process.

## Translucency with Watercolors

Another thing that is important to remember in watercolors is the dynamic between the pigment and water. If you have never used watercolors, this topic will interest you. Even if you are comfortable with watercolors, I would suggest that you still read, if only to look out for any additional tips.

I love doing this exercise and I know you are going to love it too.

Pick any color pan (generally, it is best to start with a darker color). Here, we are going to use indigo, which is such a favorite in the watercolor industry.

Now, take a clean, damp brush and a palette to mix your paints. With your damp brush, take a little indigo and mix it with some water droplets. This will give a light translucent wash. Swatch it onto the paper. This can be called a light wash of indigo or a less activated wash of indigo.

Next, add a little more indigo to the mixture and paint another swatch for a medium wash.

Continue the process to finally reach an opaque wash of deep indigo. This is also referred to as a highly activated wash of indigo and is therefore much darker in color.

As we work on our paintings, this is how we will be approaching layers in order to darken a color: from a translucent light wash to an opaque dark wash.

You can try this with different colors, and you will notice that with colors like yellow, the range is much smaller.

## Tints, Tones and Shades

Next, let's mix tints, tones and shades of paints.

**Tints:** Mixing a pigment with white will give varying tints. Adding more white will create lovely pastel colors.

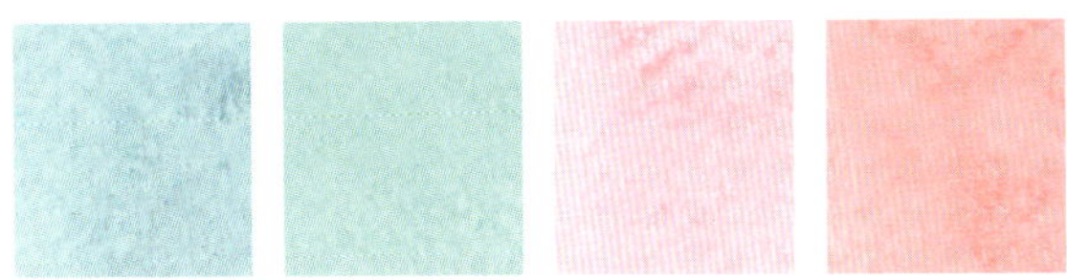

**Tones:** Mixing a pigment with gray will give you tones. These create a vintage color palette.

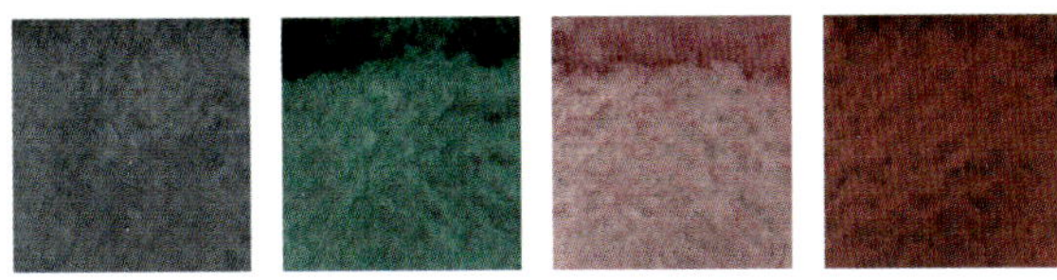

**Shades:** Mixing a pigment with a little black will give darker shades. More black will give you darker colors.

## Choosing Color Palettes

Let's go a bit deeper into warm and cool colors. The color wheel can be divided on either side for the warm and cool colors. Think warmth and the colors that come to mind are orange, red and yellow, while cool colors are blue, purple and violet.

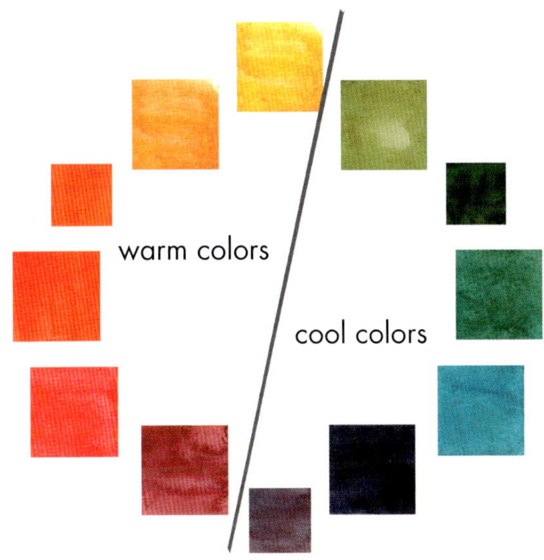


On the next page are some examples of how to use this information to create a balanced color scheme.

In our projects, we will be using warm and cool colors.

**Pro-Tip:** Use a mix of tints, tones and shades of these colors.

For a four-color combination, we can choose two colors that are warm and two colors that are cool. Using our Pro-Tip, we can change the colors. For example: Instead of using scarlet red, we can use a tint of scarlet red and light pastel pink. Similarly, instead of ultramarine blue, we can use a shade of ultramarine blue by adding a little black.

So, our color scheme may look something like this: a deep shade of ultramarine blue and turquoise blue for the cool colors and pastel pink and scarlet red for the warm tones.

Thus, the four colors create a lovely set.

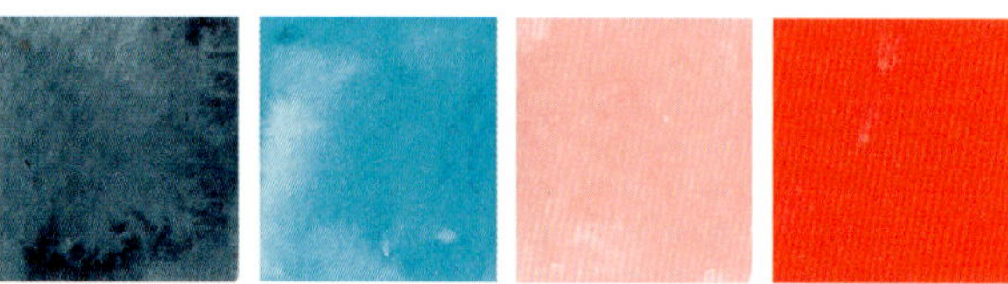

Practice creating four-color combinations by playing with tints, tones and shades as I have shared above. The more you play around with the combination, the more you will be able to naturally choose colors for your paintings.

For a three-color combination, try pairing contrast colors. Choose colors opposite each other on the color wheel—for example, blue and orange. This is a brilliant color combination.

Contrasting colors are very vibrant and need to be balanced. To balance this color scheme, use an additional third color. Use the color wheel to decide which color can be added to this pair. Generally, the color right next to one of the colors in the pair will help balance the painting. Thus, you could choose either scarlet red or bright yellow. The final three-color combination can be bright orange, bright yellow and ultramarine blue.

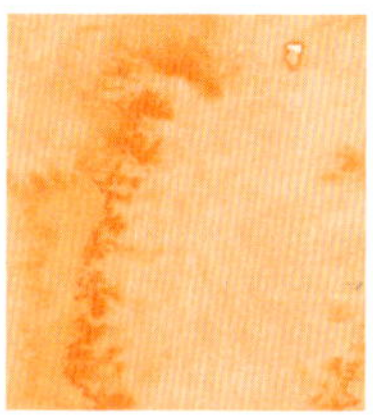

Practice this exercise a couple of times by making swatches of different color schemes. Pair contrasting colors and then add a third to balance the color combination. Don't worry if you are still figuring it out—as we move along the chapter, you will see how we play with different color palettes.

# Practice Exercises

Now that we have gone over our supplies and color palettes, let's move on to the different techniques within watercolors that we will be using in the book. All the exercises that we will explore in this chapter will help you build your skills and easily tackle the upcoming projects.

Some of these techniques will also be used within the upcoming chapters to create lovely compositions for our birds.

To start off your practice session, take a clean sheet of cold press watercolor paper.

> **Pro-Tip:** If you prefer, you can tape down your paper on the back so that it does not move around while you paint.

Keep a fresh glass of water and some dry tissues next to the paper, ready for you to use. Then, take out your watercolor paints and watercolor brushes to dabble in some exercises. Keep a dry palette as well to use to mix your paints. Now, activate your paints as mentioned in the section Activating Your Watercolor Paints on page 15. If you are using paint tubes, squeeze out a drop of your favorite paint (remember that in watercolor, a little goes a long way). Add a drop of water to the paint before starting to paint. If you are using a paint pan, simply add a drop of water to the color that you want to use and allow it to soak in before starting your exercises.

Now let's explore with watercolors.

## Single-Color Gradient Effect

In this technique, we will be creating a gradual gradient of a single color. The gradient will start from an opaque layer of paint to a clear layer of water. This gentle effect will be used mainly when we paint the base of the birds. We might also use this technique in the background for our birds.

For this technique, use your dampened size 000 mop brush and glide a layer of ultramarine blue paint on the paper as seen below. This is also known as the wet-on-dry technique—a wet wash of watercolor paint on dry paper. Be sure to use more paint for a vibrant wash.

first wash of ultramarine blue

water layer added

Clean your brush using the cup of water. Dab the excess water on your tissue before adding a layer of clear water below the previous layer. Keep in mind that you should not paint over the previous layer but slightly below it so that only the tip of the brush glides through to that previous layer. Immediately, you will see the blue paint flow into the water layer to create a gradual gradient effect as seen above.

## Dual-Color Gradient Effect (Wet-on-Wet)

In this technique, we will be using multiple colors to create a gradient effect. This is very useful for background compositions. Using a size 000 damp mop brush, paint a thin layer of paint at the top of the page. Next, clean the brush and dab out the excess water before gliding on a secondary color. This is known as the wet-on-wet technique, where a wet layer of paint is added to wet paper. Keep in mind to paint below the previous layer, slightly touching it so that the colors merge together.

**Pro-Tip:** Work quickly so that the layer is still wet when the next color is added for a wet-on-wet technique.

first wash of ultramarine blue

wash below

Finally, after cleaning your mop brush, take some clear water and add a third layer at the bottom of the page, slightly touching the edge of the previous layer. The previous paint will flow into this new layer, creating a gradient effect of multiple colors.

clear water to blend the previous layers

## Easy Practice Exercises

Now, let us practice painting some simple elements. These exercises are meant for you to get used to handling your brush and exploring the flow of watercolors as mentioned in the section Translucency with Watercolors, on page 16.

### Spokes

For our first exercise, we will be painting simple spokes by making eight lines that crisscross at their center, not unlike a snowflake. I would like you to experiment with using both your size 4 round brush and size 0 script liner brush. If you are finding it hard to understand the proportions, draw the spokes in pencil first. Try to draw thin and thick spokes.

Next, load either brush with activated scarlet red paint and paint inside the drawing. With the thicker-width spokes, the round brush is much easier to use since it quickly covers a lot more surface, while the thinner spokes are easier to paint with a script liner brush.

Practice these a couple more times to get used to the amount of water each brush can hold.

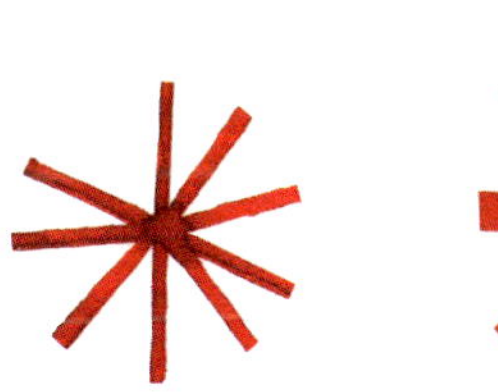

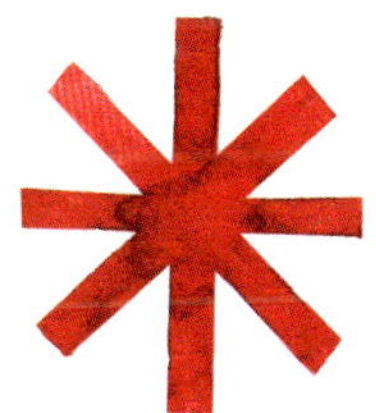

### Circles

For the next exercise, we can use both a size 000 mop brush and a size 4 round brush. Here, you can skip the pencil drawing, since circles and oval shapes are easier to paint.

First, load your mop brush with scarlet red paint and paint some circles and outlines of circles. Notice the amount of paint the brush can hold in relation to its size. This exercise will help you to really understand your brushes and the differences between them. Try the same exercise with your round brush, gently painting the outlines for the circles as well as filling in some of the circles.

With the round brush, you will be able to paint much smaller circles compared to the mop brush, while with the mop brush, you can easily paint much bigger radius shapes.

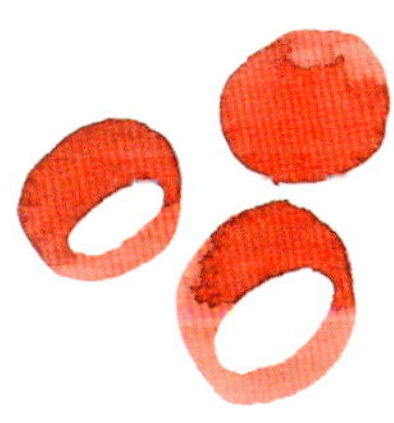

## Thin and Thick Lines

For our final simple exercise, we will be practicing some basics lines with the round brush. Load your brush with red paint and start by gliding the tip of the brush on the paper. While your brush is still touching the paper, press it down more onto the paper while gliding your brush. You will notice your line increases in width.

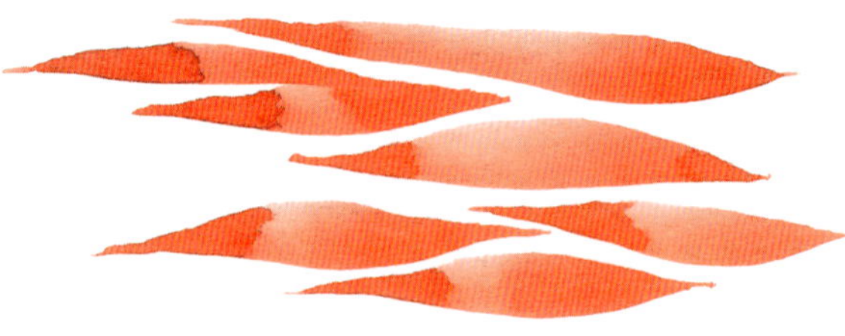

Finally, lift your brush to its tip to reduce the width of the line. Practice this technique a couple of times, as we will be using this often in our projects.

You can also try this with your mop brush to see the difference in the width.

## Simple Florals

I love Practice Exercises that are really fun to paint. While painting washes can be fun, what is even more fun is painting florals, so I wanted to show you how to paint some simple ones. We will be using these floral designs in further chapters to add to the background for the birds. There are many ways to paint florals. However, to keep our focus on birds, we'll keep our florals simple.

Start by drawing a simple flower using a pencil. As you can see in the image below, I have drawn a circle for the center of the flower. Next, I have added W-shaped petals around it. I prefer to use five or six petals for my flowers.

> **Pro-Tip:** If you don't have space to add all five petals, use a simple U-shape for one of the petals. This creates dimension within the painting.

Next, paint a light wash of scarlet red on the flower, using a damp size 4 round brush. I use a round brush here so that I can fill the areas of the flower easily. Allow this layer to dry naturally or use a hair dryer to speed up the drying process.

Once the layer is dry, we'll use a thin script liner brush to add more details. Let's use a darker maroon color to intensify the painting. Simply paint the inner filaments of the flower and outline the petals. For the filaments, paint circles around the previously drawn center circle, and then use thin lines to connect them to the middle of the flower.

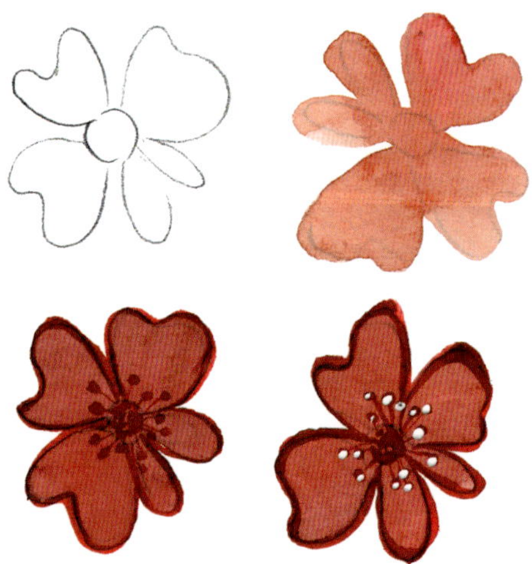

Allow the layer to dry before adding white acrylic paint to the center of the dots from the previous layer. To add the dots, I continue using my script liner brush so that I can control the placement. Notice how the white acrylic paint creates an interesting contrast and makes the flower really pop.

Practice this flower a couple of times before moving on to painting leaves.

## Exploring Leaves

Another exercise that is great when starting your watercolor journey is painting leaves. Leaves are so interesting and can really help you build your skills. Even now, whenever I am not sure what to paint, I paint leaves and this gets my creative juices flowing. We are not only going to learn how to paint leaves and experiment with them; we are also going to use this information in our upcoming projects. Leaves make great background elements for birds and can really add to the paintings.

To begin, I suggest using a round brush to paint leaves. For our purpose, we will be using a size 4 round brush since it is a user-friendly size. A size 6 or size 8 round brush is much larger and thus leads to larger leaves, while a size 0 or size 1 round brush is very small and can create very small leaves.

### Round Leaves

For this style of leaves, we will be using a rounded edge. In addition to that, we will be using the single-color gradient effect technique that we explored on page 19.

Until you get comfortable with the shape of the leaves, I suggest drawing them with a pencil. Start by drawing a curved stem, and then add drop-shaped leaves along the stem on either side.

> **Pro Tip:** Make sure that the leaf starts with a thin line for the stem, followed by a rounded edge. This will help keep the leaves separated from each other as we move on to the next step.

For the leaves, I have used hunter's green. Take your round brush and dip it in water, and then dab out the excess water on the dry tissue paper. Now load your brush with the activated hunter's green paint and paint along the stem and the middle of the leaf.

While the paint is still wet, take a clean, damp brush and paint the edges of the leaves. Make sure to gently touch the green with this clean water brush for a gentle gradient effect (see the wet-on-wet technique on page 20).

> **Pro Tip:** Make sure to keep the stem thin to contrast with the roundness of the leaves.

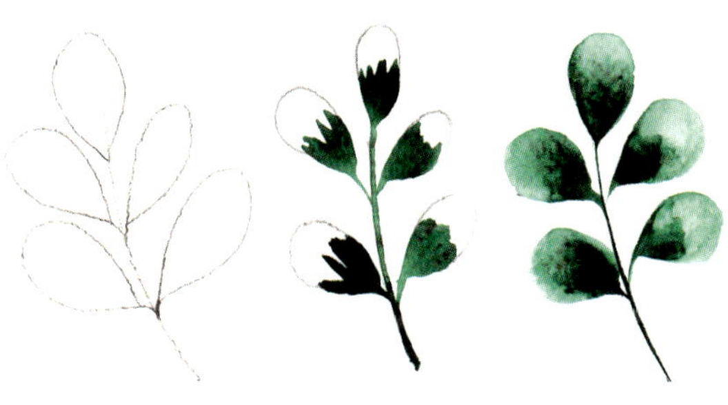

## Pointed Leaves

For this style, we will use the exact same technique as we did for the rounded leaves. However, we will be changing the shape of the leaves. The reason I wanted to add this variation to our list of Practice Exercises is because even the simplest change in shape can create a completely different style of leaf.

Start by drawing a curved line for the stem of the leaf. Next, draw pointed leaves along either side, making sure the right and left side leaves are not along the same line. This creates an asymmetrical look.

Start by painting the stem, and then continue midway through the leaf as painted above. Then, clean your brush and dab out the excess water. Using this clean brush, paint the remainder of the leaf. This creates a lovely gradient effect within the leaf, as seen in the figure below.

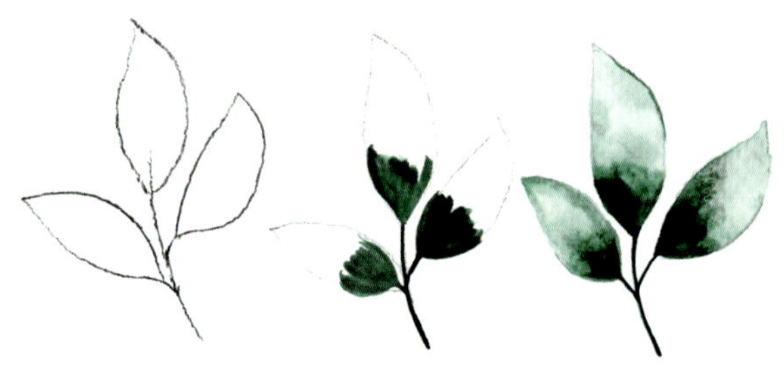

Now let's try the opposite gradient effect. Start by drawing your leaf. Once you are happy with the leaf shape, use a damp brush loaded with hunter's green to paint the stem and the pointed edges of the leaf.

Next, clean your brush. Then, using this damp brush, paint along the bottom of the leaves. Gently glide the edge of the brush along the previously painted layer. You can see the paint gently move down the leaf, creating a lovely gradient.

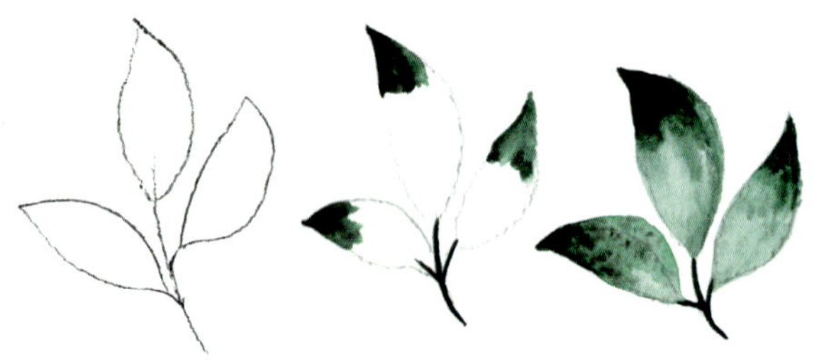

Now that we have covered the basic styles, you can go ahead and play around with combining multiple styles. I would suggest doing this over and over again because it will help you practice gradients and mixing colors.

Now, let's go over a couple of ways to create contrast within leaves.

One really fun way is to use the outlines of leaves along with the gradients of leaves. To easily paint only the outlines of leaves, I would suggest using a thin script liner brush size 1 or 0. Script liner brushes are very user-friendly and easy to control for painting outlines and smaller details.

For this motif, start drawing the simple leaves with a pencil. Once you are happy with the shape of the leaves, start painting them using a single-color gradient effect as described on page 19. Allow this layer to completely dry before moving on to more details.

Now, take your thin script liner brush and load it with a deeper color. Here I have chosen ivory black for the details. Paint the simple outline of the leaves along the stem of the previous layer. I also went a step further and added a stem with rounded leaves.

As you can see, the contrast in colors creates a lovely motif.

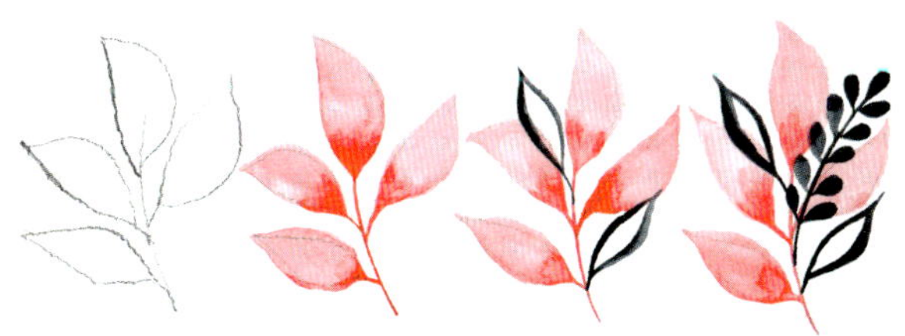

Another way to play around with leaves is to add outlines to existing gradient leaves. To do this, start by painting a lovely set of leaves following the steps from the previous Practice Exercise. Now, allow the layer to dry before adding more details using a script liner brush. Next, move on to adding outlines to the leaves and other fun details as seen in the image.

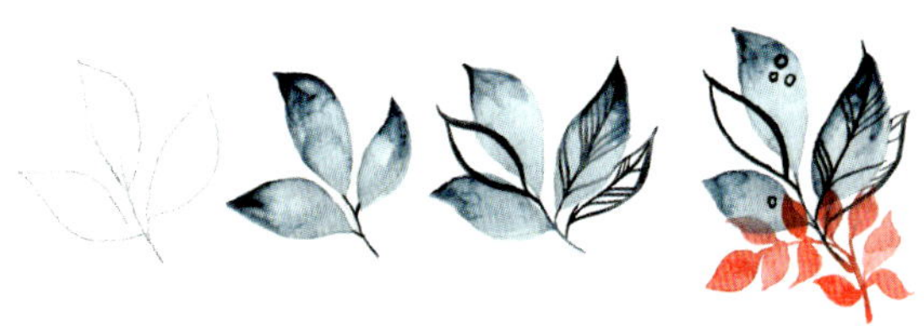

There are no limits to the various motifs you can create with these exact same techniques. Have fun and let loose. Because this section is all about play, I haven't gone into too much detail on how you should paint but have focused instead on what is possible to do.

Now that we have gone through some fun Practice Exercises, I would suggest going over them multiple times and learning the names, as these are common terminologies within watercolors. Keep these exercises in mind as we move on to painting our birds.

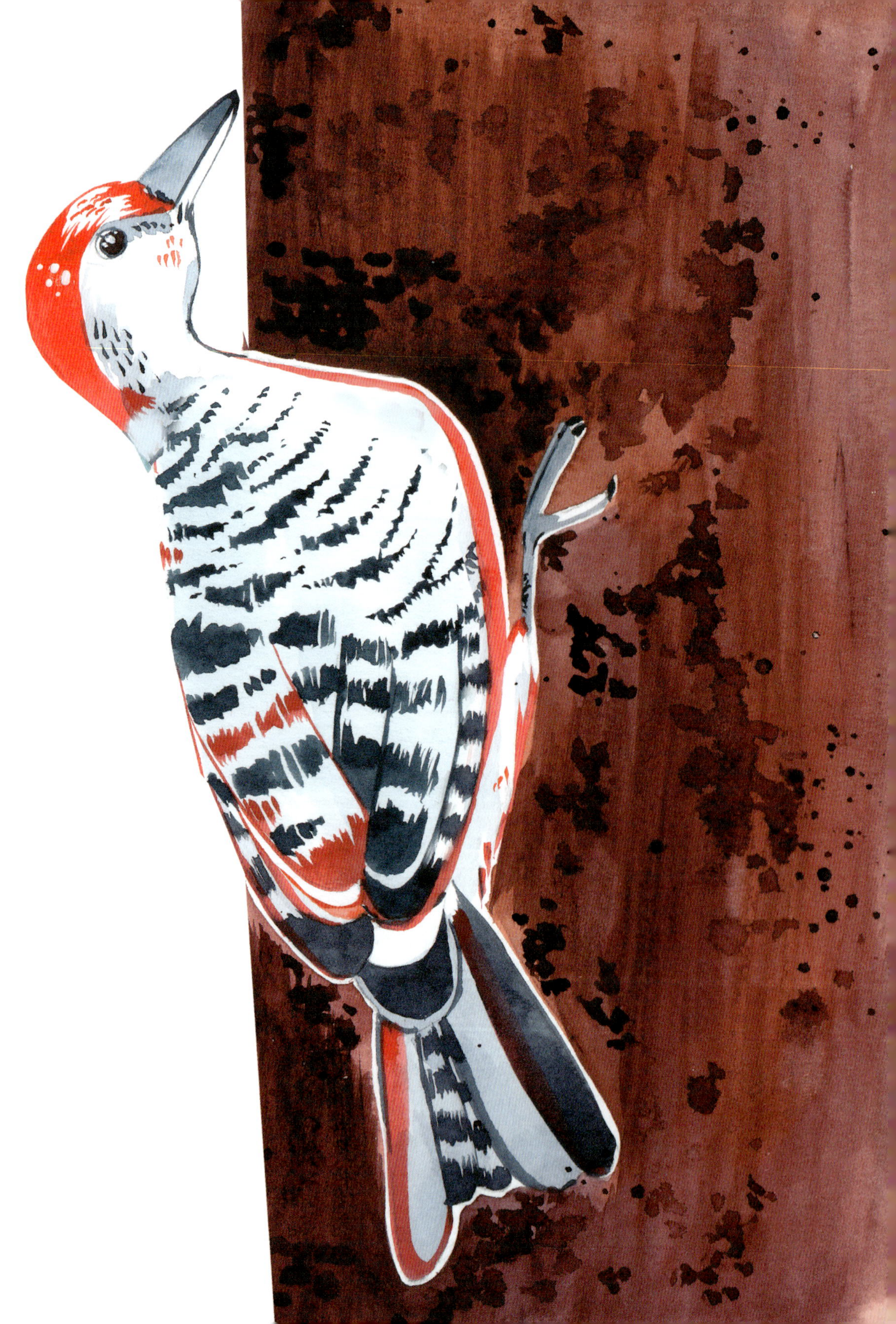

# Garden Birds

The first category of birds we will be tackling in this book is garden birds. Garden birds are so lovely, perched all around us. They are part of our lives and are so important in our daily activities. Garden birds generally tend to be smaller in size and are usually similar in color to the gardens they attend. These birds are adorably cute and known for their cheery bird calls, and I want to bring this cheeriness to each and every one of our projects within this category. As an artist, it is important not only to capture the bird's shape and proportions, but also its playful spirit.

I specifically chose garden birds as our first chapter because I find them much easier to draw. With a few basic geometric shapes, you can easily capture their proportions. Also, most garden birds are monotone or two-toned. Because of the limited color palette, they are also much simpler to paint.

Bringing that light into our cute, chirpy friends is going to make these paintings very unique. We will start by painting red cardinals on page 28, which are much simpler to paint since they are monotone. Next, we will move on to painting American robins on page 33 and red-bellied woodpeckers on page 38, both of which will focus on adding simple textures. After that we will move on to the goldfinch on page 44, another small and vibrant bird. Finally, we will play around with colors as we paint brown sparrows on page 49 and barn swallows on page 55. Brown sparrows and barn swallows are more difficult to paint as well, since we will be layering more colors and textures.

To complement each project, we will be selecting multiple elements that have already been explained in the Practice Exercises chapter on page 19.

Brushes in hand, I can't wait to get started–let's dive right in.

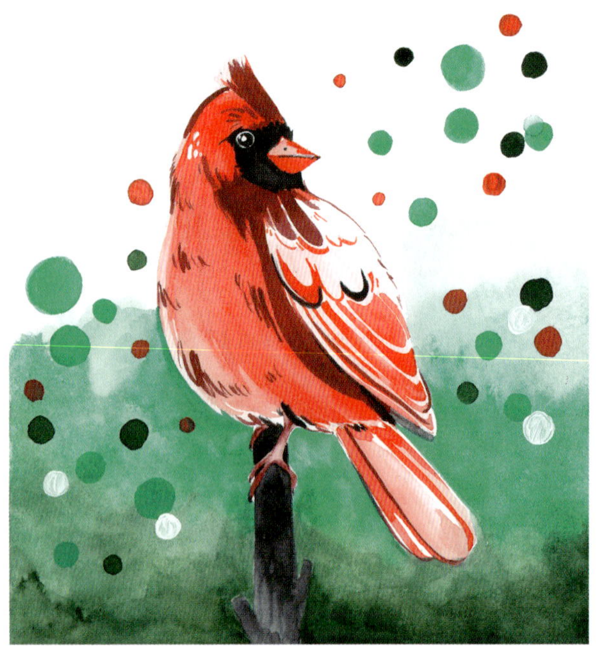

# Red Cardinal

*Somewhere in the distant past, cardinals were named Christmas birds. Nowadays, they are seen all over Christmas greeting cards and decorations. In this painting, along with capturing the lovely bird, we will be playing around with the background. As this is the first project in this book, it is definitely going to be a memorable one. Red is already a bright color, and using a contrasting green color will enhance our composition. Furthermore, red and green are classic Christmas colors.*

## MATERIALS

Watercolor cold press paper, 200gsm (95lb)
Pencil
Kneadable eraser
Palette
Glass cup
Watercolor mop brush, size 000
Round brush, size 4
Script liner brush, size 0
Tissue paper

## COLOR SCHEME

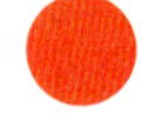 Scarlet Red

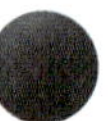 Ivory Black

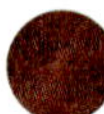 Maroon (can be created by mixing a dash of Ivory Black with Scarlet Red)

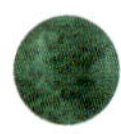 Hunter's Green

 Viridian Green

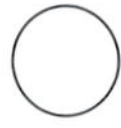 White acrylic paint

## CHALLENGE LEVEL

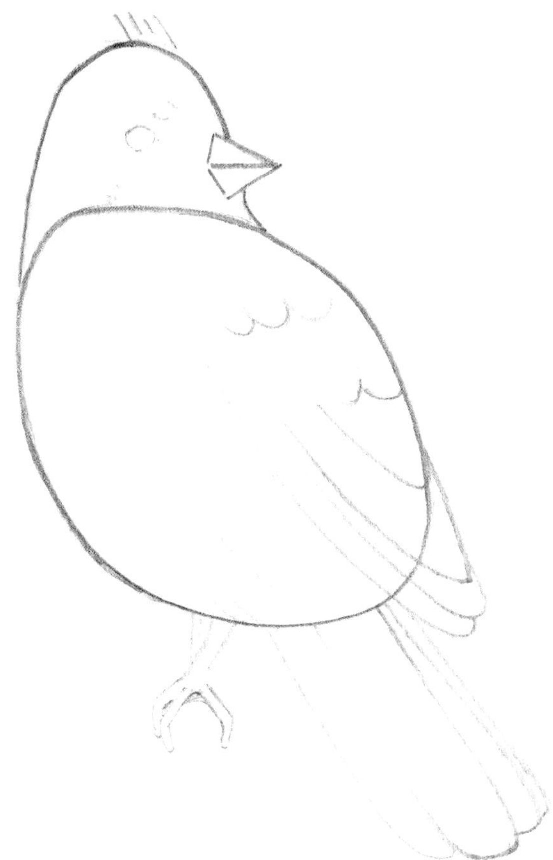

Figure 1.1

**Step 1:** Let's start drawing our cardinal with a pencil. It is important to simplify drawing the bird by using easy shapes. Start with an egg shape for the bird's body, followed by an inverted U-shape for the cardinal's face. Use triangle shapes for the beak.

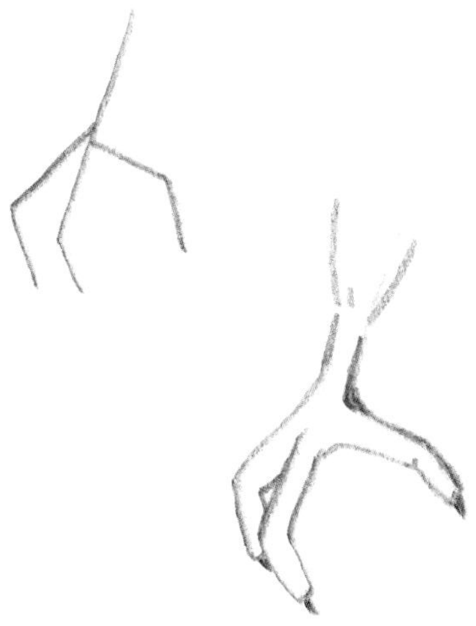

drawing the foot

Now, draw the feet using simple lines. Use a center line for the main leg and connect three L-shaped lines for the claws. Draw two of the L-shaped lines closer together for the front claw. Next, draw parallel lines for a 3D effect. I also like to add small V-shapes for the nails as seen in Figure 1.1.

Use U-shaped lines for the wings, starting with smaller U-curves at the top, and longer lines at the bottom. Use the same for the tail feathers by overlapping multiple U-lines as seen in Figure 1.1. Erase any dark pencil lines with a kneadable eraser before moving on to the next step.

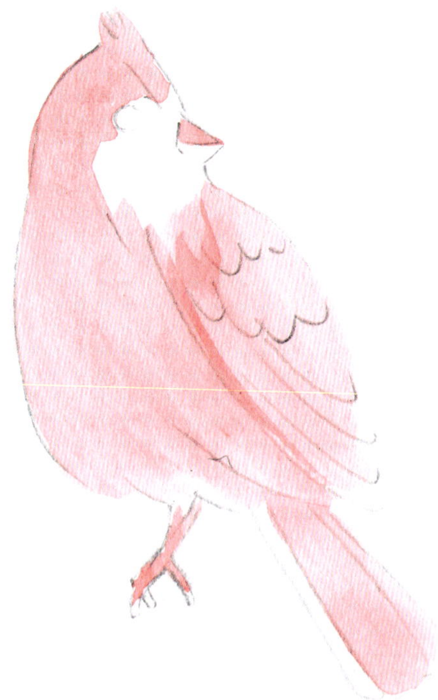

Figure 1.2

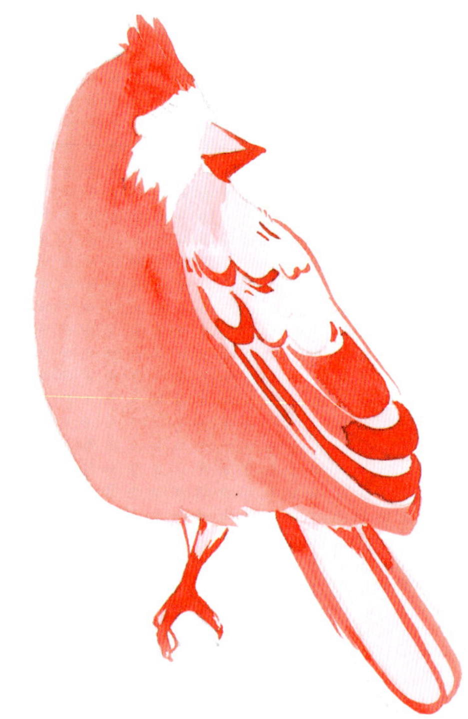

Figure 1.3

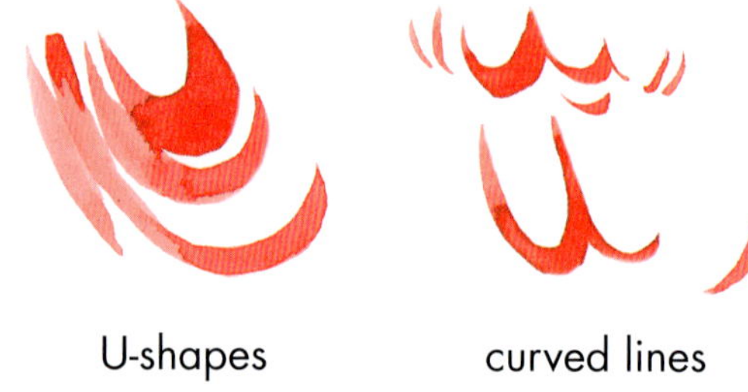


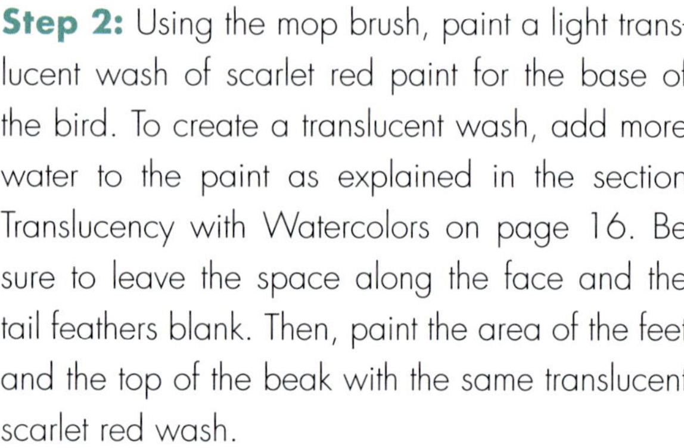

**Step 2:** Using the mop brush, paint a light translucent wash of scarlet red paint for the base of the bird. To create a translucent wash, add more water to the paint as explained in the section Translucency with Watercolors on page 16. Be sure to leave the space along the face and the tail feathers blank. Then, paint the area of the feet and the top of the beak with the same translucent scarlet red wash.

Allow the layer to dry before moving on to the next step.

**Step 3:** In this step, we will be adding another layer of scarlet red using a round brush. Start with a gentle single-color gradient effect from the top of the head to the body of the bird. For more on how to do this, see the section on single-color gradients on page 19. Paint the bottom of the beak as well.

Next, add curved lines at the top of the wing and longer U-shapes at the bottom of the wing. Finally, paint the outlines of the tail feathers, alternating between thin and thick lines as seen in Figure 1.3.

Allow the layer to dry before moving on to the next step.

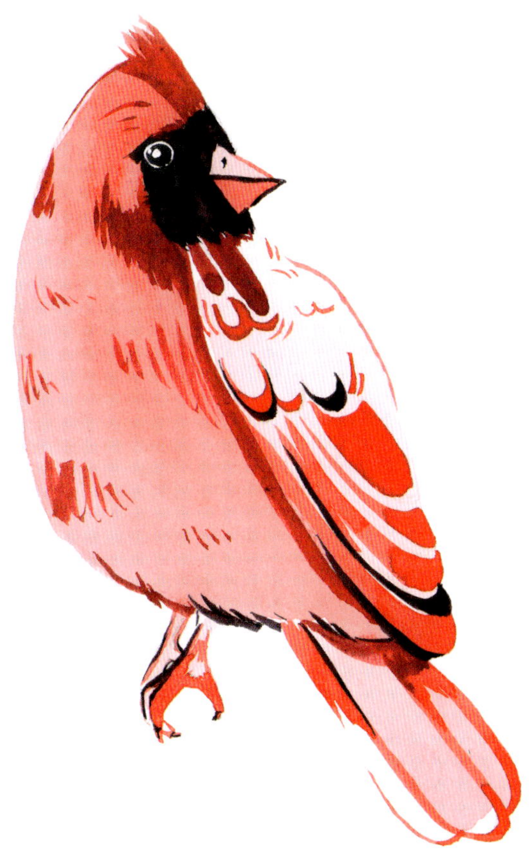

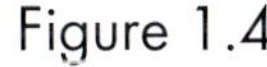

Figure 1.4

**Step 4:** In this step, we will be adding details. For details, it is easier to use a script liner brush for better brush control. Start with ivory black and paint the face of the bird. Use concentric circles for the eye and a thin line for the beak.

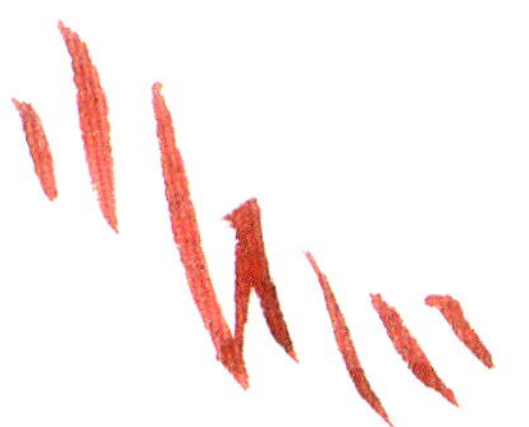

thin strokes

Additionally, use ivory black to paint curved lines along the wings and thin strokes along the underbelly of the bird. This creates a lovely depth to the painting.

Now, clean your brush completely before loading it with maroon paint. Refer to the color scheme section at the beginning of the project to mix a lovely shade of maroon on your palette. Gently add jagged maroon strokes along the body of the bird. Follow this step by adding maroon at the top of the head, the neckline and the curve of the wing. Add maroon to the feet of the bird as seen in Figure 1.4.

**Pro-Tip:** Paint multiple thin strokes from short to long for the body. This gives an interesting texture to the painting.

Let the painting dry before moving on to the next step.

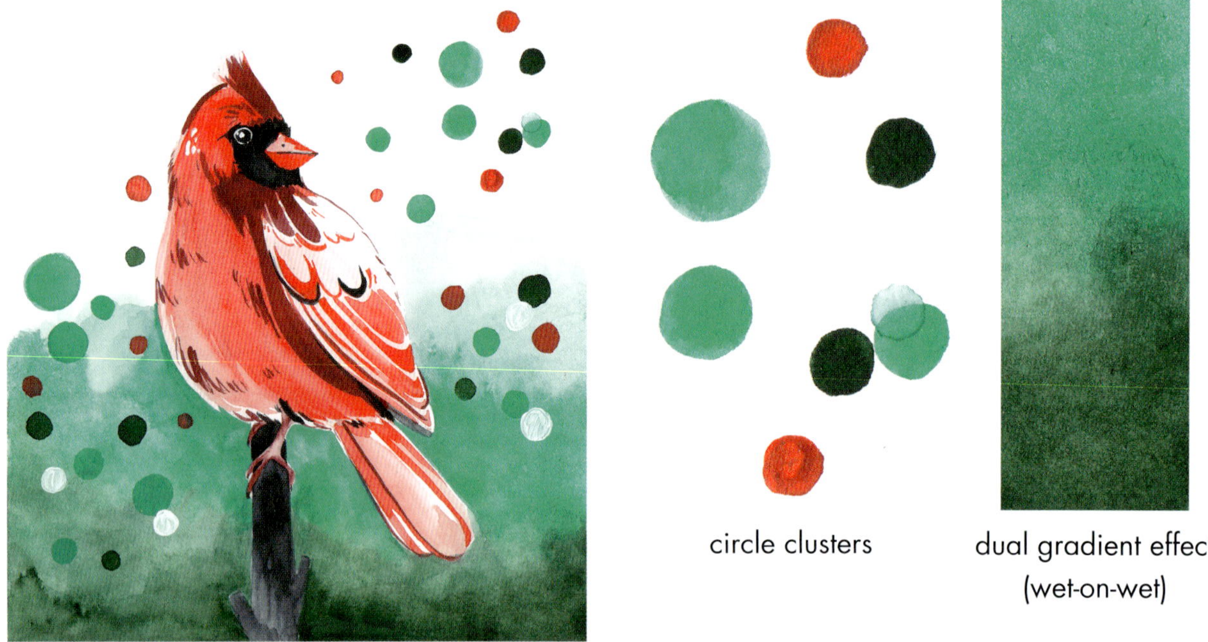


Figure 1.5

**Step 5:** Now that our cardinal is complete, let's use a simple composition to balance the painting. Start with a lovely dual-color gradient effect for the background as explained in the Practice Exercises chapter on page 20 by using your mop brush, which allows you to quickly cover a larger surface area. Start with a deep hunter's green at the bottom of the page, then move to viridian green and then clear water for a gradual wash.

Once the gradient layer has dried, add some fun multicolored circles. This can be done by using your round brush as described in the simple Practice Exercises chapter on page 19. The reason I add these circles is not only to add a pop of color to the painting, but to also bring a playful look to the composition. For the circles, we will be using scarlet red, acrylic white, viridian green and hunter's green.

**Pro-Tip:** Use a cluster of small and big circles instead of individual circles.

Clean your round brush before loading it with ivory black to paint the wooden stump for the bird to perch on.

# American Robin

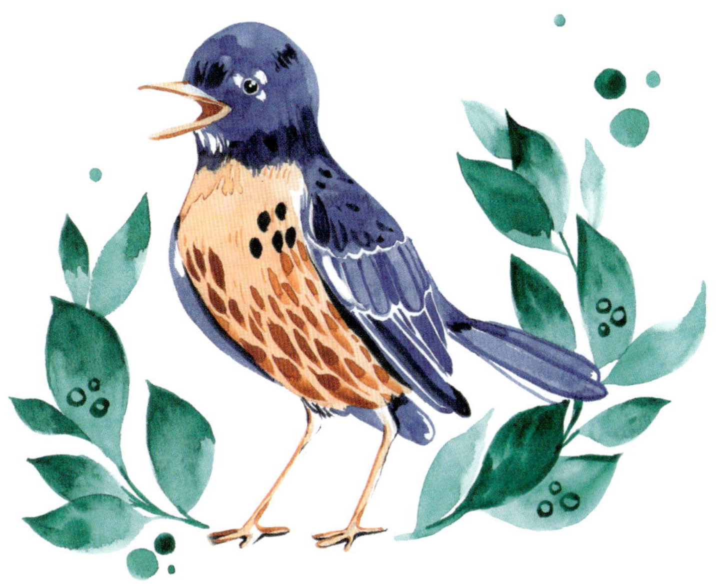

*American robins are common garden birds that are seen all over the world. Generally, robins also symbolize new beginnings across different cultures. For this project, instead of using the actual brown shades of American robins, we will be using violet to further enhance our painting. This can be tricky but can create a lovely final composition. Take your time to play around with step 5 as we add more details to our bird. Now let's begin!*

## MATERIALS

Watercolor cold press paper, 200gsm (95lb)
Pencil
Kneadable eraser
Palette
Glass cup
Round brush, size 4
Script liner brush, size 0
Tissue paper

## COLOR SCHEME

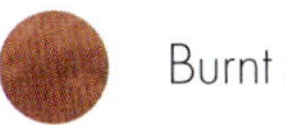
Burnt Sienna
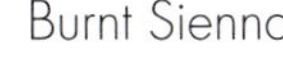
Ultramarine Violet

White acrylic paint
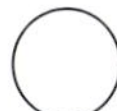
Hunter's Green
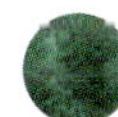

## CHALLENGE LEVEL

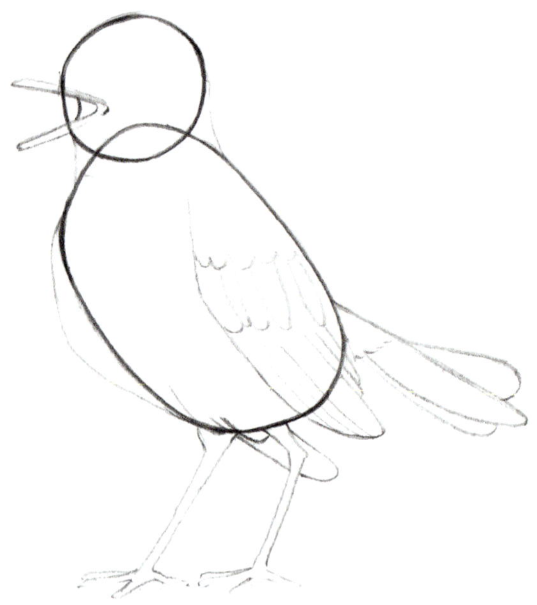

Figure 1.1

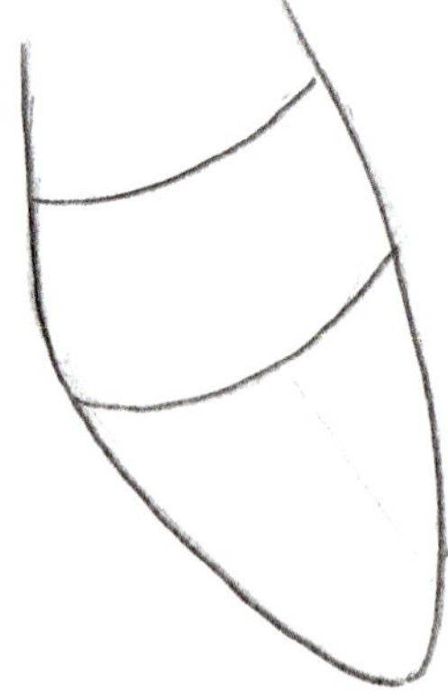

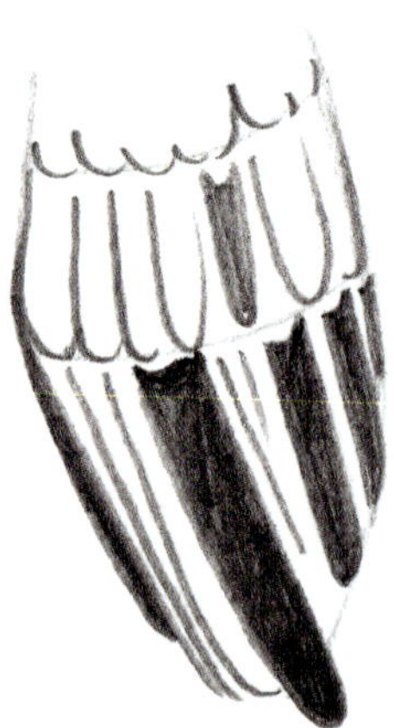

wing shape

**Step 1:** To draw an American robin, use a pencil to first draw an oval shape for the body of the bird. Next, draw a lovely circle for the face of the bird. Connect the two with curved lines for the shape. Create an open beaked bird by using simple triangle shapes.

For the wings of the bird, draw a V-shape as seen in Figure 1.1. To fill in the feathers, draw U-shaped curves for the top of the wing and a deeper U-shape for the bottom of the wing. Next, draw the tail feathers of the bird using U-shapes. Finally, draw the feet with simple parallel lines as seen in Figure 1.1.

Erase any dark pencil lines with a kneadable eraser so that they don't affect the painting in the next steps.

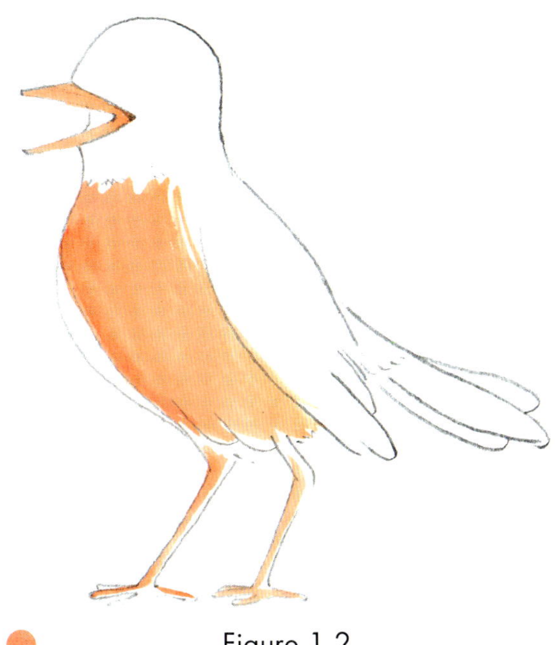

Figure 1.2

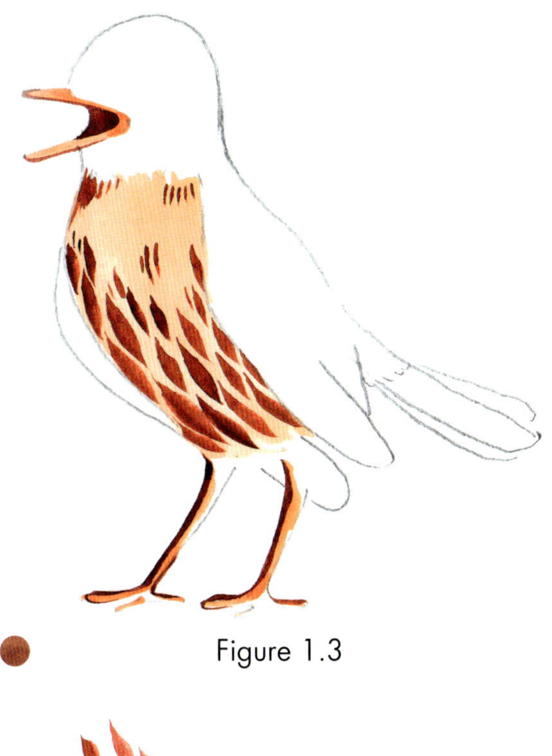

Figure 1.3

**Step 2:** Let's start by painting a simple base layer for the bird. Use a light burnt sienna wash and a round brush for this step. We will be using a very translucent wash of burnt sienna, which means more water mixed with the paint. This is further explained in the Translucency with Watercolors section on page 16.

Now, with this light wash of burnt sienna, paint the beak and the body of the bird by using jagged lines. This helps create textures within the painting. Next, paint the feet of the bird as seen in Figure 1.2.

**Step 3:** After the painting has dried, let's add texture to the bird. Using a round brush, start with diamond shapes for the chest of the bird. Make sure you wash your brush and dab out the excess water before loading it with the burnt sienna paint.

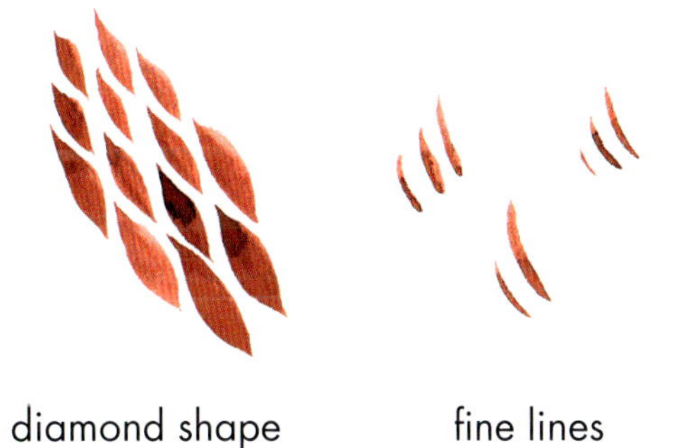


Here, we will be using a more opaque layer of burnt sienna as shown in the Translucency with Watercolors section on page 16.

**Pro-Tip:** For the diamond textures, vary from small shapes to larger shapes, and then back to smaller shapes again at the end of the underbelly.

Switch to a script liner brush for better control while adding some fine line strokes along the neckline, the beak and the feet, using burnt sienna.

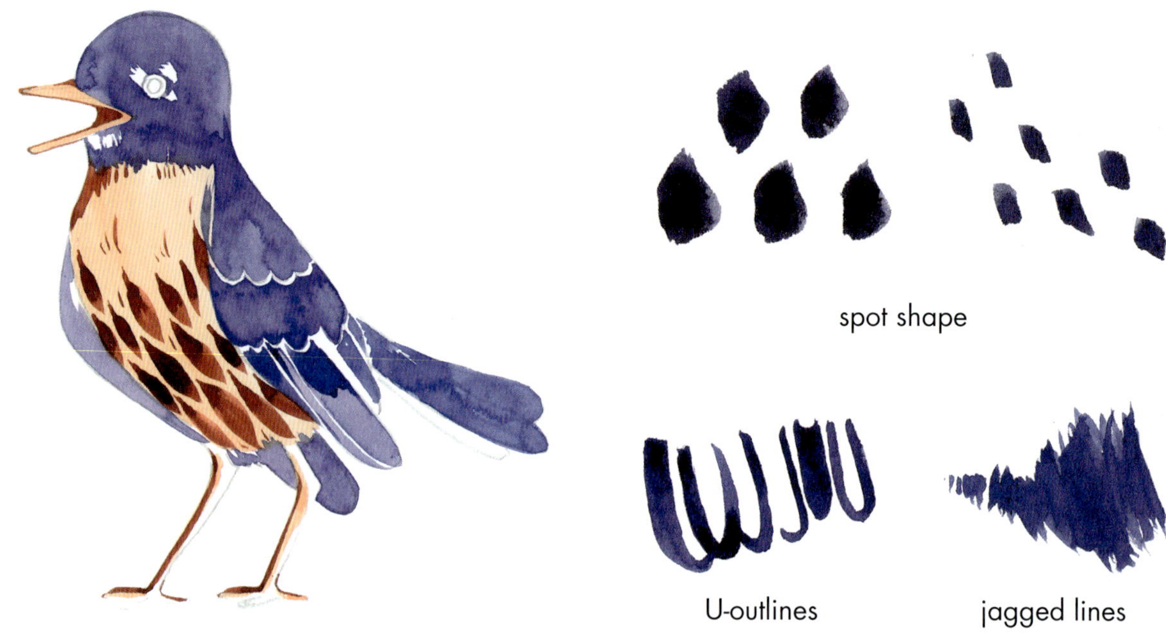


Figure 1.4

**Step 4:** Next, let's paint the body of the bird with a lovely shade of ultramarine violet. Paint a translucent watered-down layer by simply adding water to the paint as explained in the Translucency with Watercolors section on page 16. Use a round brush for this step to cover a larger portion of the bird quickly. Keep in mind to clean the brush of any previous color before loading it with translucent ultramarine violet. Notice the gaps left at the bird's eye and the bottom jaw line—this is to mimic the white feathers in American robins.

Also, leave space between the layers of the wing and the feathers of the tail feathers. This creates more visual appeal as the white of the page shines through the wing.

**Pro-Tip:** For smaller areas, feel free to switch to a script liner brush for easy control.

Keep note of all spaces since these will be very important as you move on to the next step. Allow the painting to dry before moving on to the next step.

**Step 5:** Using a script liner brush loaded with saturated opaque ultramarine violet, go ahead and add more texture to the painting. Start with jagged lines along the neckline, the top of the beak and the top of the tail feather.

Next, add deep U-outlines at the wings and tail feathers as seen in Figure 1.5. Continue loading the brush with ultramarine violet and begin to paint thin, fine strokes at the top of the head. Here, add some circle shapes along the chest as well. All these miniature details bring the bird together as we move on to the next step to complete it. I also make sure to paint the eye in this step as well as some spot shapes on the side of the wing.

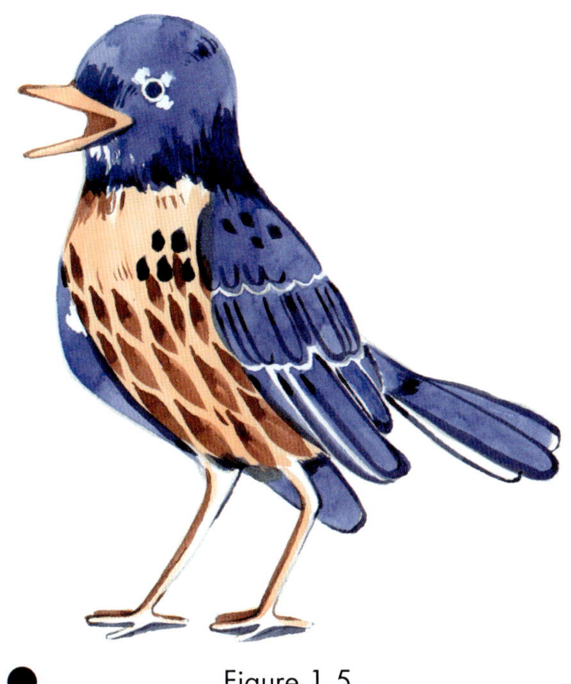

Figure 1.5

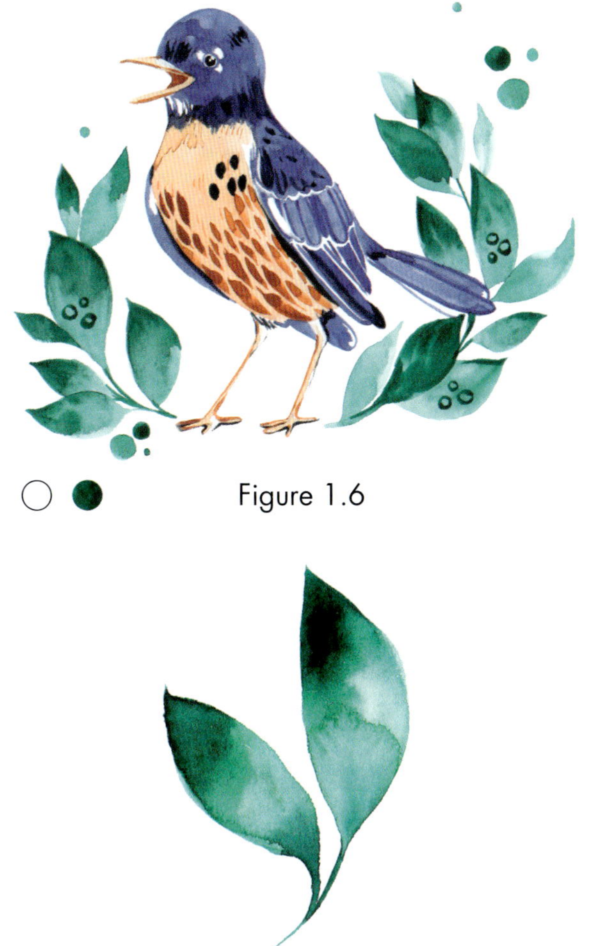

Figure 1.6

opposite gradient leaves

Additionally, use ultramarine violet to outline the legs and create a shadow for the bottom of the feet. Allow the layer to dry before moving on to the finishing touches.

**Step 6:** First, add white acrylic spots to the eye using the script liner brush. Make sure to clean your brush from the previous step before loading it with acrylic paint.

Complete the painting by using elements from our Practice Exercises chapter on page 19. We will use some gradient leaves and circles for this step. Start by drawing a stem of leaves with a pencil on the right and left sides of the bird. Next, load your round brush with hunter's green to paint the leaf ends. Then, use clear water along the bottoms of the leaves to gently create a lovely gradient. Connect adjoining leaves with a branched stem by using a script liner brush. This gradient effect gives a stunning look and complements our bird painting.

Additionally, add some cute spots outside and inside the leaves to balance the composition (see Figure 1.6).

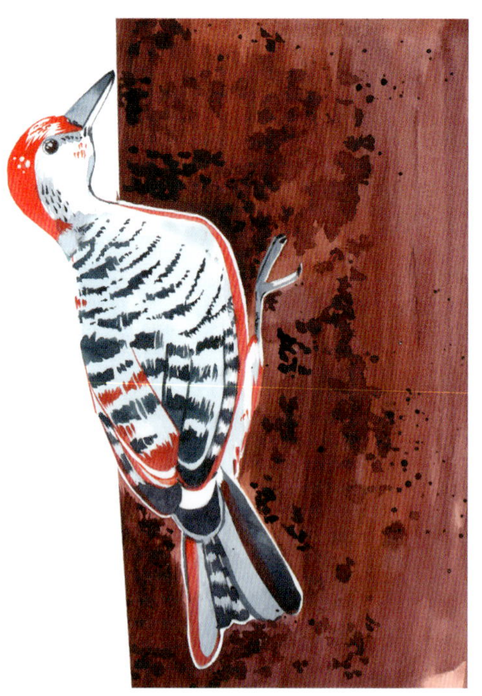

# Red-Bellied Woodpecker

*Woodpeckers are perfectionists and will peck a perfect circle on the trunks of trees. Therefore, this bird is relatable to any perfectionists out there. However, watercolors are not the perfect medium. Accepting its imperfection is part of the charm of watercolors. For this painting, we will be trying a fun new technique (dry brush-strokes) to add texture to the tree trunk. Don't worry—I will be sharing what this is in step 6 as we dive into the technique.*

## MATERIALS

Watercolor cold press paper, 200gsm (95lb)
Pencil
Kneadable eraser
Palette
Glass cup
Watercolor mop brush, size 000
Round brush, size 4
Script liner brush, size 0
Tissue paper

## COLOR SCHEME

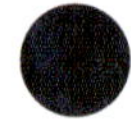 Indigo Blue

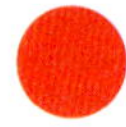 Scarlet Red

 White acrylic paint

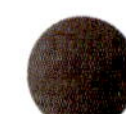 Burnt Umber

## CHALLENGE LEVEL

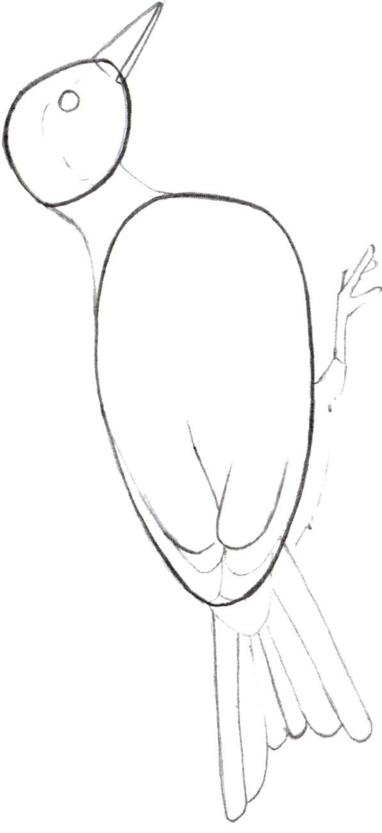

Figure 1.1

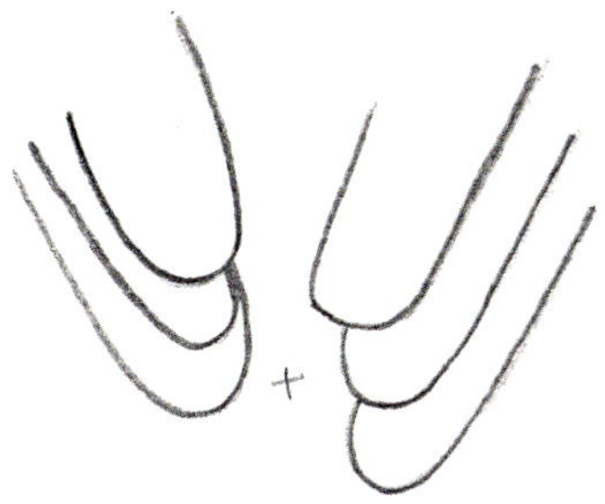

back feather details

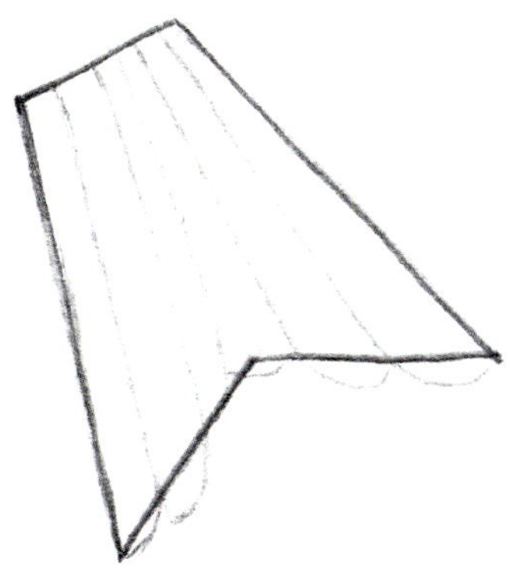

tail feathers

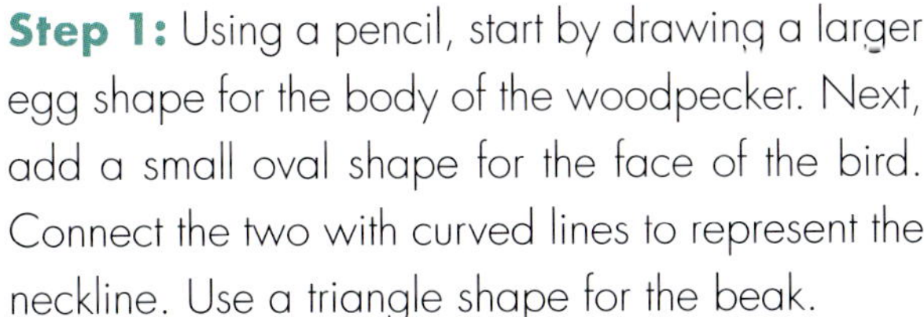

**Step 1:** Using a pencil, start by drawing a larger egg shape for the body of the woodpecker. Next, add a small oval shape for the face of the bird. Connect the two with curved lines to represent the neckline. Use a triangle shape for the beak.

For the back body wings, use U-shapes as seen in Figure 1.1 above. The back wings are created by overlapping the right and left sides. Together, these form the back feathers. Next, use geometric shapes to draw the back tail feathers by overlapping the feathers, along with the foot of the bird.

Erase any harsh pencil lines with the kneadable eraser so that they do not affect your final painting.

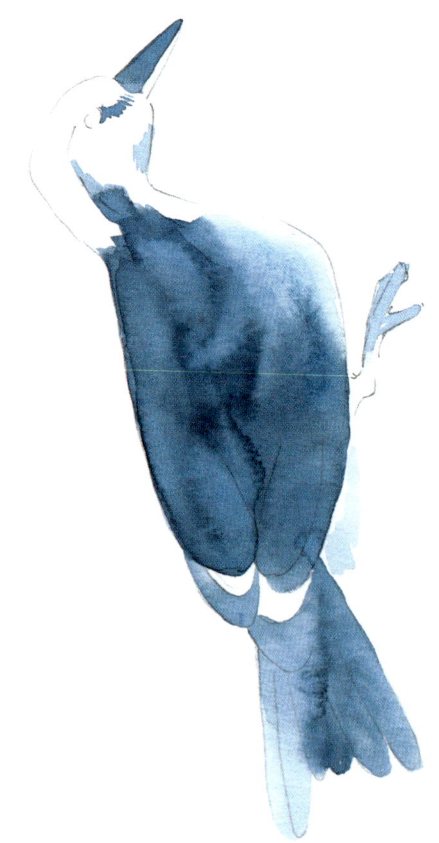

Figure 1.2

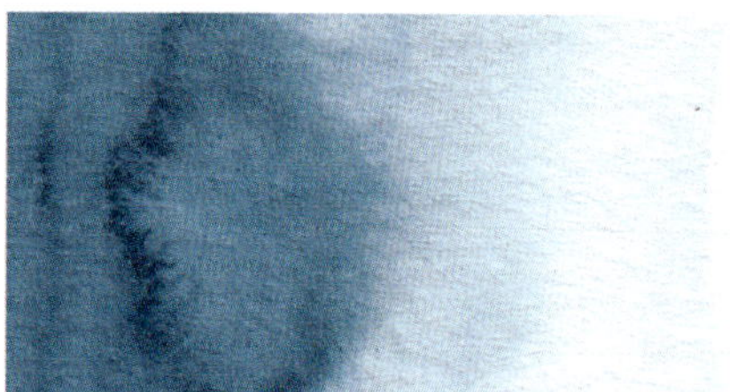

gradient effect

indigo translucency

**Step 2:** In this step, we will be adding a light translucent indigo wash with a mop brush to cover more area. To prepare a light translucent wash, simply add more water to the paint as explained in the Translucency with Watercolors section on page 16.

Instead of adding a continuous layer of paint, I suggest adding some clear water and blending to create a single-color gradient effect as explained on page 19. This creates a lovely base to our painting as we add more layers.

As you can see in Figure 1.2, I use a gradient wash for the body of the bird by using water to blend along the chest area and the edge of the tail feathers.

**Pro-Tip:** Avoid using saturated deep indigo in this step.

Allow the layer to dry before proceeding to the next step.

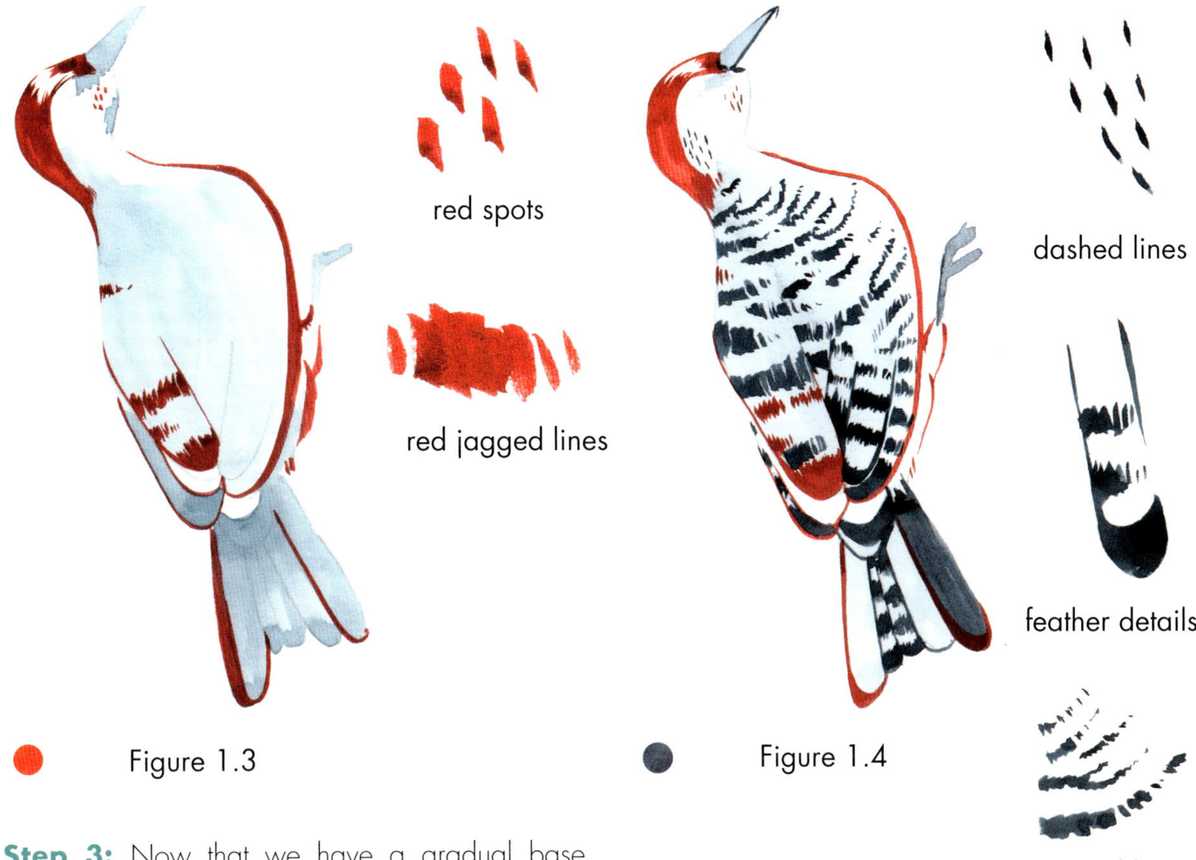


Figure 1.3

Figure 1.4

**Step 3:** Now that we have a gradual base wash, let's go ahead and add scarlet red details for the woodpecker with the script liner brush. Focus on the top of the head and the outline at the bottom of the bird.

Next, add in some red spots and jagged lines to give the painting a playful effect. First, add small spots along the cheeks of the face. Then, add the jagged-lined feathers along the back feather wings. Use Figure 1.3 as a reference point for this step.

**Step 4:** Once the painting is dry from the previous step, add a saturated indigo layer using a script liner brush. Make sure the script liner brush is completely clean before loading it with indigo paint.

Start with jagged curved lines from the neckline to the back wings. The lines should start smaller at the top near the neck, and become longer towards the back of the body. Fill in some of the feathers and the bird's chest as well with jagged lines. I have also filled in U-shapes for some of the feathers to complete the look.

**Pro-Tip:** Add in some thin dashed lines along the head, and then outline the beak as seen in Figure 1.4 for a more interesting look.

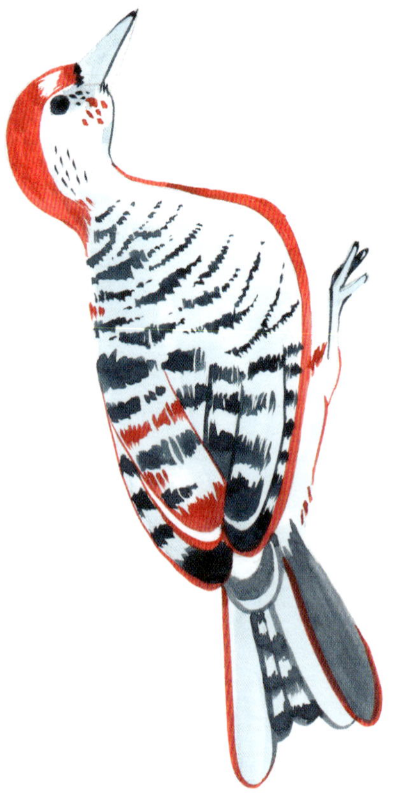

Figure 1.5

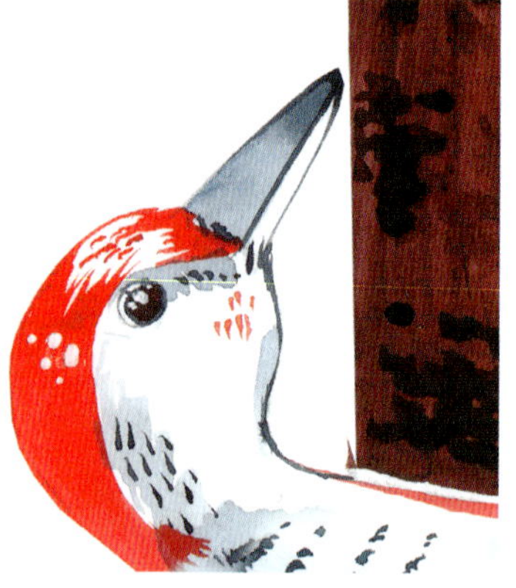

**Step 5:** Once the previous layer has dried, go ahead and use the script liner brush to add more details. We will continue to use indigo paint to fill in the eye as well as the foot outline.

**Pro-Tip:** Use a broken outline for the foot as seen in Figure 1.5. This gives an incomplete asymmetrical look.

I also added some circle shapes near the beak to create texture within the painting. The reason I do this is because birds are full of feathers and texture. To translate that aspect of them on paper, adding quirky spots, dashes and lines can bring a similar feel to the painting. Allow the layer to dry before proceeding to the next step.

**Step 6:** In the final step of our painting, let's first complete the bird by adding white acrylic spots for the eye, head and body. To make this process easier, let's use a script liner brush. Make sure that your brush is cleaned completely before loading it with acrylic paint.

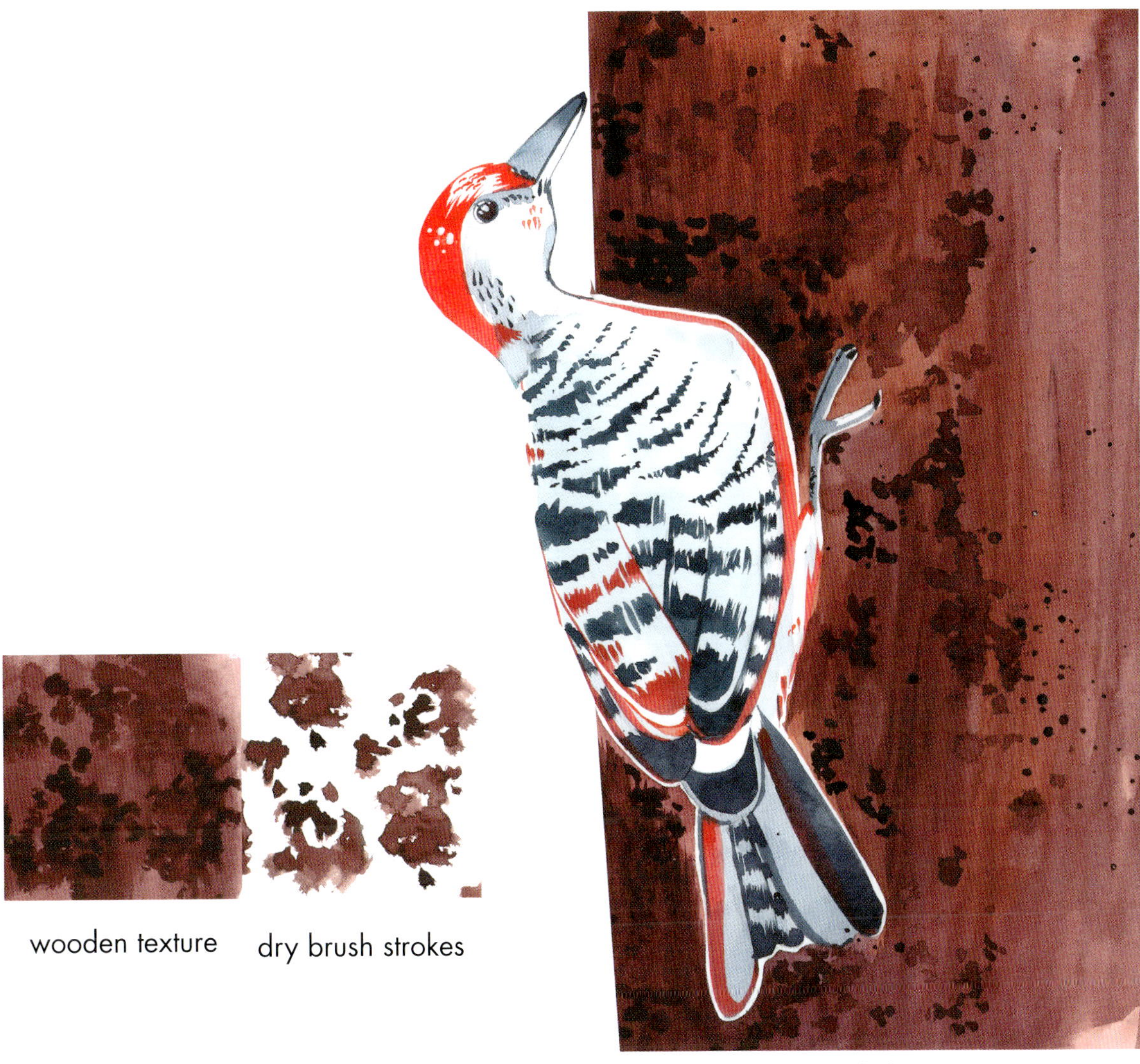


Figure 1.6

Now for the background details, let's combine some simple elements. Since our bird is already textured and has so many other features, let's keep our background simple. Start by painting the tree trunk for the bird to perch on by using a deep burnt umber wash. This can be done using a damp round brush so that we can cover more area and easily paint around the foot of the bird. Allow this layer to dry and then add a dry brush effect. Dry brush is exactly what it sounds like–use a dry round brush and dab it in your burnt umber. Next, stamp the brush on the paper for a dry brush effect as seen in Figure 1.6.

# Goldfinch

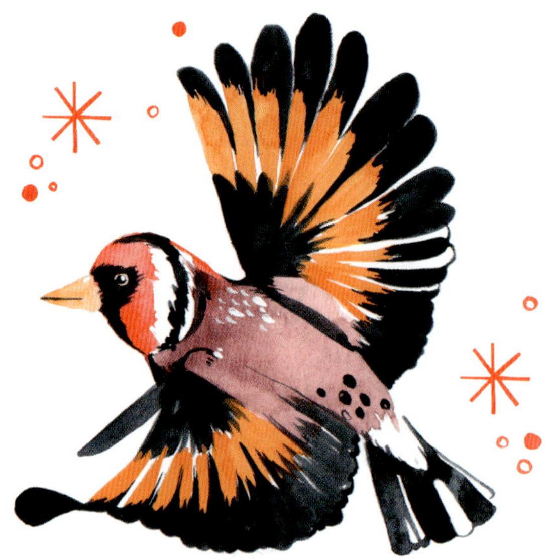

*Goldfinches are so common that I had to add them to this lovely book. I especially love the fact that their bright yellow wings are because of the carotenoid pigments they consume. After nesting season, they drop their old feathers and grow brown feathers, and we will be exploring all those colors in this piece. For a striking painting, I have chosen a slightly more interesting pose: a flying goldfinch. Hence, watch out for step 4 as we tackle each feather.*

---

## MATERIALS

Watercolor cold press paper, 200gsm (95lb)
Pencil
Kneadable eraser
Palette
Glass cup
Round brush, size 4
Script liner brush, size 0
Tissue paper

## CHALLENGE LEVEL

## COLOR SCHEME

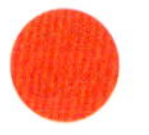 Scarlet Red

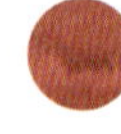 Mahogany (can be made by mixing Scarlet Red with a dash of Ivory Black)

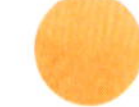 Chrome Yellow

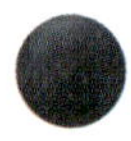 Ivory Black

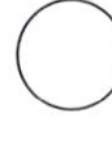 White acrylic paint

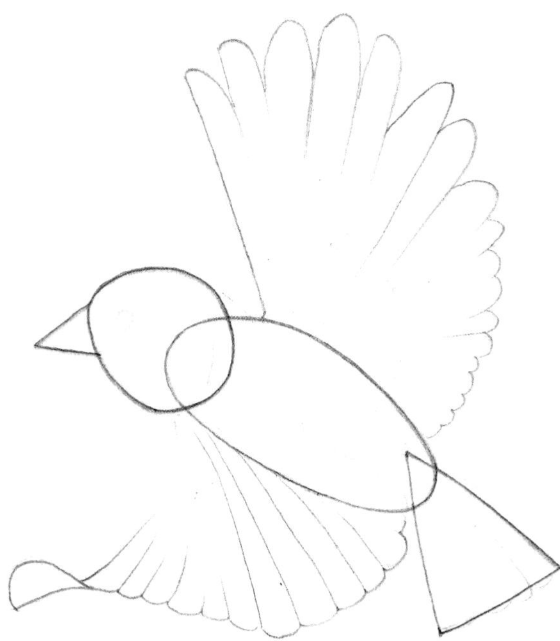

Figure 1.1

**Step 1:** Let's start by drawing our goldfinch with simple geometric shapes using a pencil. For the body, use an elongated oval shape and overlap a small oval circle for the face. Connect the two for the neckline. The beak can be easily drawn using a triangle shape. Add U-shapes to complete the overlapping tail feathers (Figure 1.1).

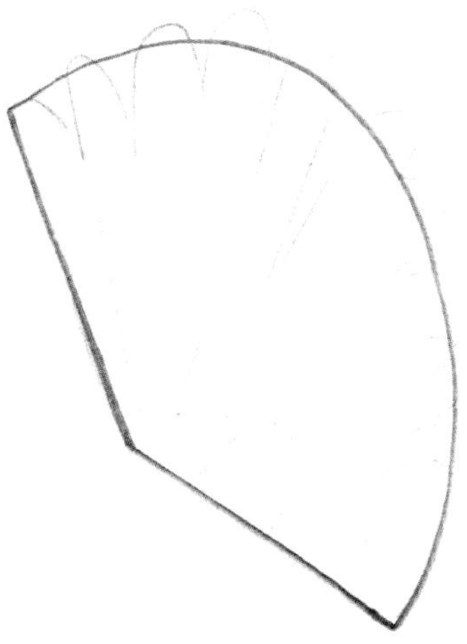

wing shape

Finally, for the wings, we are going to use semi-circles as seen in Figure 1.1. For the right wing, try to separate the feathers on top and make them more prominent. For the left wing, add a 3D effect with an opposing semicircle at the end. Always try to separate the feather toward the top of the bird and make the feathers smaller and less prominent near the body of the bird.

Erase any dark pencil lines with a kneadable erase before painting the goldfinch.

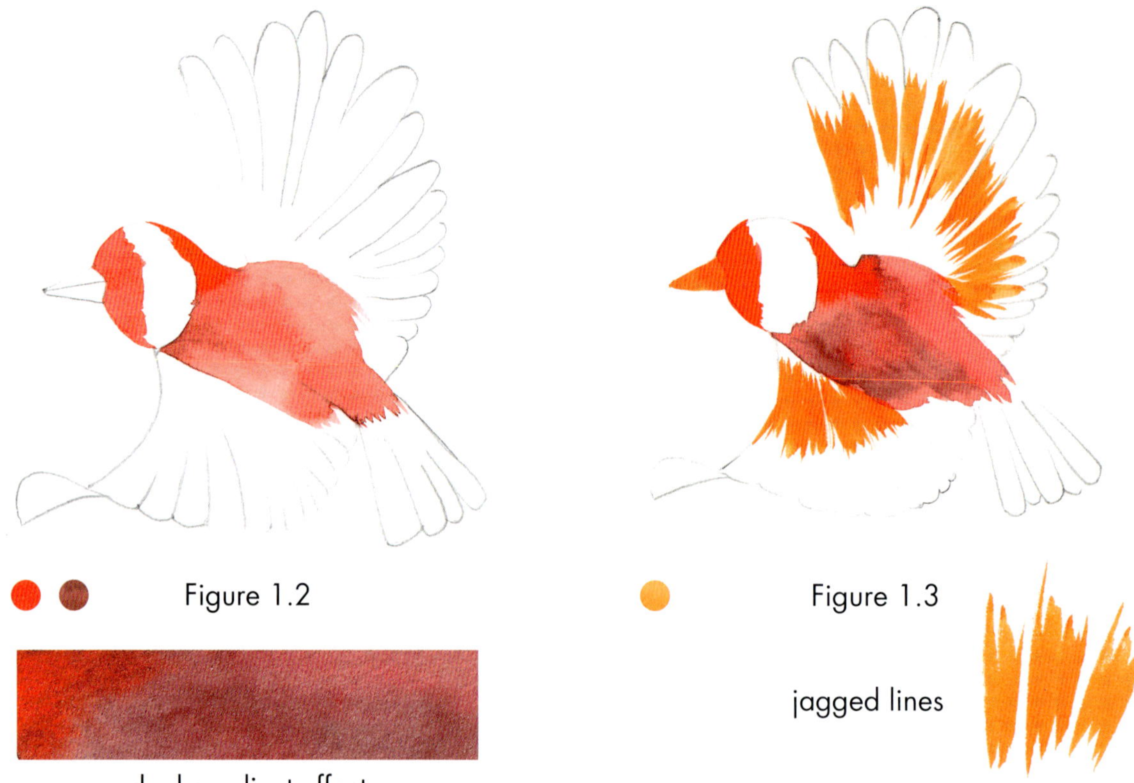

Figure 1.2

dual gradient effect

Figure 1.3

jagged lines

**Step 2:** First, paint a scarlet red patch along the bird's face near the beak using your damp round brush. Use jagged lines to give a textured effect along the edge. Next, use the same scarlet paint for the back of the head and neckline as seen in Figure 1.2.

Wash your brush and load it with mahogany. To mix mahogany, refer to the color scheme section at the start of this project. While the paint is still wet, use mahogany to paint the body of the goldfinch for a wet-on-wet technique as mentioned in the Dual-Color Gradient Effect section of page 20. This will automatically create a gradient effect as the color swishes through.

Allow the layer to dry before moving on to the next step.

**Step 3:** In this step, we are going to be adding a bold chrome yellow to the painting using your round brush. Make sure to clean your brush from the previously used mahogany color before loading it with chrome yellow. Start with painting the beak of the bird followed by the wings of the bird, as seen in Figure 1.3. Let us use jagged lines throughout this process, which will create an asymmetrical look.

Notice in Figure 1.3 how the yellow lines take more space in the front of the wings and less at the back of the wings, as the wings there are also smaller in size.

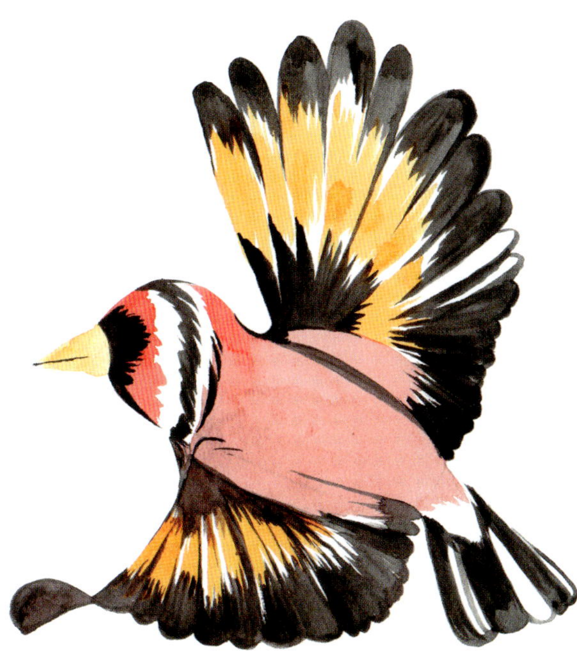

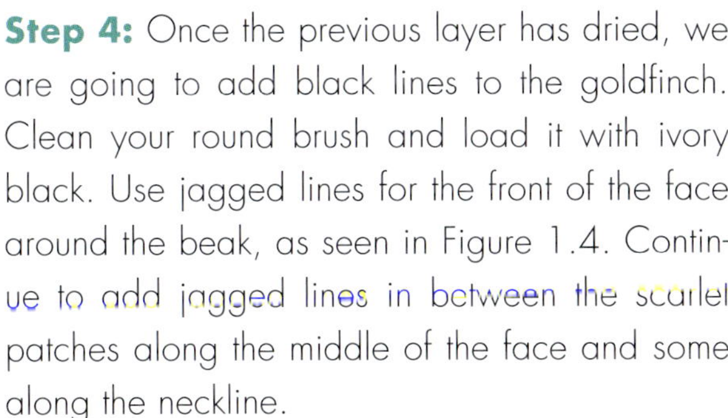

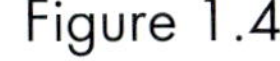

Figure 1.4

jagged lines (wing edge)

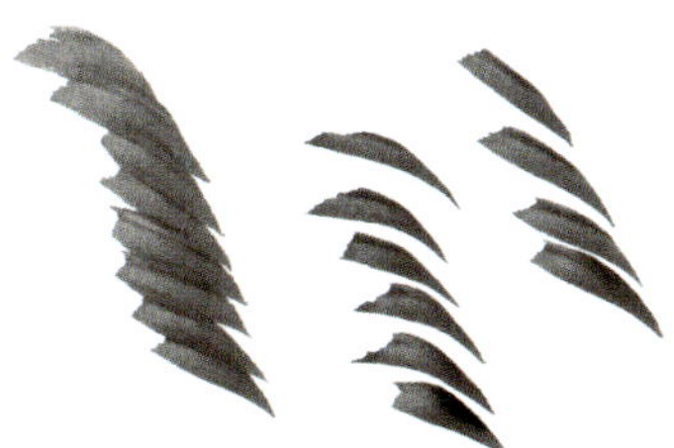

jagged lines

**Step 4:** Once the previous layer has dried, we are going to add black lines to the goldfinch. Clean your round brush and load it with ivory black. Use jagged lines for the front of the face around the beak, as seen in Figure 1.4. Continue to add jagged lines in between the scarlet patches along the middle of the face and some along the neckline.

Now move on to the wings. Use black at the inner wings and the edges of the wings. Take your time in this step and tackle each feather individually for the best results. One at a time, slowly fill in the inner and outer edge of the feathers. Keep loading more ivory black paint through the process for vibrancy. Once you have completed the bottom wing, move on to the top wing. Follow Figure 1.4 for placement of these details.

Finally, once you are happy with the wings, move on to the tail feathers, filling some, while leaving others empty.

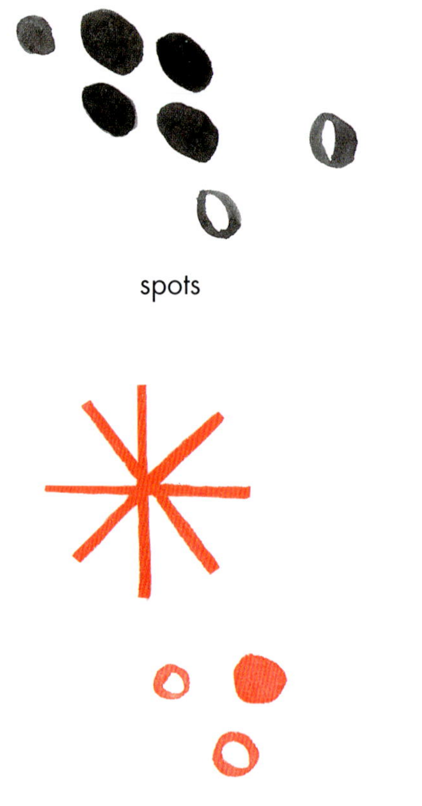

spots

spokes and circle shapes

**Step 5:** This is our last step, where we will be adding white acrylic spots for the eye of the goldfinch as well as along the back neckline. Take your script liner brush and load it with white acrylic paint. Add white details to create a rather interesting texture for the bird.

Clean your script liner brush, load it with ivory black and add some black spots for the back of the bird as well.

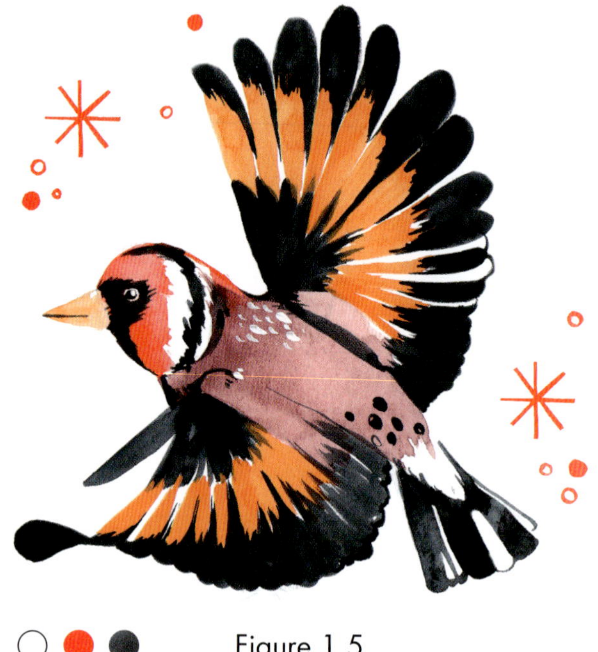

Figure 1.5

Complete the bird composition with simple spoke shapes and circles, using scarlet red as seen in Figure 1.5. I chose these small elements since they finish off the painting and complement the bird without overpowering it. These different shapes can be painted using your script liner brush loaded with scarlet red paint. For more details on how you paint these elements, refer to the chapter Practice Exercises on page 19.

**Pro-Tip:** Balance the spokes and circle elements by placing them on opposite ends of the bird instead of clustering them on one side to create an asymmetrical look.

# Brown Sparrow

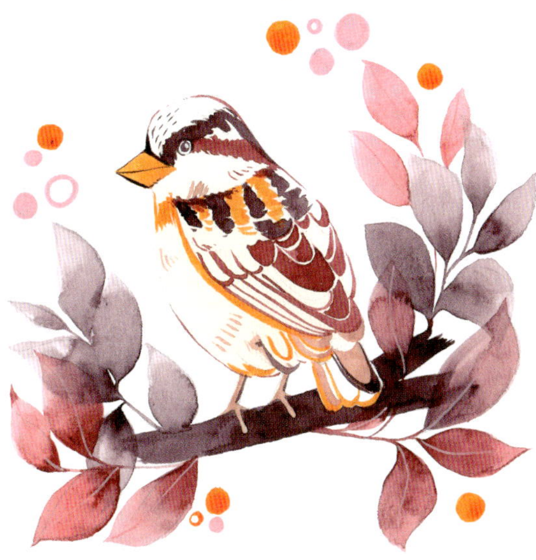

*Sparrows are among the most common garden birds. This small brown bird is so adorable and cute–it is also the reason why my audience loves my sparrow paintings, stickers and notebooks. From an artistic perspective, brown can be a bit boring. Hence, to increase the vibrancy, we will be adding lovely shades of mahogany, crimson and chrome yellow. Also, step 5 can be more intricate as we add details to the bird's feathers, so take your time in this step.*

---

## MATERIALS

Watercolor cold press paper, 200gsm (95lb)
Pencil
Kneadable eraser
Palette
Glass cup
Round brush, size 4
Script liner brush, size 0
Tissue paper

## CHALLENGE LEVEL

## COLOR SCHEME

Shell Pink (can be made by mixing Scarlet Red with a dash of White watercolor paint)

Chrome Yellow

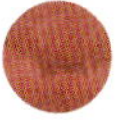
Mahogany (can be made by mixing Scarlet Red and a dash of Ivory Black)

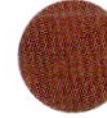
Crimson (can be made by mixing Scarlet Red and Burnt Sienna)

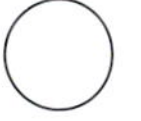
White acrylic paint

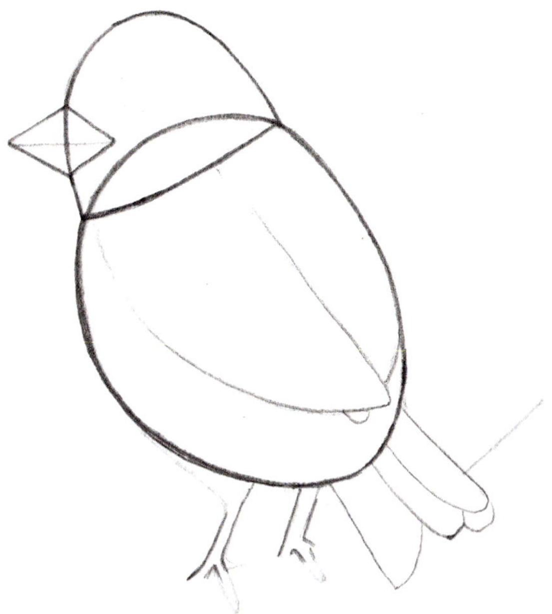

Figure 1.1

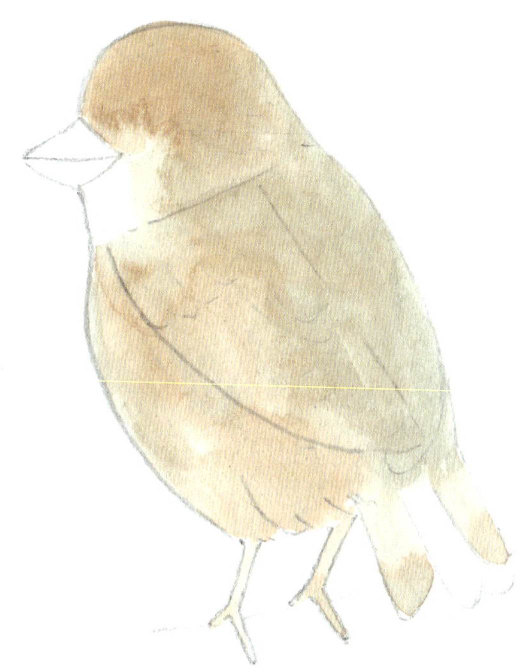

Figure 1.2

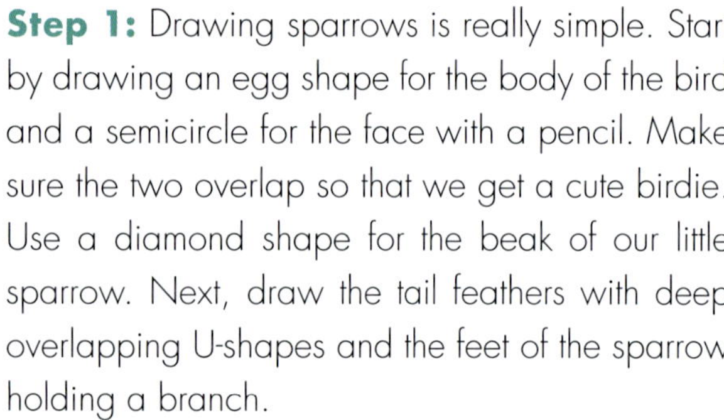

**Step 1:** Drawing sparrows is really simple. Start by drawing an egg shape for the body of the bird and a semicircle for the face with a pencil. Make sure the two overlap so that we get a cute birdie. Use a diamond shape for the beak of our little sparrow. Next, draw the tail feathers with deep overlapping U-shapes and the feet of the sparrow holding a branch.

In this three-quarter view of the wings, both the right and the left sides will be visible. Accordingly, draw them overlapping with U-curves on either side as seen in Figure 1.1.

Erase any dark pencil marks using a kneadable eraser to avoid it affecting the final painting.

**Step 2:** For the base layer, let's use our shell pink mixture as shown in the color scheme section of this project. Load your round brush with shell pink so that you can quickly fill the base of the bird. Use shell pink around the bird's body while skipping the beak and some of the tail feathers (see Figure 1.2).

Allow the layer to dry before moving on to the next step.

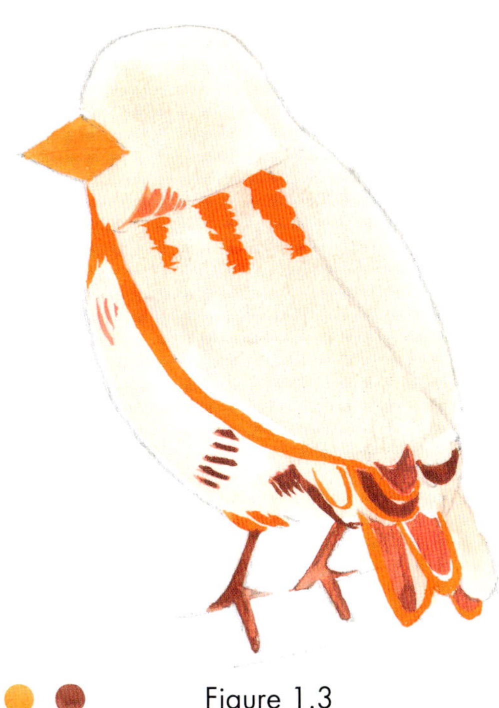

Figure 1.3

jagged lines

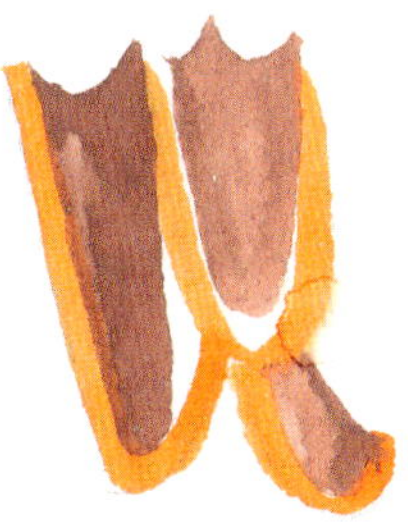

tail feather details

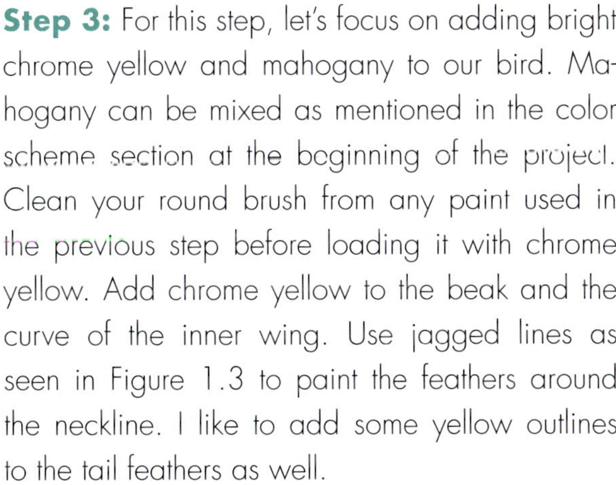

**Step 3:** For this step, let's focus on adding bright chrome yellow and mahogany to our bird. Mahogany can be mixed as mentioned in the color scheme section at the beginning of the project. Clean your round brush from any paint used in the previous step before loading it with chrome yellow. Add chrome yellow to the beak and the curve of the inner wing. Use jagged lines as seen in Figure 1.3 to paint the feathers around the neckline. I like to add some yellow outlines to the tail feathers as well.

**Pro-Tip:** For a more playful effect, add some thin strokes along the chest and neckline of the bird. All these mini details add to the final look of the painting.

Now, clean your brush and load it with mahogany. Using mahogany, paint U-shapes along the tail feathers and paint the legs. Add some grouped parallel lines along the underbelly as well, as seen in Figure 1.3.

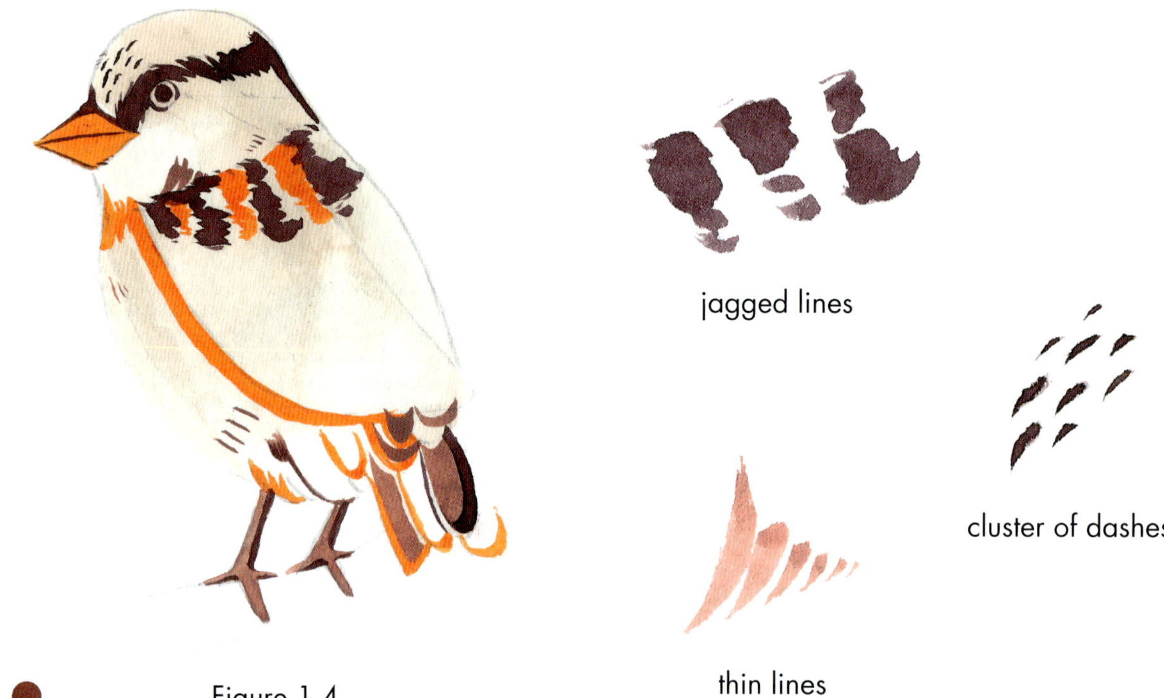


Figure 1.4

**Step 4:** Let's add more details in this step by using a script liner brush. First, load your script liner with crimson paint. Crimson can be prepared as mentioned in the color scheme section at the start of this project. Now, add a jagged crimson line starting from the beak and continuing to the back of the head. Next, add vertical jagged lines along the back wings of the sparrow, as seen in Figure 1.4

Use this as an opportunity to add an outline for the feet and some of the tail feathers. Finally, for added texture, add a cluster of dashes above the beak, as shown in Figure 1.4, using the script liner brush.

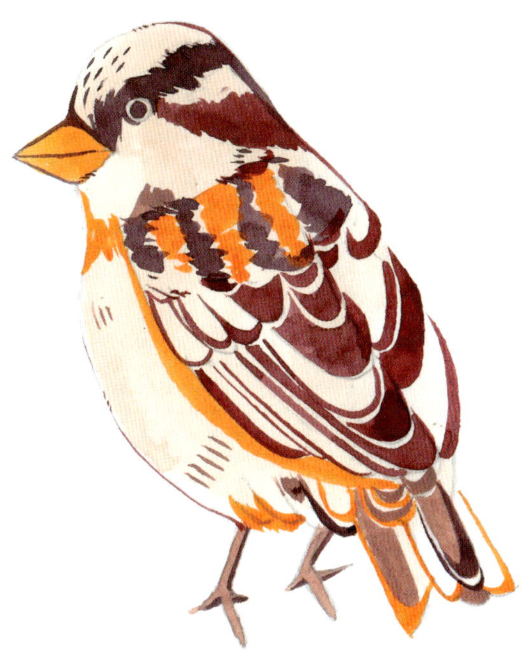

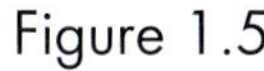

Figure 1.5

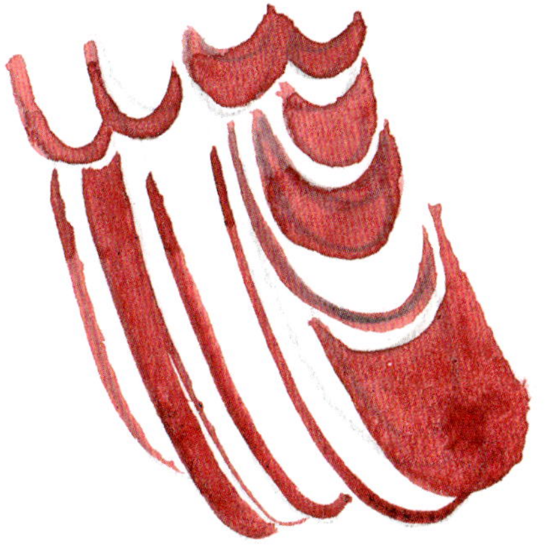

curved shapes for the wing

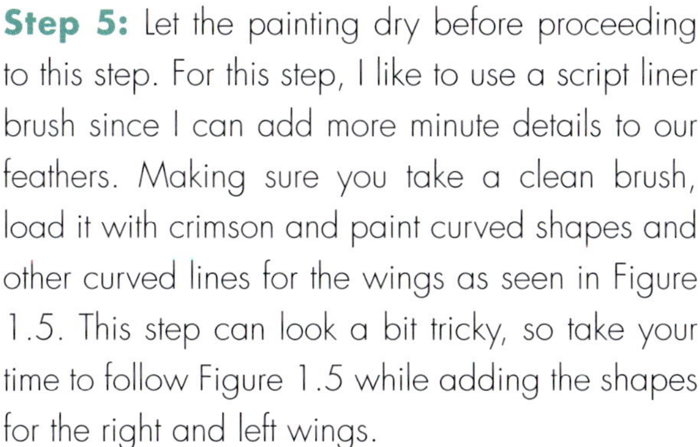

**Step 5:** Let the painting dry before proceeding to this step. For this step, I like to use a script liner brush since I can add more minute details to our feathers. Making sure you take a clean brush, load it with crimson and paint curved shapes and other curved lines for the wings as seen in Figure 1.5. This step can look a bit tricky, so take your time to follow Figure 1.5 while adding the shapes for the right and left wings.

**Pro-Tips:** Start with smaller U-shapes at the top of the wings near the neck and move to longer, deeper U-shapes at the edge of the wings.

For the bottom feathers of the wings, layer them by adding half U-shapes as well.

Using jagged lines from the previous step, add a crimson line from the eye to the back of the head. Allow the painting to dry before moving on to the next step.

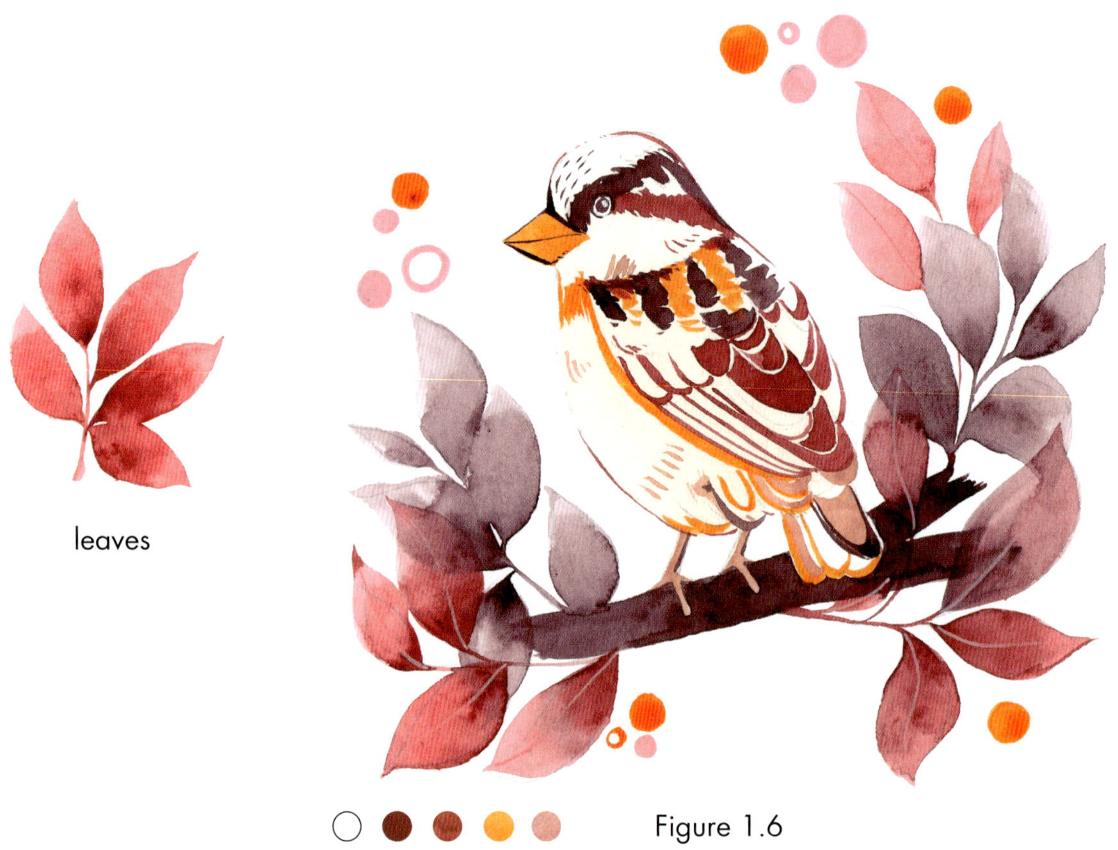


Figure 1.6

**Step 6:** This is the most important step to complete the painting. Let's choose a lovely backdrop that complements the painting.

Before we move to that step, let's add a simple white acrylic dot to the eye using a script liner brush. Make sure the brush is cleaned from the previous steps before loading it with bright white.

For our sparrow, I decided to choose a very simple backdrop with lovely leaves using my round brush. As seen in the Practice Exercises chapter on page 19, draw simple pointed leaves on either side of the branch with a pencil. Next, paint the leaf using the single-color gradient technique. To make the painting more interesting, use both crimson and mahogany to paint your leaves.

While the leaves are drying, add some circles in chrome yellow and shell pink by using a round brush. These circles help balance the painting and give it a cheerful effect.

Next, using a round brush loaded with mahogany, paint the branch for our little birdie to perch on.

Finally, after the leaves have dried, I add a thin white stem line to some of the leaves using a script liner brush loaded with white acrylic paint.

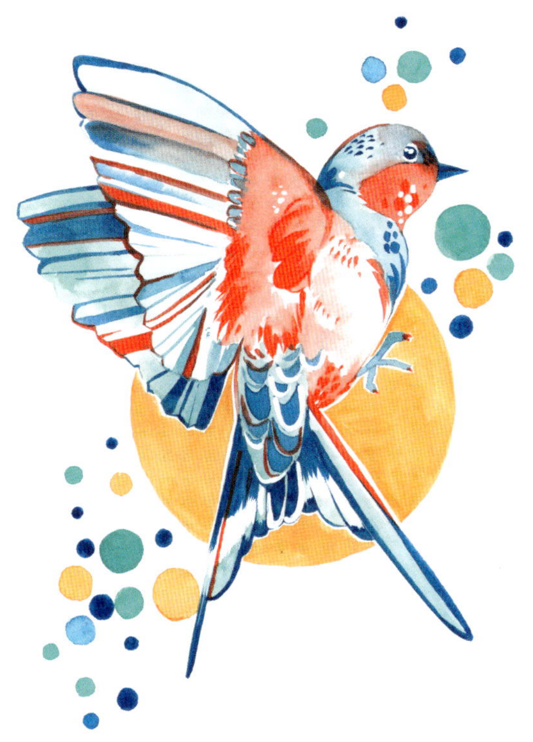

# Barn Swallow

*Swallows are very common in folklore. Swallows were associated with Aphrodite, the goddess of love, and were believed to bring good luck and happiness. From the viewpoint of this painting, we will be adding vibrancy to the swallows by playing with the complementary colors of blue and yellow. This is going to be amazing in bringing your painting to life. I would also suggest taking your time with steps 4 and 5, since we are adding so many details and quirky elements.*

## MATERIALS

Watercolor cold press paper, 200gsm (95lb)
Pencil
Kneadable eraser
Palette
Glass cup
Watercolor mop brush, size 000
Round brush, size 4
Script liner brush, size 0
Tissue paper

## COLOR SCHEME

 Bright Orange

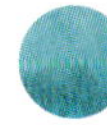 Ultramarine Blue

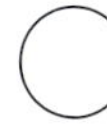 White acrylic paint

 Chrome Yellow

## CHALLENGE LEVEL

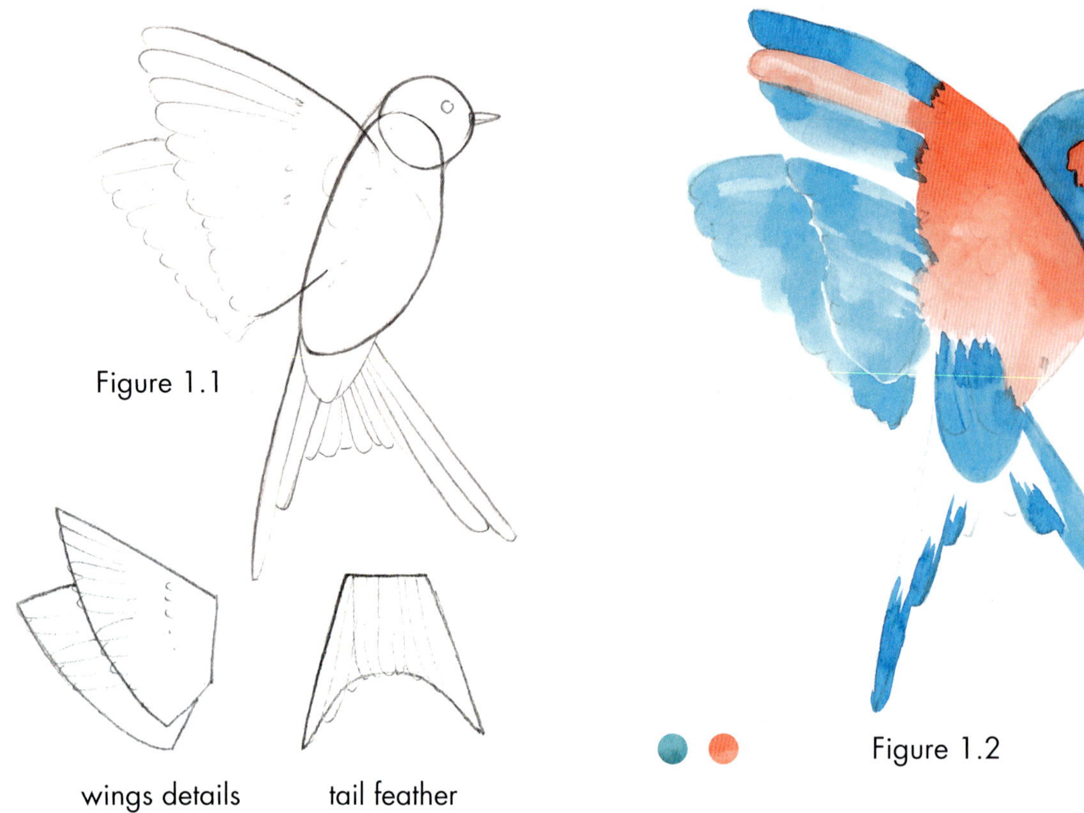


Figure 1.1

Figure 1.2

**Step 1:** Swallows are small birds with prominent forked tails. For this painting, I decided to choose a swallow that is in flight to capture the essence of the bird.

Using a pencil, start your drawing with an elongated egg shape for the bird's body overlapped by a circle for the face. Quickly complete the face with a triangle for the beak. Connect the face and body with curved lines for the neckline. Next, use some quadrilateral shapes for the wings. I like to separate the feathers at the top of the wings. Use U-curves along the wings and tail feathers to complete the drawing.

**Pro-Tip:** Draw longer feathers for the ends of the tail feather to create a forked tail.

Once you have a base drawing as shown in Figure 1.1, erase any darker pencil marks with a kneadable eraser. This is very important because when we paint, it will affect the final painting.

**Step 2:** Let's start with the base colors, ultramarine blue and orange. Use the mop brush to paint the body and the bottom half of the face with a translucent layer of orange. Simply add more water to the paint for this light wash, as shared in the Translucency with Watercolors section on page 16. Use jagged lines along the edges to

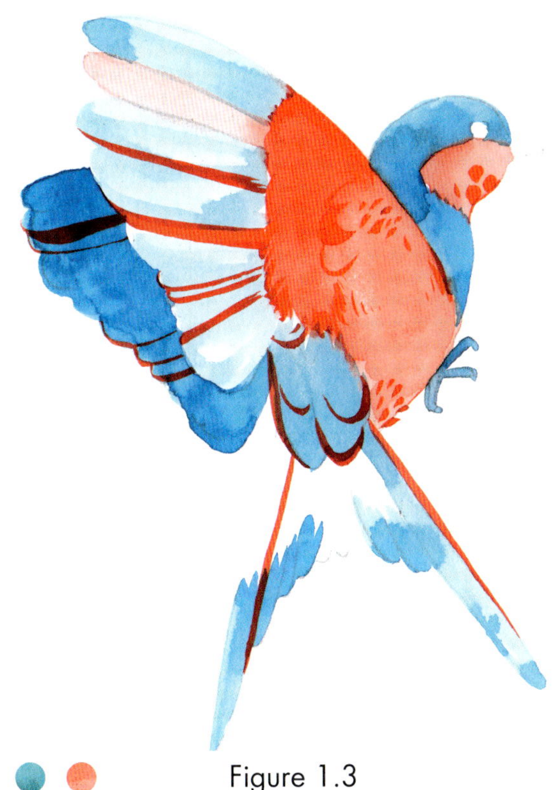

Figure 1.3

create texture within the painting. For the area around the body, use a simple single-color gradient effect as explained in page 19.

Now clean your brush and load it with a watered-down translucent ultramarine blue and paint the bird's head, chest, wings and tail feathers, as seen in Figure 1.2. To prepare a translucent layer of ultramarine blue, simply add more water to the paint as explained in the Translucency with Watercolors section on page 16. Add jagged U-shapes along the edges of the wing feathers.

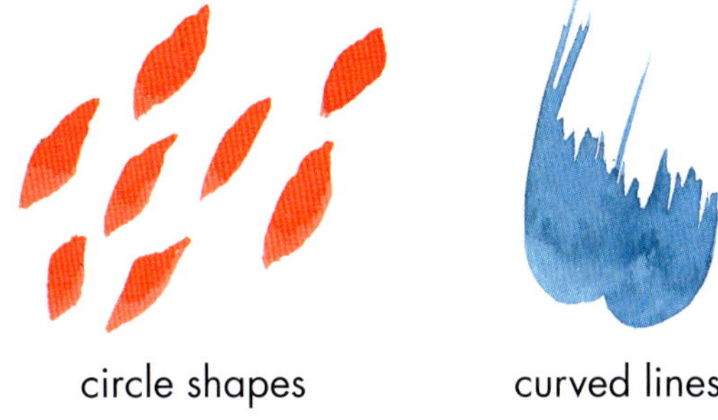


Continue this along the tail feather and the bottom of the bird. Make sure to use jagged lines through the edges of the shape. Add more of the blue along the wings.

Allow the layer to dry before moving on to the next step.

**Pro-Tip:** Paint the back wing slightly darker by using a more saturated ultramarine blue.

**Step 3:** This is my favorite step, adding texture to the painting using a script liner brush. In this step, we are going to be playing with lots of shapes and miniature details using bright orange. Use circle shapes along the bottom of the face, wings and underbelly. Use jagged lines along the edges of the inner wing details. Add curved lines along the tail feathers, and outline the wing feathers and forked tail.

Bring all these together for a textured painting as seen in Figure 1.3.

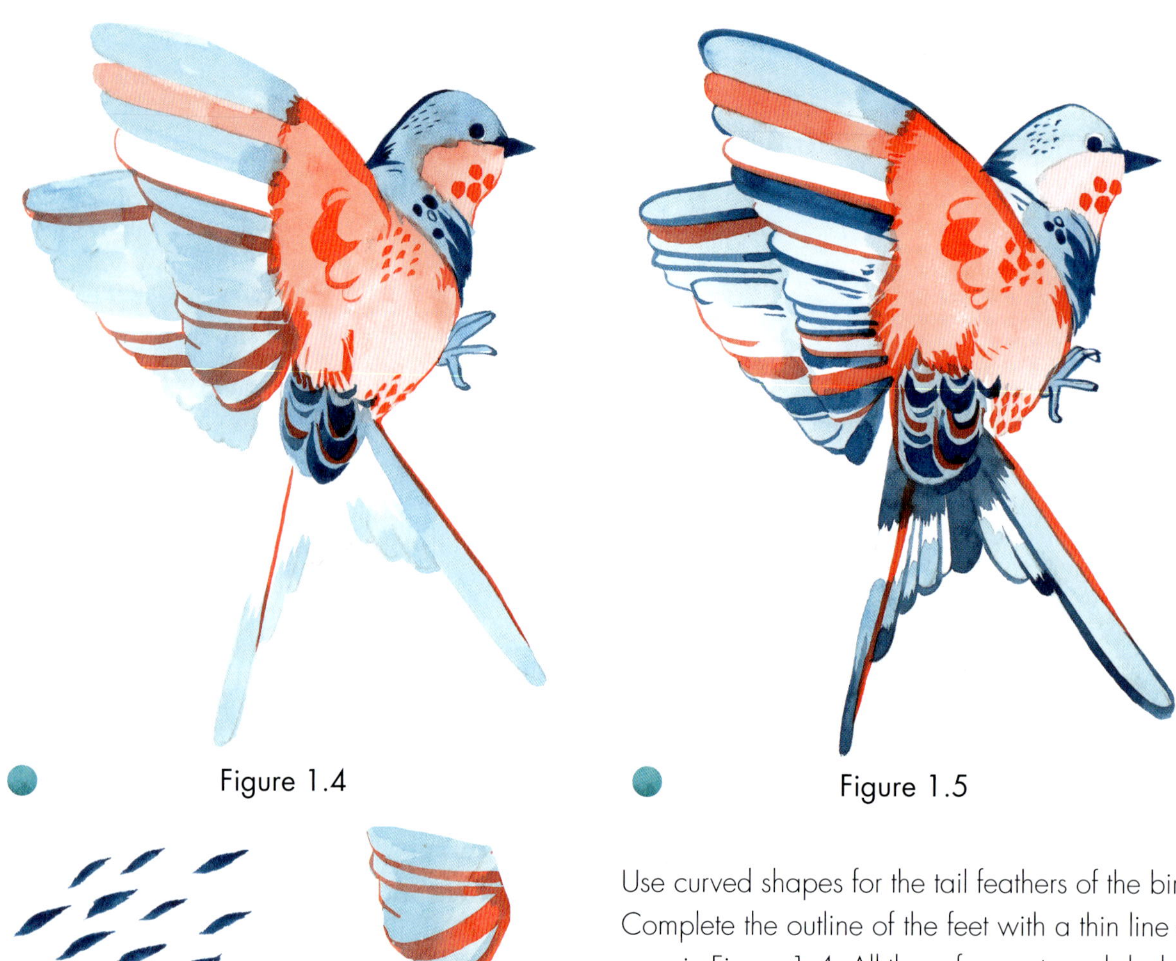

Figure 1.4

Figure 1.5

indigo details

wing details

**Step 4:** In this step, we are going to add ultramarine blue textures on the body by using a script liner brush. Make sure to wash your brush of the orange used in the previous step and load it with blue. First, add jagged details at the bird's chest. Then, add an outline for the top of the head, eye and beak. Add in some ultramarine blue dashed details for the top of the head.

Use curved shapes for the tail feathers of the bird. Complete the outline of the feet with a thin line as seen in Figure 1.4. All these fun spots and dashed texture will add to the painting and really bring it to life.

**Step 5:** Let's add finishing touches to the swallow by completing the wings of the bird with a round brush using ultramarine blue. The trick here is to use a random approach that plays with filling the entire feather shape, skipping some of the feathers and using simple outlines for the rest. This gives it an interesting effect.

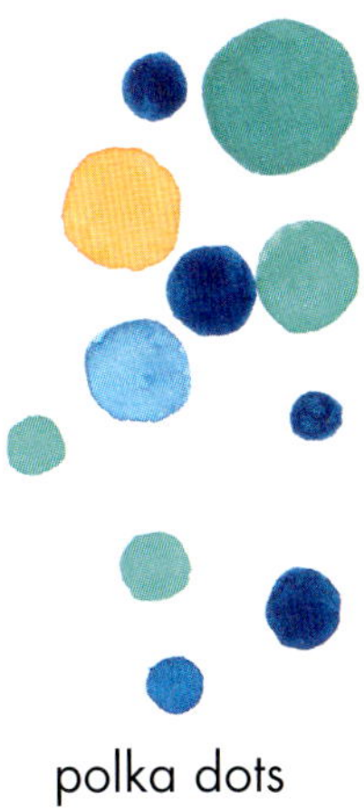

polka dots

Add jagged lines to the tail feathers. Paint each feather one at a time, only at the top and bottom of the tail feather. Make sure to keep the space in the middle blank.

Overall, you should have a lovely swallow as shown in Figure 1.5.

Allow the painting to dry before moving on to adding white acrylic details and the backdrop.

**Step 6:** Our final step for painting the swallow is to add the white acrylic details for the eye with a script liner brush. Make sure that the brush is clean of any other color before loading it with white. I like to add some white spots below the face and the inner wing for more texture.

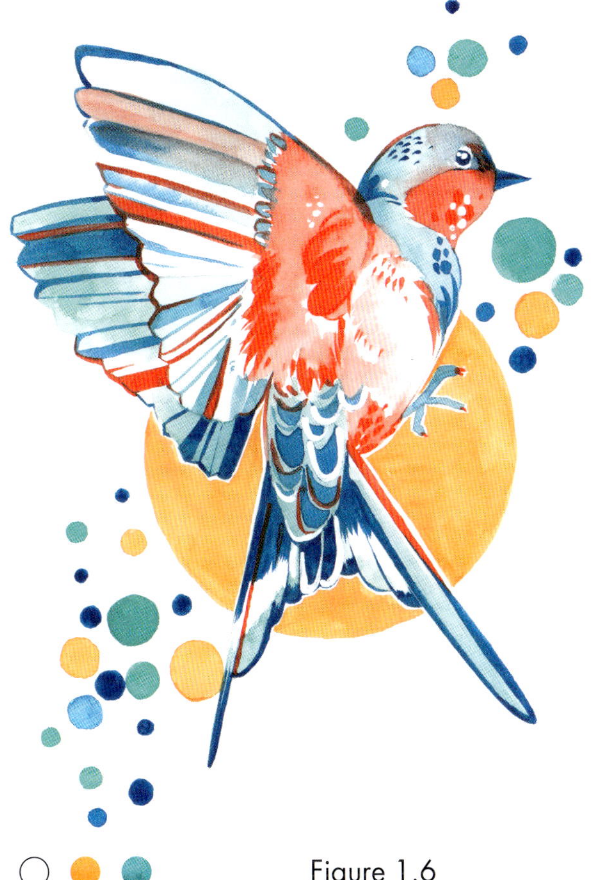

Figure 1.6

Finally, for a simple background, add a bright complementary chrome yellow with a round brush. Make sure that you wash the brush before loading with chrome yellow. Try to leave a small gap between the background circle and the bird as seen in Figure 1.6. The gap adds to the final composition. Finally, add some fun circles around the bird for a complete frame-worthy painting. I make sure to balance the circles on either side as seen in the Figure 1.6.

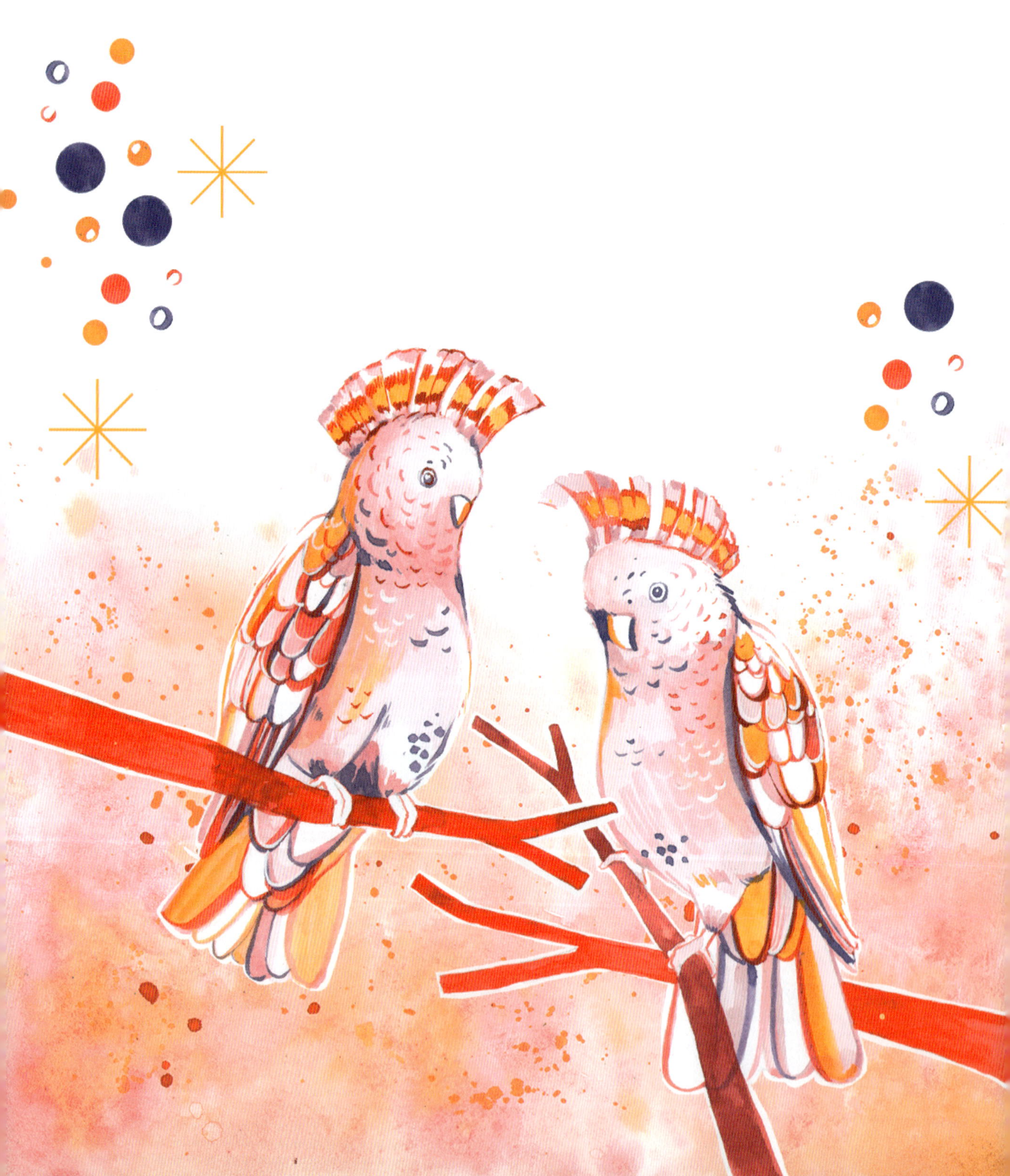

# Tropical Birds

There is so much to say about tropical birds. These are the birds that symbolize vacation to me. Every time I even think of parrots, I imagine being in some exotic place, while toucans remind me of rainforests. I can't get enough of these birds, and I am sure you are as thrilled as I am for this specific chapter.

As an artist, I love painting tropical birds because they are just so pretty to capture. I love mixing the bright colors of their plumage with a simple background to highlight the composition.

We will start our chapter with toco toucans on page 62; these are the easiest to paint since they are mainly black with a vibrant beak. Next, we will be painting two beautiful parrot varieties—the scarlet parrot on page 66 and the smaller military macaw on page 71. These beautiful birds are striking and bold and choosing colors to complement the composition will take a bit of exploration. Next we will be painting cockatoos on page 77. Pink cockatoos are stunning and one of my favorite birds to paint. I especially love capturing their features through an array of colors, textures and shapes. Next, we will be painting kingfishers on page 82 and experimenting with complementary colors. These bright-spirited birds have captured the hearts of many, and now it's time for us to paint our version.

Finally, to end the chapter on a high note, we will be painting cute budgie parakeets on page 86. These sparks of pure excitement are just such a joy to paint. They also include a couple of interesting textures and hence are labeled as an intermediate level project.

Talking about colors, let's take our brightest set of paints and get started.

# Toco Toucan

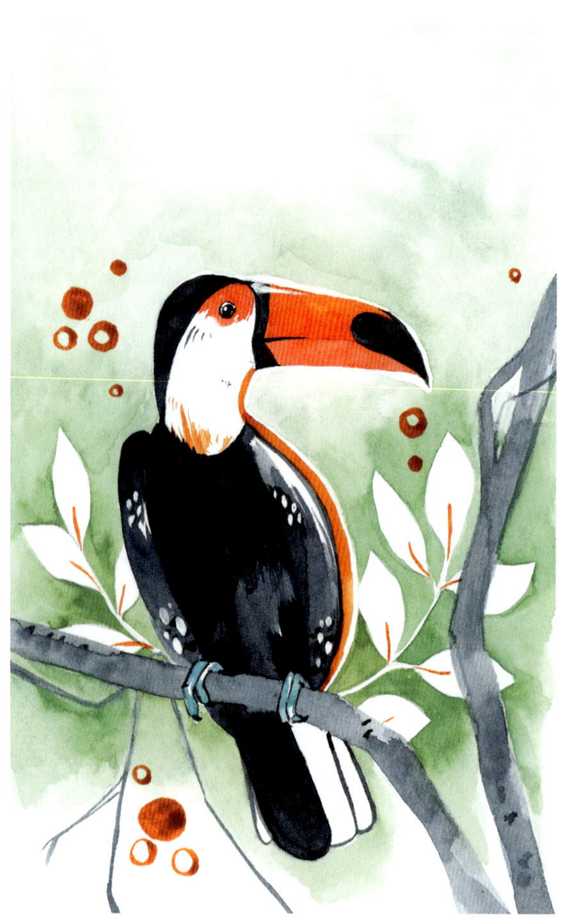

*These lovely ivory black birds with their bright orange beaks can be easily spotted anywhere in rainforests. Toco toucans are the largest and most well-known toucan species. In terms of painting, toucans can be slightly more difficult to paint because they are black. Another aspect is to ensure that the background doesn't overpower the painting. If we choose the wrong color, it could make the painting dull. Hence, we need to plan the color scheme carefully.*

## MATERIALS

Watercolor cold press paper, 200gsm (95lb)
Pencil
Kneadable eraser
Palette
Glass cup
Watercolor mop brush, size 000
Round brush, size 4
Script liner brush, size 0
Tissue paper

## CHALLENGE LEVEL

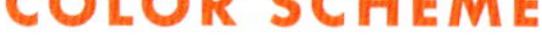

## COLOR SCHEME

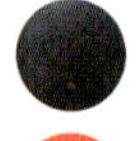 Ivory Black

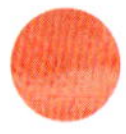 Bright Orange

 Chrome Yellow

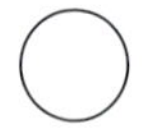 White acrylic paint

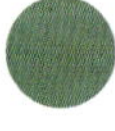 Sea Foam Green (can be made by adding a dash of White watercolor paint to Hunter's Green)

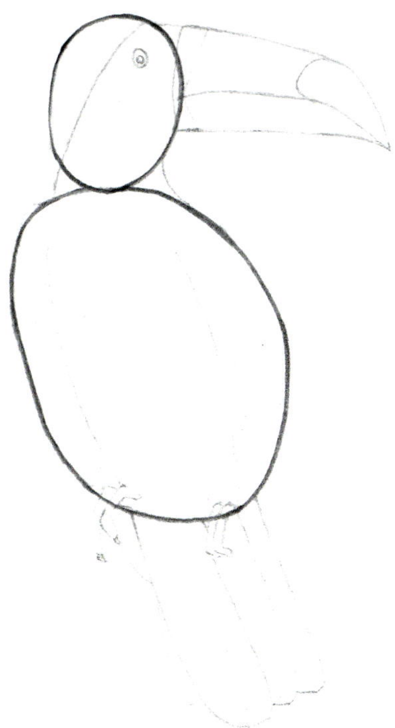

Figure 1.1

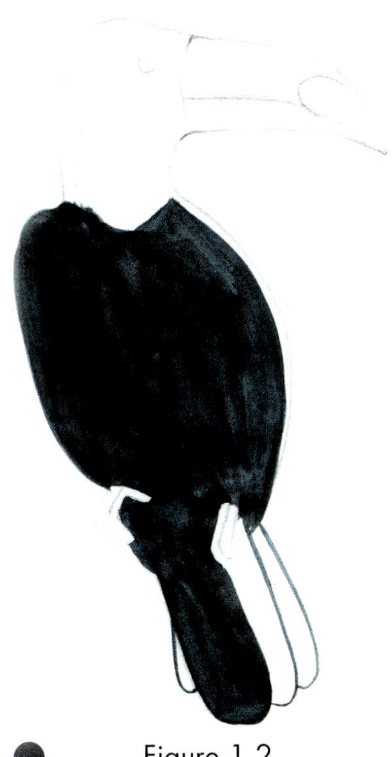

Figure 1.2

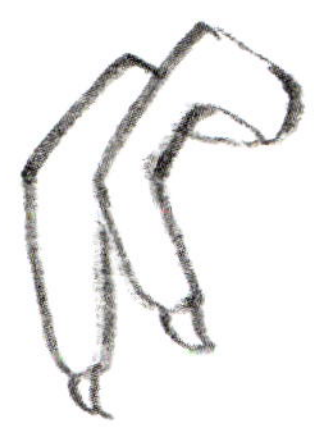

feet drawing

**Step 1:** Drawing toucans is fairly simple. With a pencil, start with an oval for the face of the bird and a larger oval shape for the body of the bird. Next, add a big, elongated beak. Add the eye and a line across the face for the top part of the head. Now for the bottom part of the body—draw in the feet details as shown in the highlight image. Then, complete the tail of the bird with long U-shapes. Erase any darker lines with a kneadable eraser so that it doesn't affect the final painting as we move on to painting our first layer.

**Step 2:** Let's start painting our first layer of the bird by using a round brush. This is a very easy step. Simply paint a translucent layer of black for the body of the bird. This light wash can be created by mixing more water into the paint as explained in the Translucency with Watercolors section on page 16. With the same brush, outline the bird's tail feathers.

Allow the layer to dry before moving on to the next step.

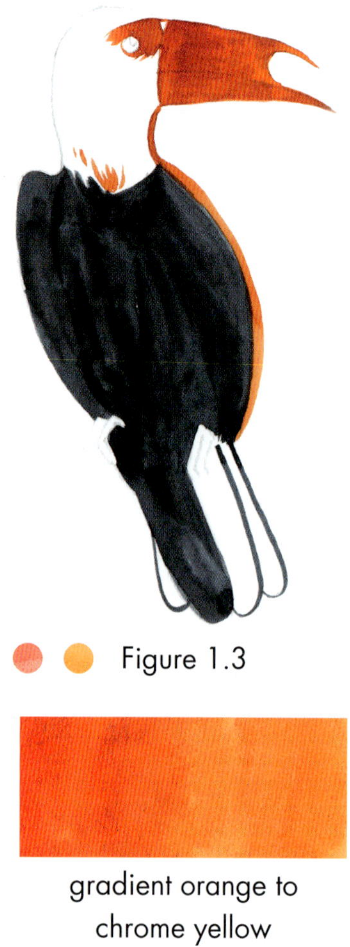


Figure 1.3

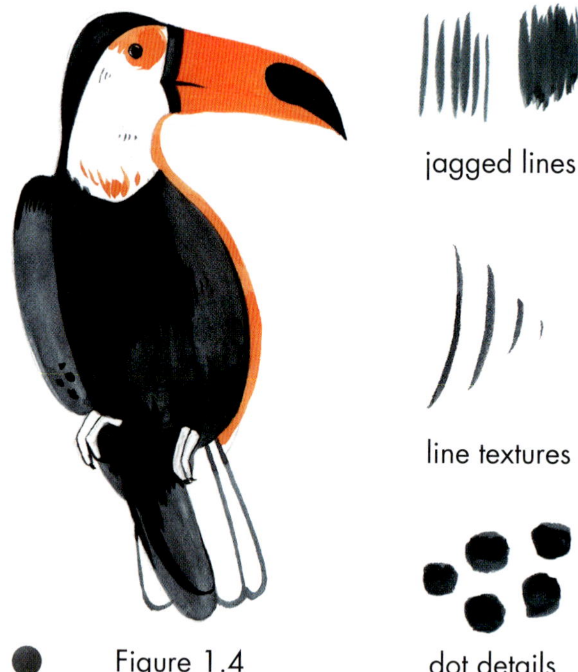


Figure 1.4

**Step 3:** In this step, let's add orange and yellow details for the bird using a script liner brush for better control. Start with loading your clean brush with bright orange and paint the beak and the eye. For the beak, I like to use a dual-color gradient of bright orange to chrome yellow as explored in the Practice Exercises chapter on page 19. Make sure to wash your brush completely before loading it with a new color. That way, the colors remain vibrant and not mucky. Next, paint some simple jagged lines along the neckline. Finally, paint the outline of the bird along one side. This outline creates the effect of shadow and depth. Allow the layer to dry before moving on.

**Step 4:** In this step, we are going to add more depth to the black part of the bird using your script liner brush. We will be using a saturated layer of ivory black. Before loading the brush, make sure to wash it of any previously used colors. Now, for the second layer of ivory black, use jagged lines along the left shoulder, the body and the tail feathers, as seen in Figure 1.4. I also like to add some spot textures for wing feathers.

Next we can paint the eye, top of the head and small parallel lines around the face. Complete the beak shape by filling in the remaining areas and the middle line. You can paint the bird's feet whatever color you'd like (I chose a bright blue). Allow the layer to dry before moving on to the next step.

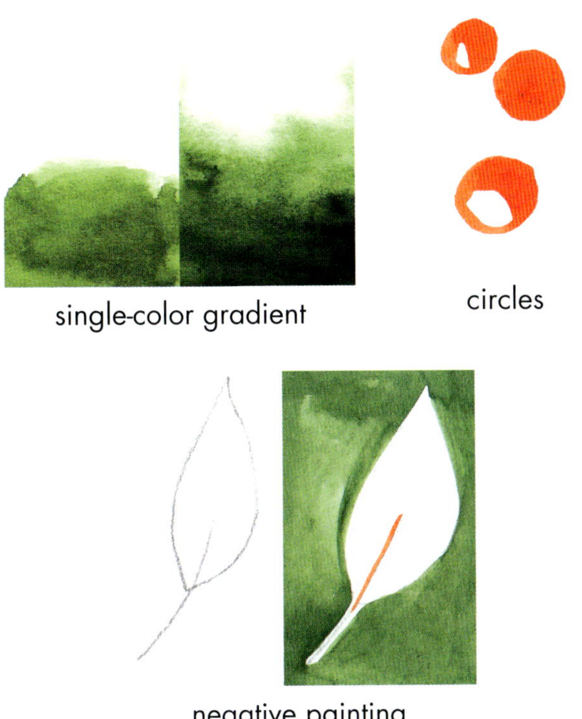


**Step 5:** Let's complete the painting by adding the background. Before that, it is important to add white acrylic details for the bird by using the script liner brush. Make sure to wash it before dabbing it in white acrylic paint. Now, add dots for the eye and a cluster of spots for the wings of the bird.

For the background, let's try a different technique. Instead of painting inside the leaf, let's paint around it. This is also known as the negative painting technique. To start, draw the branch and the leaves around the bird lightly, using a pencil. I like to draw large leaves to balance out the thin branch. Next, use the mop brush loaded with sea foam green to paint around the leaves and the branch to create an effect as seen in the highlight image. So that we aren't left with a flat sea-foam green wash, clean your brush and glide it along

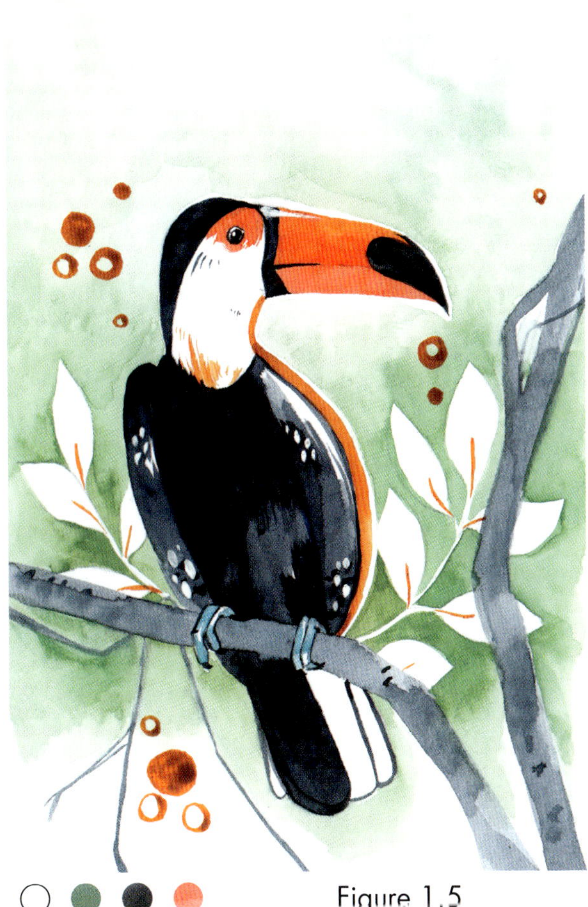

Figure 1.5

the edge of the sea foam line. This will create a single gradient effect (see Practice Exercises chapter, page 19).

Allow this effect to completely dry before loading your round brush with some ivory black to paint the branches. Finally, switch the color in the brush by cleaning out the black paint and loading it with bright orange. Use bright orange to add circles around the bird and to add thin stems to the inner leaves.

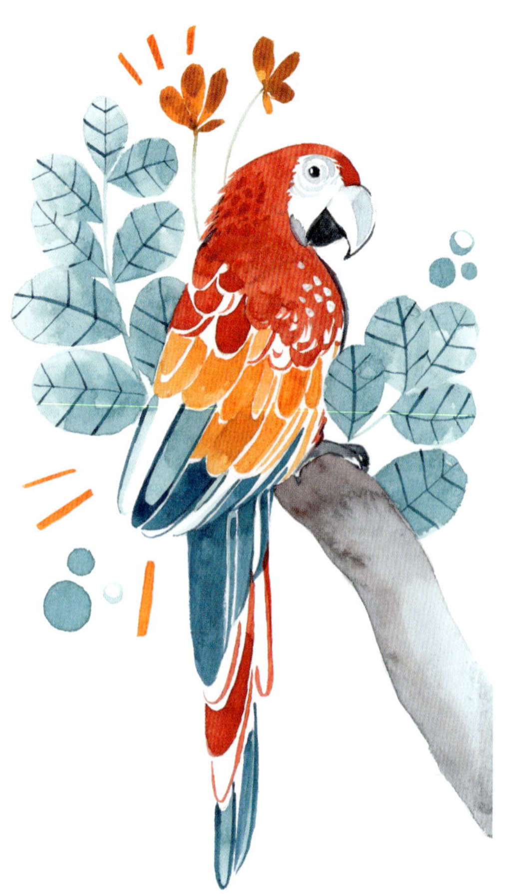

# Scarlet Parrot

*In a book about watercolor birds, parrots are a must! I love the fact that these birds talk and are also in every pirate movie. Full of color, these birds can be fairly simple to paint. However, let's keep in mind to compose a simple background to complement this brilliant bird. Also, since we will be switching colors often, be sure to always clean your brush before loading it with a new color to avoid muddy colors.*

## MATERIALS

Watercolor cold press paper, 200gsm (95lb)
Pencil
Kneadable eraser
Palette
Glass cup
Round brush, size 4
Script liner brush, size 0
Tissue paper

## COLOR SCHEME

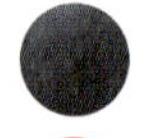 Ivory Black

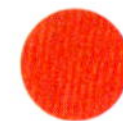 Scarlet Red

Chrome Yellow

 Ultramarine Blue

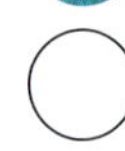 White acrylic paint

## CHALLENGE LEVEL

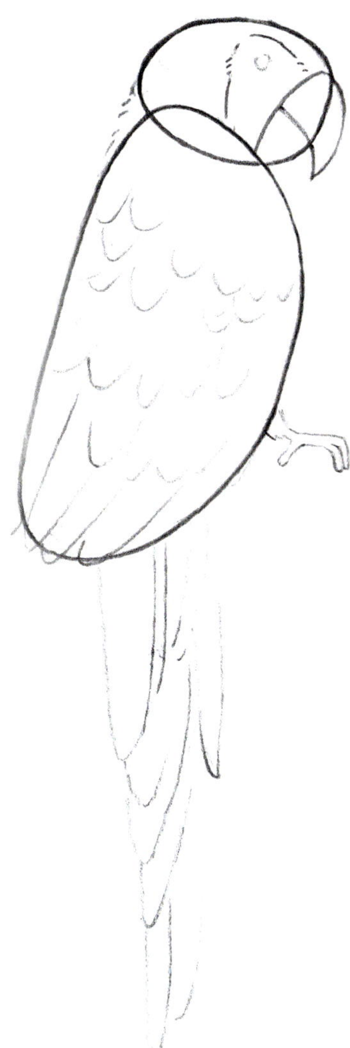

Figure 1.1

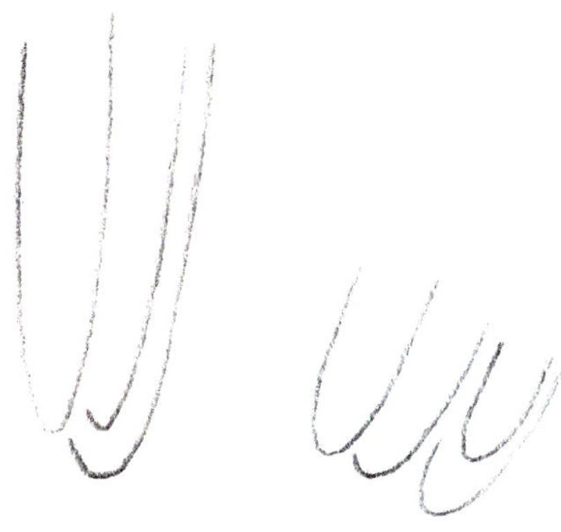

U-curve feather details

U-curves for the bird's wings

**Step 1:** Let's start by drawing our base for the parrot by using a pencil. Draw an oval for the body of the parrot. Next, draw an overlapping oval shape for the face. Connect the two shapes with rugged lines to represent the neckline. Let's go ahead and add the eye, as well as the curved beak.

Complete the body of the parrot by drawing the feet. Finally, add in the lovely, curved details for the wings of the bird, as well as the tail feathers. Use U-curves as seen in the highlight image for the feather details.

**Pro-Tip:** Use small U-curves at the shoulder and longer U-curves at the end of the wings as seen in Figure 1.1.

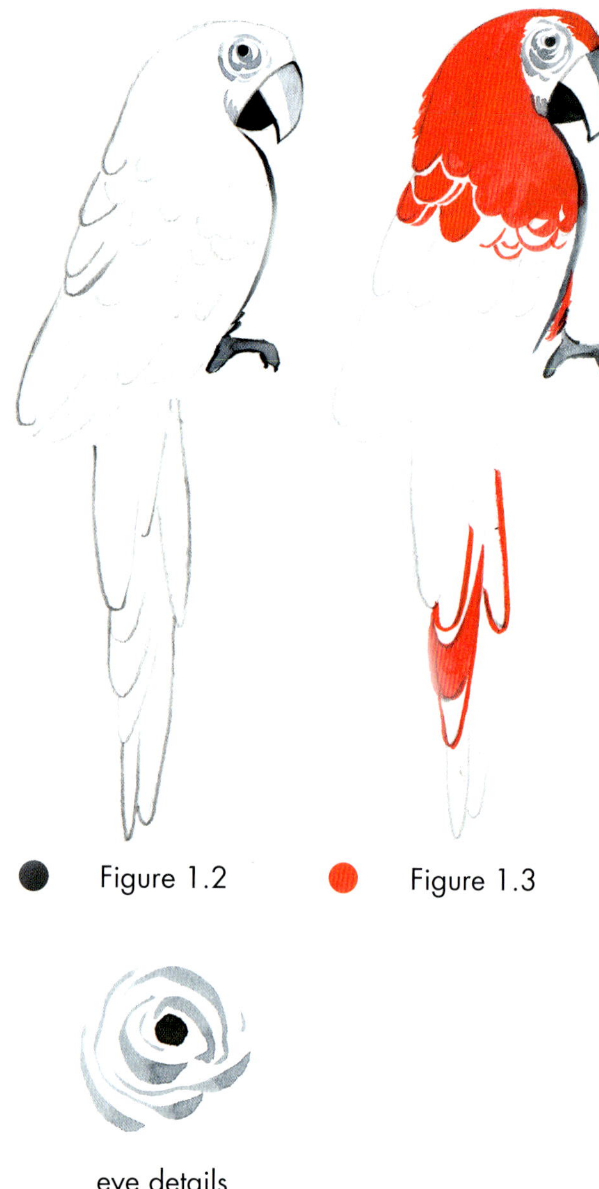

Figure 1.2

Figure 1.3

eye details

**Step 2:** For this step, let's paint our eye details for the parrot. Using a script liner brush, prepare a translucent wash of ivory black by using more water. This is further explained in the Translucency with Watercolors section on page 16. Focus on the eye details first, as seen in the highlight image. Paint in the circle for the eye and then the broken curved lines around the eye.

Use ivory black for the beak. For the top beak, use a translucent black wash and for the bottom beak, use an opaque saturated wash. Paint the outline for the bird and the feet as well. Since we are using a script liner, it will be easy to control when adding these fine lines. Allow the layer to dry before moving on to the next step.

**Step 3:** In this step, we are going to paint the top of the face and the tail feathers using scarlet red. For the top of the head and the top half of the body, paint the entire shape using a round brush. Be sure to use scalloped edges for a feathery look. Then, paint in the curve shapes for the feathers and outline for some of the feathers. Balance the two out as seen in Figure 1.3. Use the same technique for the tail feathers. Paint the outlines and some curved U-shapes for the feathers.

**Pro-Tip:** There is no fixed way to choose which feathers to paint and which to outline, so follow a random approach. This gives the painting a relaxed look.

Allow this layer to dry before moving on to the next step.

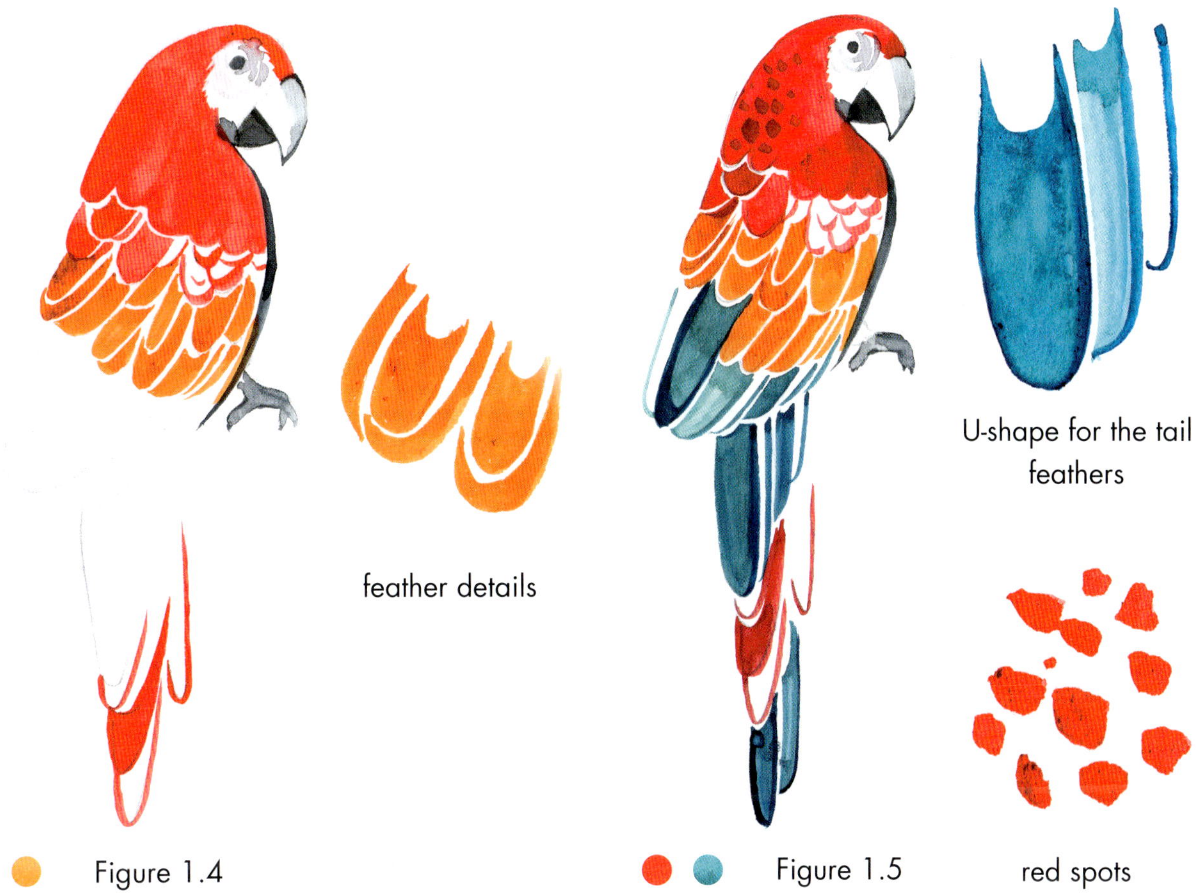


Figure 1.4

Figure 1.5

**Step 4:** In this step, we are going to dive into painting chrome yellow shapes for the feathers using the script liner brush. Make sure to wash your script liner of the ivory black from step 2 before loading it with chrome yellow. As seen in the highlight image, fill in the feather shapes in the middle of the wings. I like to keep a small gap between the feather shapes so that the white of the paper can be seen through. Allow the layer to dry before moving on to the next step.

**Step 5:** This is one of final steps in the painting of our scarlet parrot. Let's start with adding some scarlet spots to the bird's head to add texture to the painting, using the script liner brush. Be sure to wash the brush before dabbing it with scarlet red.

Then, wash your brush and load it with ultramarine blue to paint in the remaining feather areas and the tail feathers. I like to mix between filling in the shapes with a U-shape as well as U-shaped outlines. Mixing the two gives an asymmetrical effect, as you can see. Allow this layer to dry before moving on to the next step.

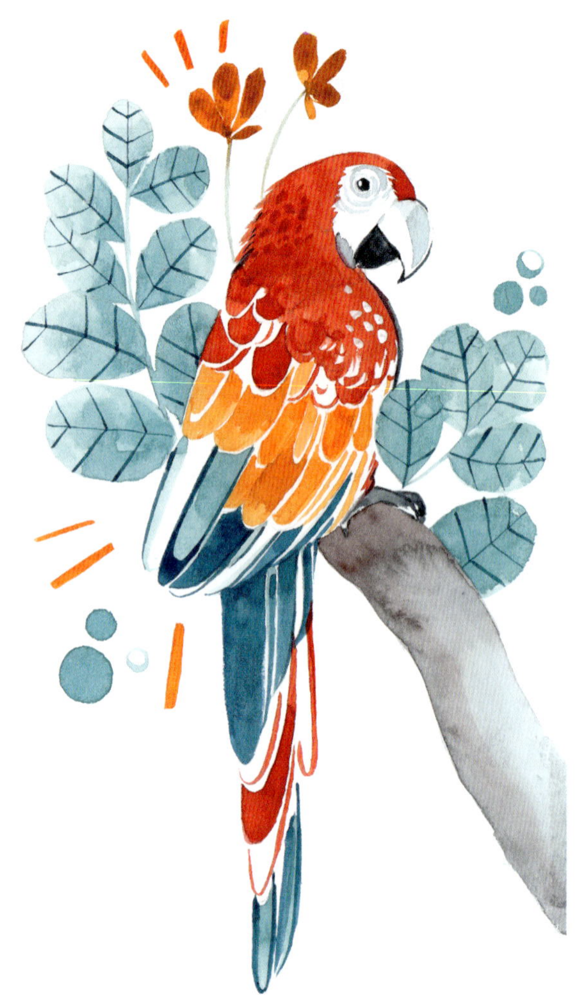

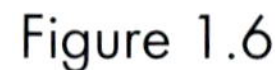

Figure 1.6

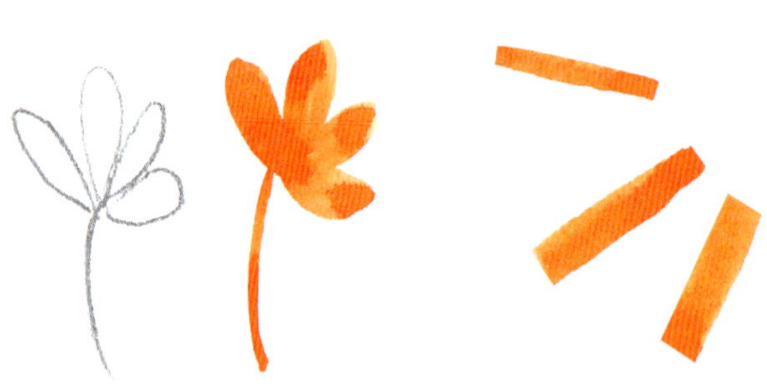

flower details

line details

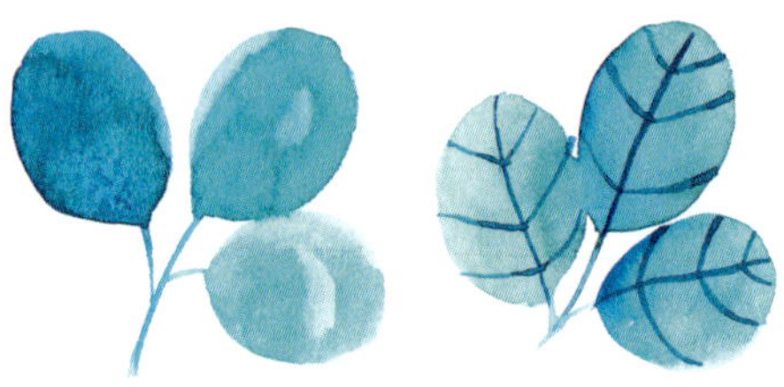

leaves

**Step 6:** Let's use white acrylic paint to add more details, such as some eye reflective spots and some more spotted textures along the shoulder of the bird. This is all done with a script liner brush for easier control.

Then to complete our painting, add branches, leaves and lovely flowers using a round brush. Start by painting the branch for the parrot to perch on using ivory black. I have used a single gradient effect along the branch, as shared in the Practice Exercises chapter on page 19. Next, add some chrome yellow flower details. I like to lightly draw the flowers first by using a pencil. Make sure you wash your round brush before loading it with chrome yellow and filling in the flower shapes and simple line details.

Next, wash your brush again and load it with ultramarine blue to paint some rounded leaves. Here, you can use a single-color gradient effect, as seen in the Practice Exercises chapter on page 19. Now allow the layer to dry completely before using a script liner brush to add the thin stem lines. You can add some fun circles as well.

**Pro-Tip:** Try to cluster the elements on the right and left sides to balance the composition. If the elements are only on either side, it can make the painting look unbalanced.

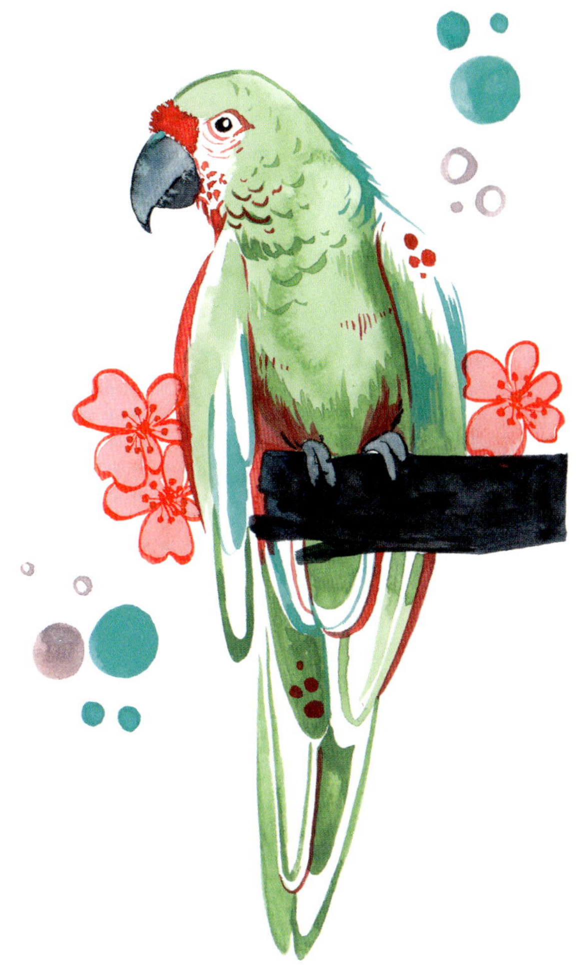

# Military Macaw

*Another gorgeous bird you must paint is the military macaw. Green, with a mix of bright blue and yellow, this bird is an array of colors. Macaws in general are very colorful—the hyacinth macaw is a mix of cobalt blue with yellow; the military macaw is a mix of green, ultramarine blue and yellow; the Catalina macaw is bright orange, ultramarine blue and green. Once you have learned to paint one variety, you can switch colors to paint the other varieties as well. So, let's dive right in and paint our military macaw using our own custom colors. In this tutorial, try to ensure that the base drawing really captures the proportions of the bird. This will lead to an amazing final result.*

## MATERIALS

Watercolor cold press paper, 200gsm (95lb)
Pencil
Kneadable eraser
Palette
Glass cup
Round brush, size 4
Script liner brush, size 0
Tissue paper

## COLOR SCHEME

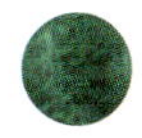 Hunter's Green

 Turquoise Blue (can be made by mixing Ultramarine Blue with a dash of White watercolor paint)

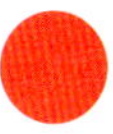 Scarlet Red

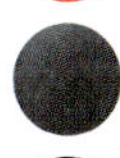 Ivory Black

 White acrylic paint

## CHALLENGE LEVEL

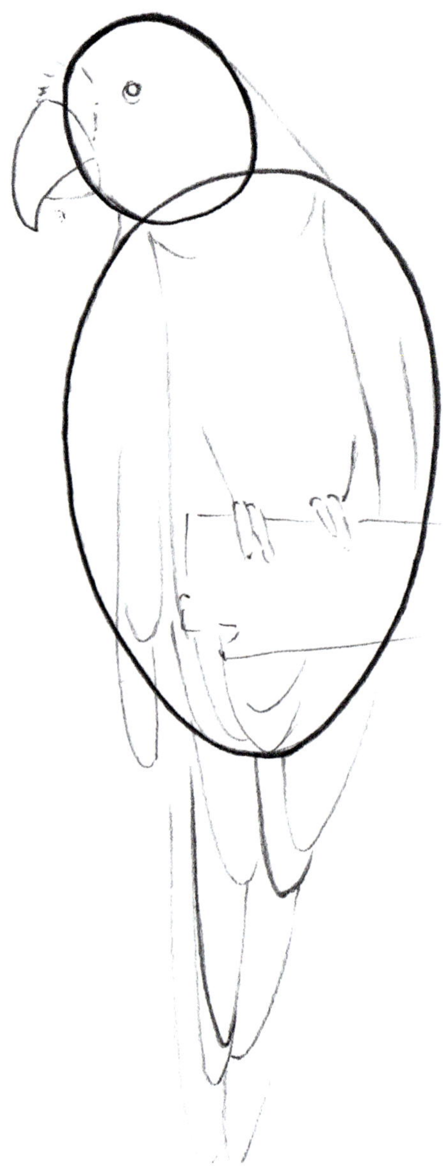

Figure 1.1

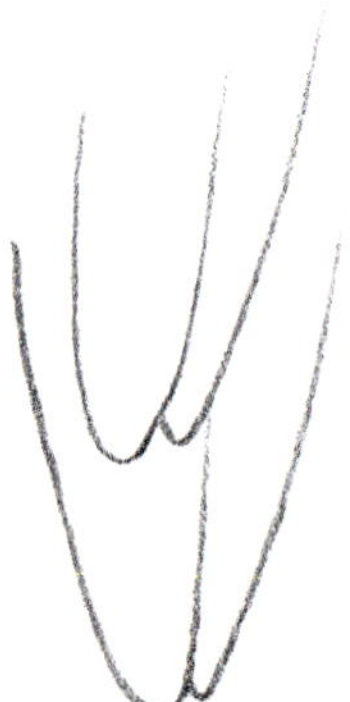

curved U-shape drawing for the tail feathers

**Step 1:** Let's start drawing the base for the macaw with a pencil. Use an inverted egg shape for the body of the bird and a simple oval shape for the face of the bird. Next, connect the two with a curved shape for the neck. Keep in mind to overlap the two shapes to give the macaw a cuter look. Add in the face details of the curved beak and the eye. For the body of the bird, draw the feet and the side wings. Keep in mind to add in the branch for the macaw to perch on.

Finally, complete the tail details with simple U-shapes. Start with shorter, more rounded shapes and continue with longer and much more pointed shapes as seen in Figure 1.1.

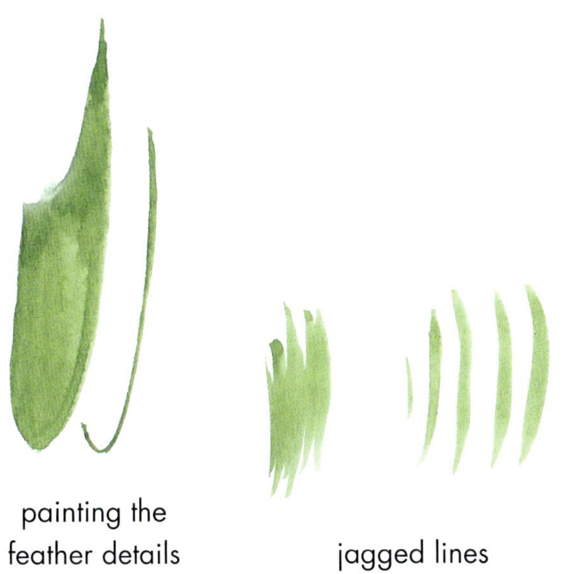

painting the feather details

jagged lines

**Step 2:** After erasing any harsh pencil lines from the previous step with a kneadable eraser, let's start painting our first layer for the bird. Use a round brush loaded with a watered-down, translucent hunter's green paint, which has been explained in Translucency with Watercolors on page 16. Then, paint the body of the bird and the face using jagged lines for the edges, as seen in Figure 1.2. Now let's add outlines for the tail feathers. Fill in some of the U-shapes for some of the tail feathers. I like to keep the cheek and shoulder empty. These white spaces add to the painting. Allow the layer to dry completely before moving on to step 3.

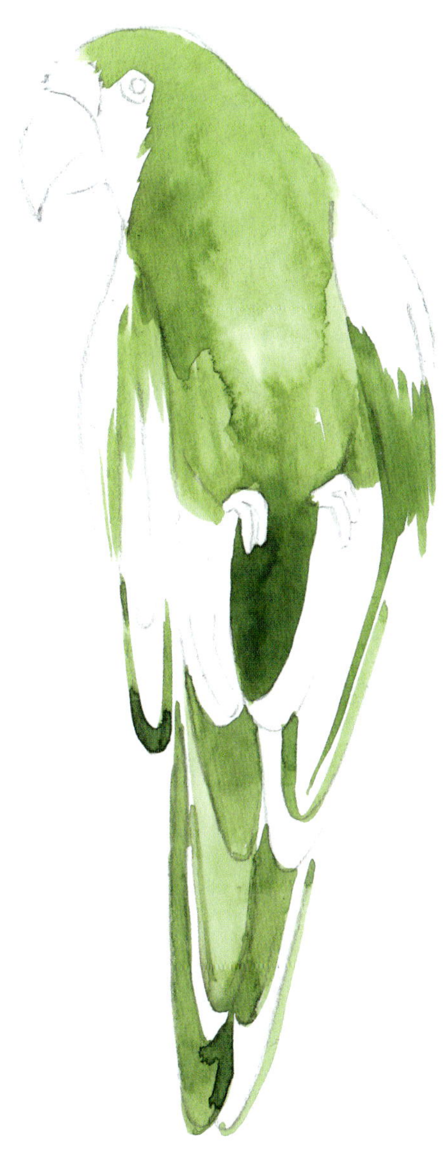

Figure 1.2

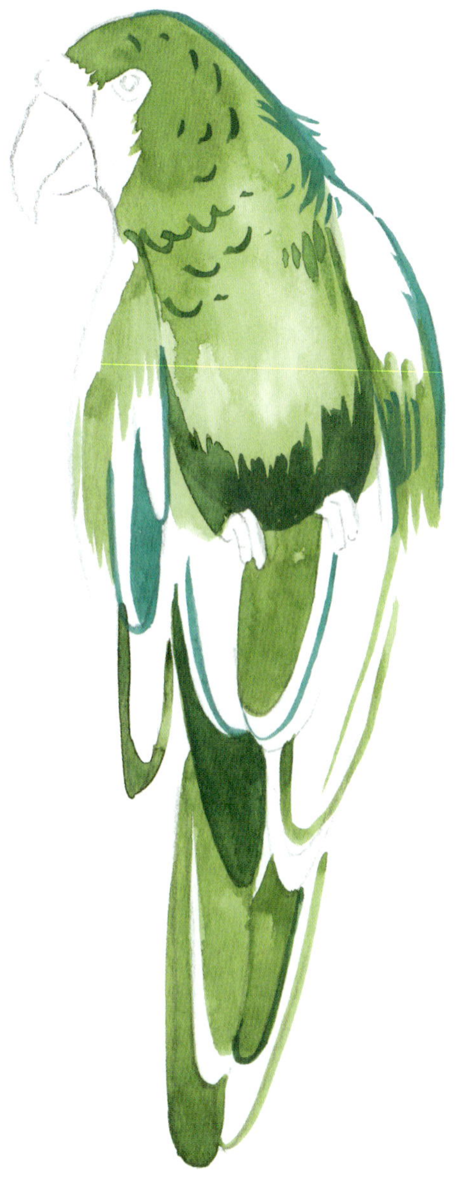

Figure 1.3

curved shape textures

**Step 3:** Here we will be adding more details for the bird. Start with a saturated layer of hunter's green using a round brush. This adds depth to the painting. First, add curved lines to the face around the eye. Add some jagged lines at the under belly and the neckline. Paint in the shape and outline of the tail feathers.

After cleaning your brush, load it with turquoise blue. Turquoise blue can be created as shared in the color scheme section at the start of the project. Use this lovely color to outline the edge of the macaw along the right side. Use bright blue along the outline and inner wing shape. Allow this layer to dry before moving on to the next step.

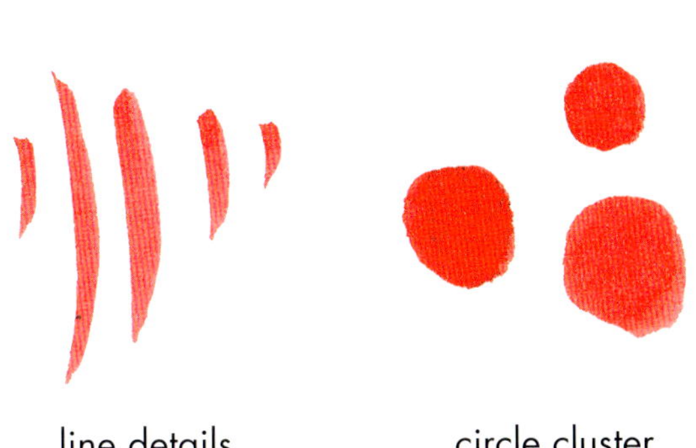


**Step 4:** In this step, we are going to dive into adding lovely scarlet red details by using a script liner brush. Start with the face detail by painting the area above the beak. Move on to adding curved lines for the eye and the lower face textures. I like to start with smaller curves near the chin and larger curves near the cheeks.

Now for the body, use line details for the body and the underbelly with a loaded script liner brush.

**Pro-Tip:** To create an interesting effect, paint parallel lines from short to long to short again.

Next, outline some of the main feathers and add circle clusters at the shoulders and tail feathers as seen in Figure 1.4.

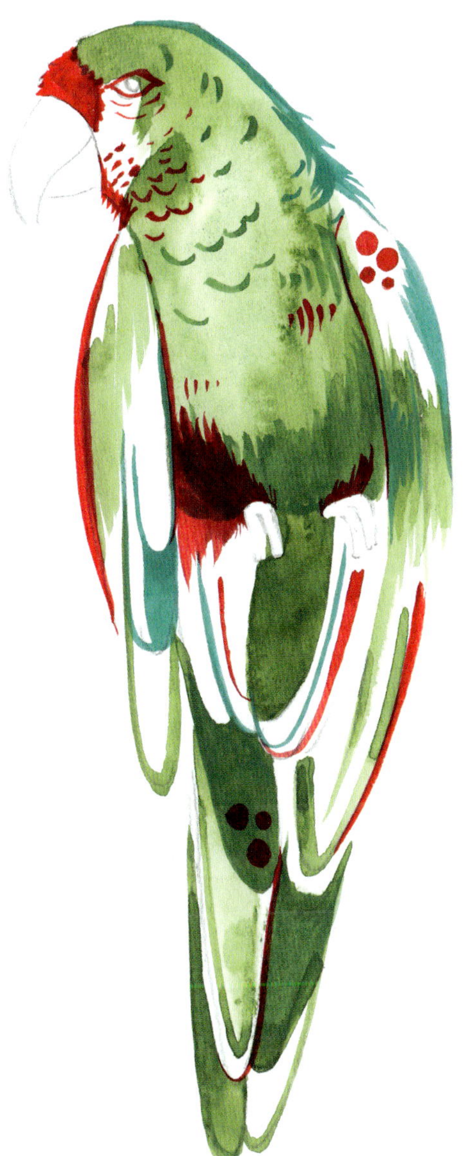

Figure 1.4

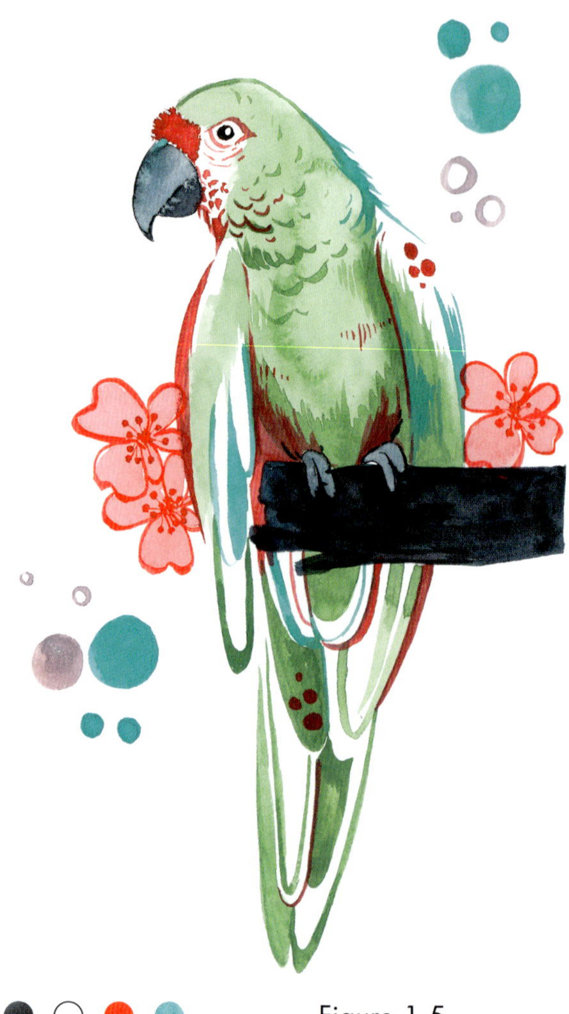

Figure 1.5

**Step 5:** Allow the layer to dry before going ahead and completing the painting. Start by painting the beak, the feet, the eye and the branch on which the bird perches, using the script liner brush loaded with ivory black. Next, wash the black from your script liner brush and load it with white acrylic paint. Once the eye is dry, go ahead and add one white spot for the eye reflection.

**Pro-Tip:** Always wash your brush before loading it with a new color to avoid the colors turning murky and dull.

To complete the background, add in some lovely flowers from the Practice Exercises chapter on page 19. Make sure you wash out the black paint from your brush before loading it with a watered-down translucent wash of scarlet red. Paint the base of the flowers. Allow the layer to dry before going in with a script liner brush loaded with scarlet red to paint the outline and the center filament for the flower. To balance the turquoise blue in the painting, add some circles around the bird by using your script liner brush.

**Pro-Tip:** Cluster multiple circles to balance the painting. Use some turquoise, as well as some diluted scarlet mixed with a dash of turquoise for the colors. Also play with small and big circles to avoid a symmetrical look.

# Pink Cockatoo

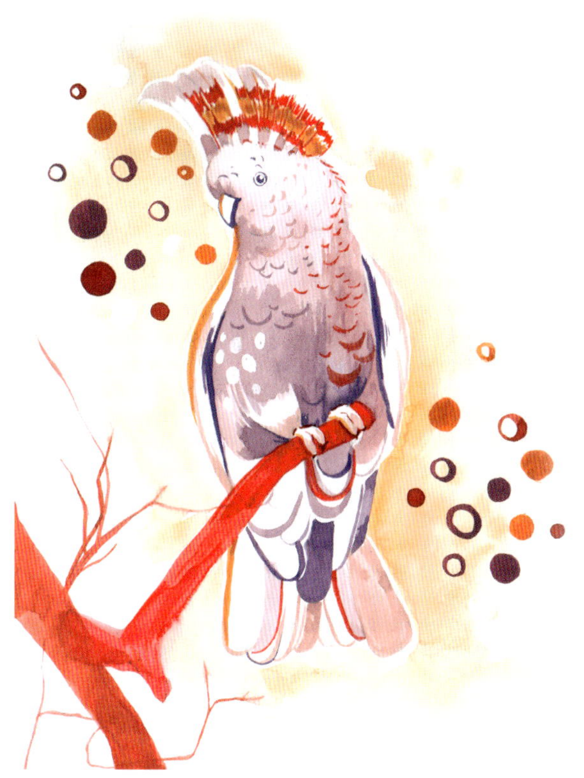

*Cockatoos are stand-out birds that are known for their pinkish color. The word cockatoo has its origins in Malay and means 'vice' or 'grip' because of their incredibly strong beak. I have always seen these lovely birds in either pink or yellow. Interestingly enough, they can also be seen in different colors, like black or brown.*

*I remember sitting on a stool in the zoo trying to take as many pictures as I could of these birds. They are so pretty that they stand out from every angle. What is also interesting is their unique shape because of the tuft of feathers on their head.*

*I am so excited to dive into this project since it is one of my favorites from the entire book. Pay attention in step 3 as we add texture to the bird. It's a really interesting step and can be part of the fun.*

## MATERIALS

Watercolor cold press paper, 200gsm (95lb)
Pencil
Kneadable eraser
Palette
Glass cup
Watercolor mop brush, size 000
Round brush, size 4
Script liner brush, size 0
Tissue paper

## CHALLENGE LEVEL

## COLOR SCHEME

Lavender (can be made by mixing Ultramarine Purple with White watercolor paint)

Light Pink (can be made by mixing Scarlet Red with White watercolor paint)

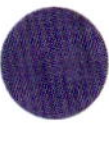
Ultramarine Purple

Chrome Yellow

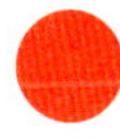
Scarlet Red

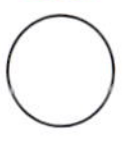
White acrylic paint

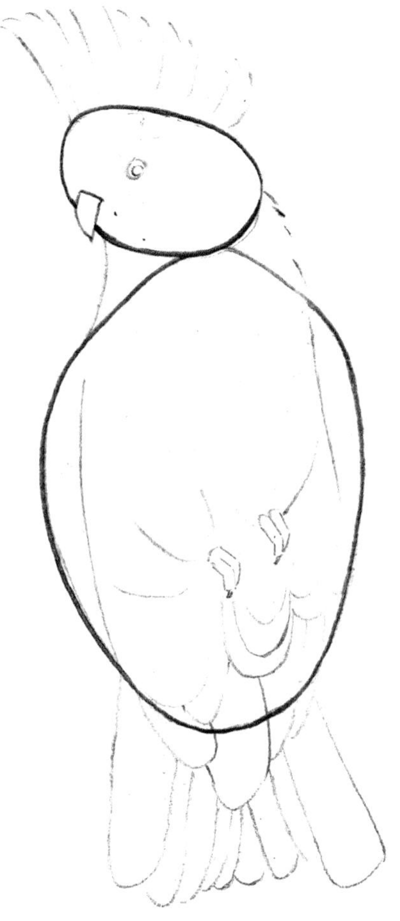

Figure 1.1

**Step 1:** I absolutely love painting cockatoos and I am excited to show you my way of approaching these vivid birds. Start by drawing the base for the cockatoo with a pencil. For the body, use a large oval shape and an elongated oblong shape for the face. Connect the two with a curved line for the neck. Next, add in the small beak with a simple triangle shape and the tuft of feathers on the head. Use a small circle for the eye. Now for the body, draw the side wings and bird's feet. Figure 1.1 shows the shape of the feet and the small triangle nails.

The final step is to add in the tail feathers with an array of U-shapes. Make sure to overlap the U-shapes to bring the tail feathers together. Also, add in curved lines for the bottom of the body as seen in Figure 1.1.

Once you are happy with the base drawing, erase any dark pencil marks with a kneadable eraser so that they don't obstruct the painting.

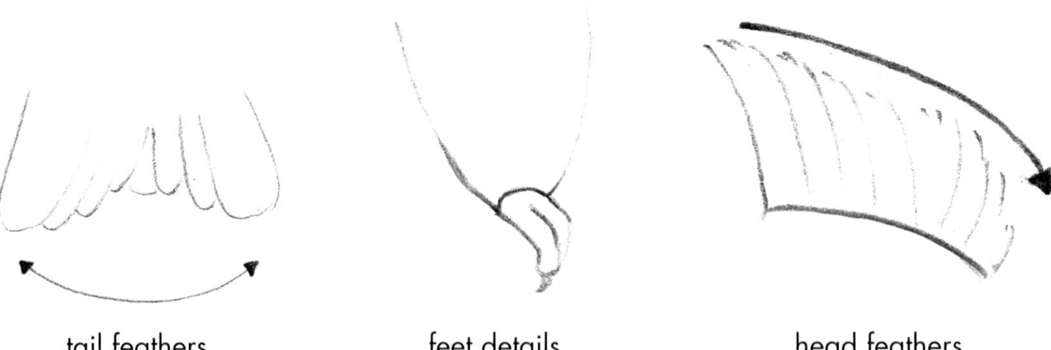

**Step 2:** Let's start painting our cute birdie using a round brush. Load the brush with lavender, which you can mix as explained in the color scheme section at the start of the project. Paint the top of the head feather tufts from the bottom and to the edge. Also, outline the edges of the feathers and the tail feathers as seen in the Figure 1.2. Add an outline to the bottom of the bird as well.

For the body of the bird, create a lovely dual-color gradient effect, starting from light pink to lavender to clean water, from right to left. This technique is further explained in the Dual-Color Gradient Effect section on page 20. Start with a layer of light pink (which can be mixed using the directions from the color scheme section at the start of the project) on the right side of the bird. Clean your brush and load it with lavender to paint a layer next to the previous one, gently touching it so that the colors blend together. Paint the face of the bird with this lavender. Finally, using clean water, add a final line along the right side of the bird to create an interesting blend.

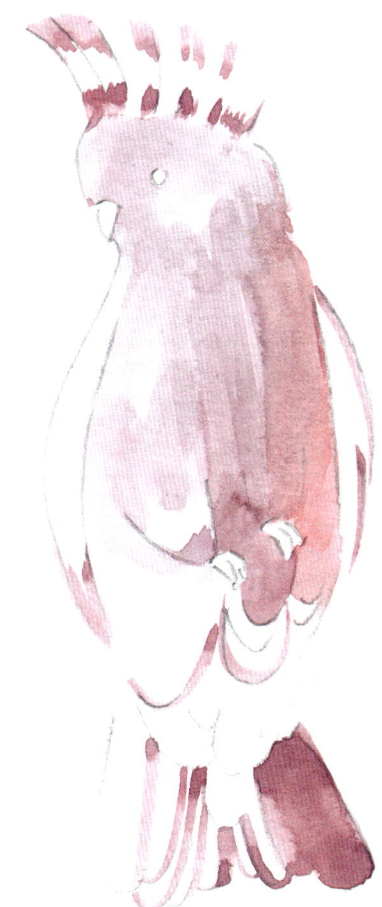

Figure 1.2

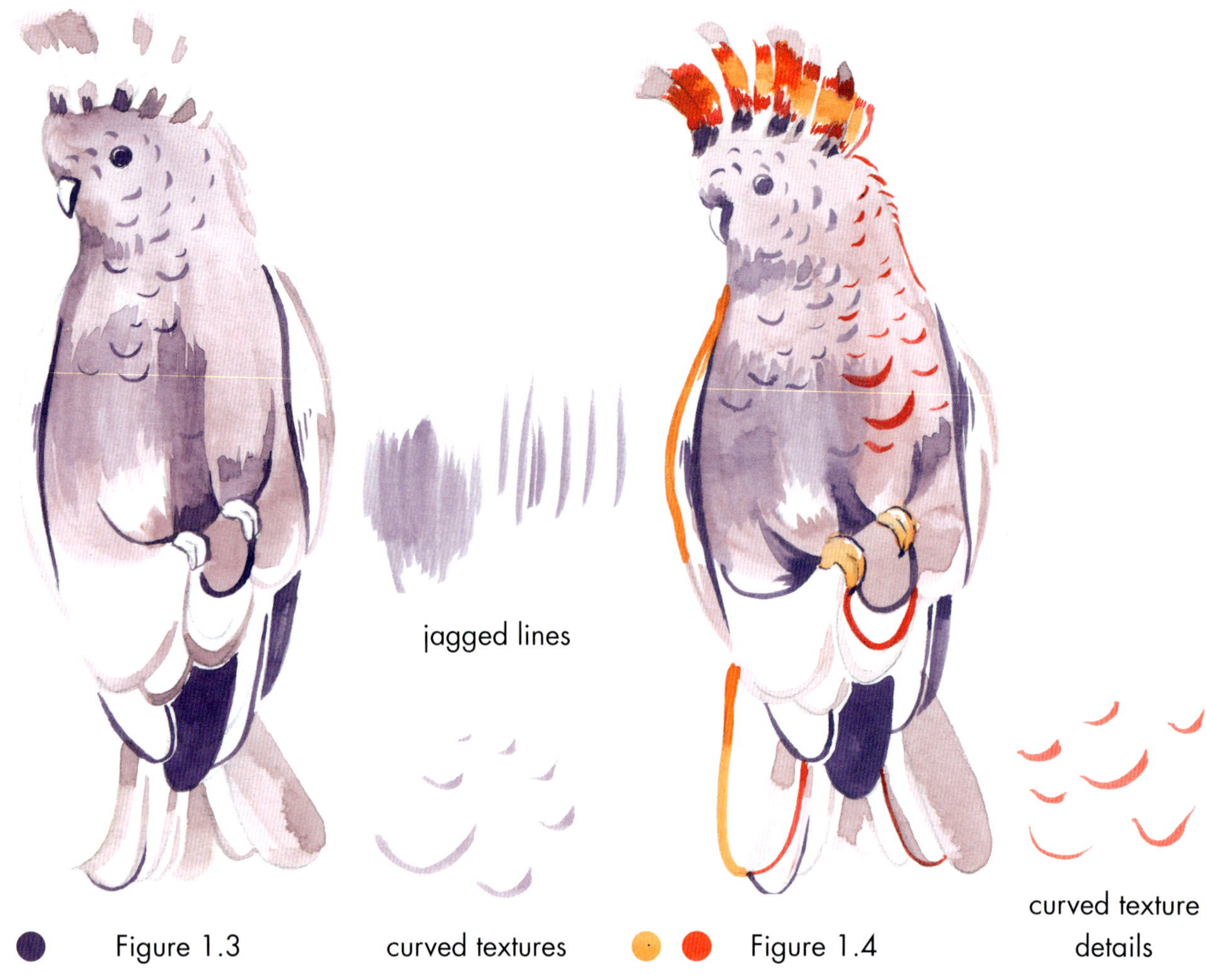


Figure 1.3

Figure 1.4

**Step 3:** Once the layer has dried, let's start adding ultramarine purple for the final details using your round brush. We will first focus on the face, painting in the eye and beak details. Paint in the tuft of head feathers. Next, add a layer of jagged lines along the bird's bottom belly and neck. This layer is meant to bring dimension to the previous layer and help define the body areas. Next, add curved lines as shown in a circle around the eye of the bird. This simple texture will really add to our bird and complete our composition. Next, use this lovely purple to outline the inner wing of the bird, the feet details and the bottom feathers as seen in Figure 1.3.

Allow the layer to dry before proceeding to the next step.

**Step 4:** In this step, we will be playing around with color. Use a script liner brush to add in some lovely chrome yellow outlines and details around the body of the bird. Start adding the yellow to the middle of the tuft feathers. Next, add the outline for the inner wing and the tail feather along the left side. Paint in the feet as well.

Additionally, add scarlet red to this process by filling in the remaining areas in the tuft feathers. Make sure to clean your script liner brush and load it with fresh scarlet paint. Now add curved lines for the body of the bird along the right side. Start with smaller curves at the top of the head and larger curves along the chest. Add some U-curved outlines for some of the wing and tail feathers.

Once the layer is dried, move on to completing the painting with some simple elements.

**Step 5:** Let's complete our painting by adding a captivating background. Before that, let's use white acrylic paint to add some reflection spots for the eye of our cockatoo. Make sure to clean your script liner brush before loading it with white acrylic paint to easily add these minute details. While we are at it, let's also add some dots along the body as well. White details create texture and help bring out the vibrancy of the painting.

For the background, start with a branch for our bird to perch on in scarlet red, using a round brush. Next, take your mop brush and load it with chrome yellow to create a single-color gradient. This is the same technique explained in the Single-Color Gradient Effect section on page 19. What I like to do is paint the area all around the bird. Then, after cleaning the brush, I use the damp brush to paint another water layer near the previous layer. That way, a gradient is created all around the bird.

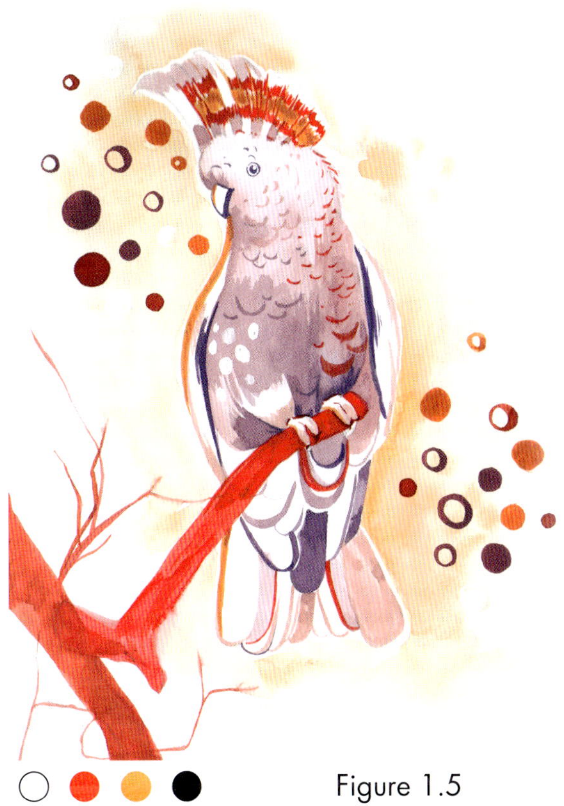

Figure 1.5

**Pro-Tip:** Keep a small white space intact when painting the background so that the colors don't mix.

Allow this layer to dry before using your round brush to add circles in ultramarine purple, chrome yellow and scarlet red. These polka dots balance the painting and make it look fun and vibrant by pulling through the colors within the bird as well.

# Kingfisher

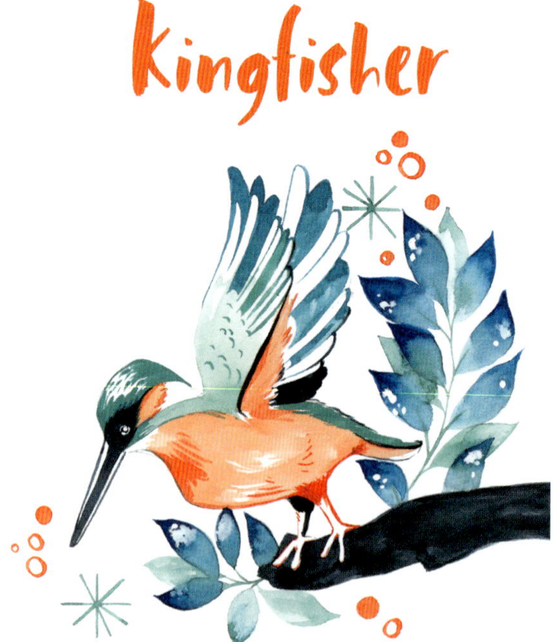

*The kingfisher is a bird whose name has been used in so many companies. Funnily, when you Google kingfisher, the beer or the airlines are what pop up. From an artistic perspective, kingfishers are fairly easy to draw. They have a similar structure to some of our other birds within this book. However, what is really unique about the bird is the mix of the complementary blue and orange. Our task here is to ensure that both colors are balanced.*

---

## MATERIALS

Watercolor cold press paper, 200gsm (95lb)
Pencil
Kneadable eraser
Palette
Glass cup
Watercolor mop brush, size 000
Round brush, size 4
Script liner brush, size 0
Palette
Tissue paper

## COLOR SCHEME

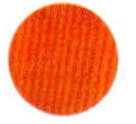 Bright Orange

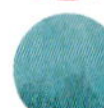 Ultramarine Blue

 Indigo Blue

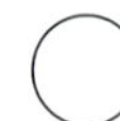 White acrylic paint

## CHALLENGE LEVEL

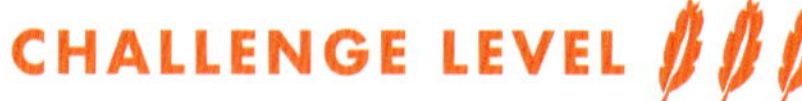

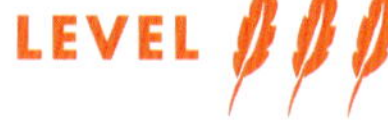

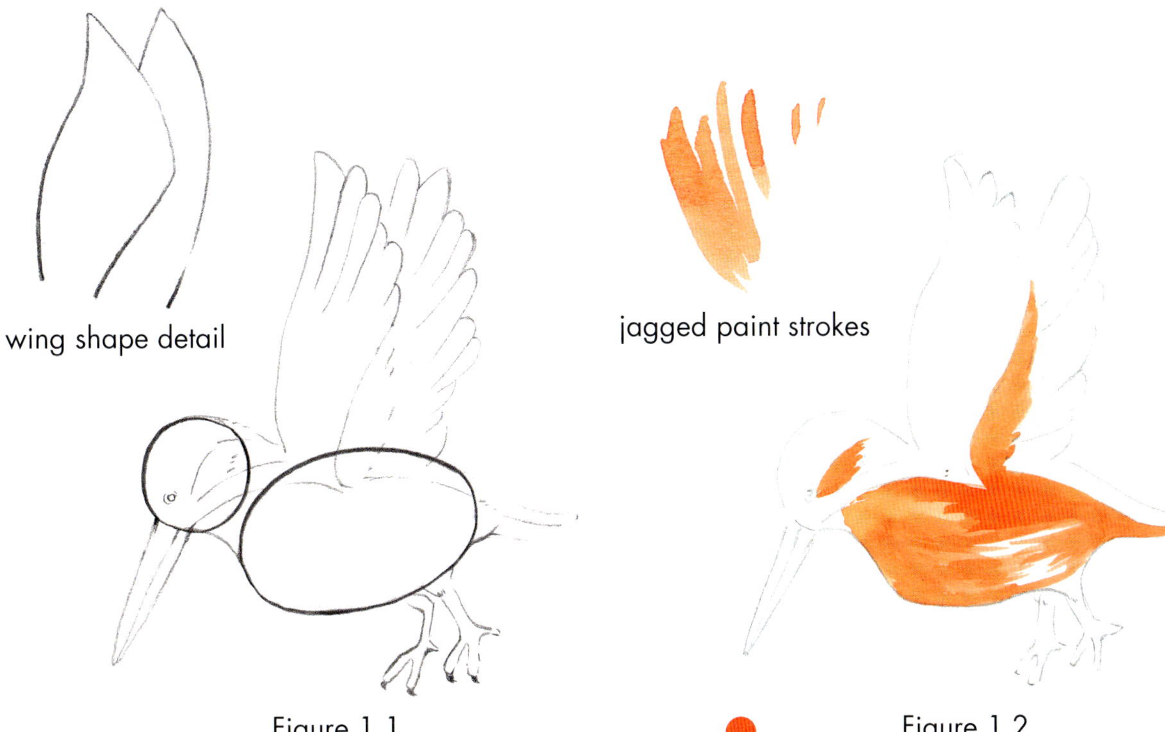


Figure 1.1

Figure 1.2

**Step 1:** Let's start drawing our kingfisher with easy shapes by using a pencil. For the body, we can use an oval shape and a circle for the face. Connect the two with curved lines for the neckline. Use a triangle shape for the beak and a simple curved tail.

Add in the feet with a focus on the shape of the feet. Next, add the wings of the bird. Follow the highlight image and draw the basic shape of the wings. Once you have completed that part, draw the curves at the edges of the wings. Use Figure 1.1 as a reference image for the base drawing

**Step 2:** Before launching into this step, erase any dark pencil lines with a kneadable eraser. Now we are mainly going to paint the orange details using a round brush. Start painting simple jagged lines near the cheeks and the inner wings. Use jagged lines for the body of the bird as well, leaving some empty white spaces as you can see in Figure 1.2.

Allow the layer to dry before adding the ultramarine details in the next step.

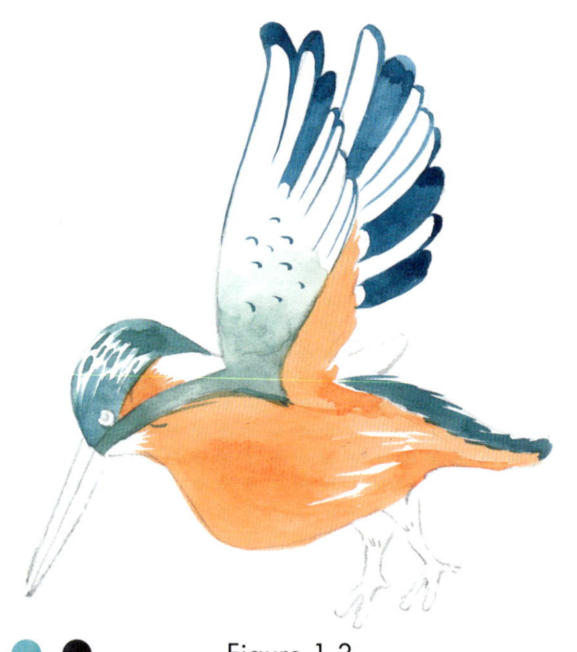

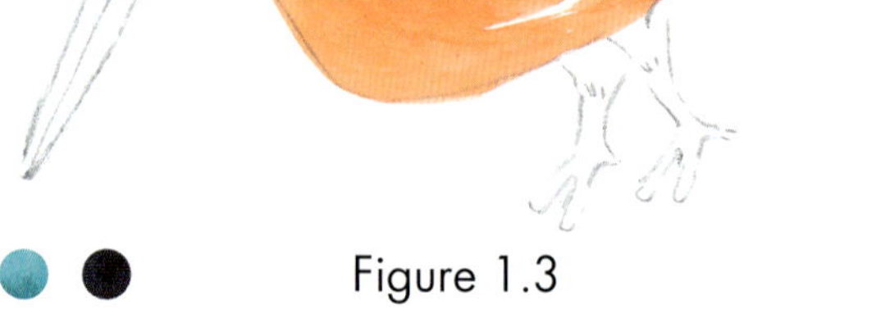

Figure 1.3

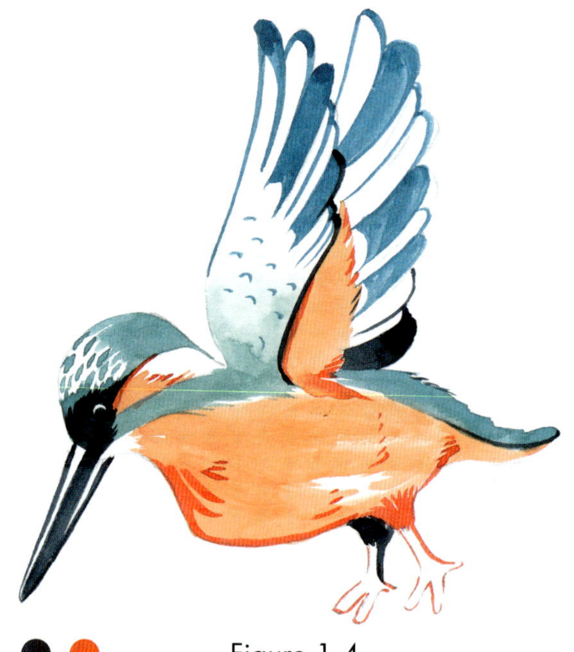

Figure 1.4

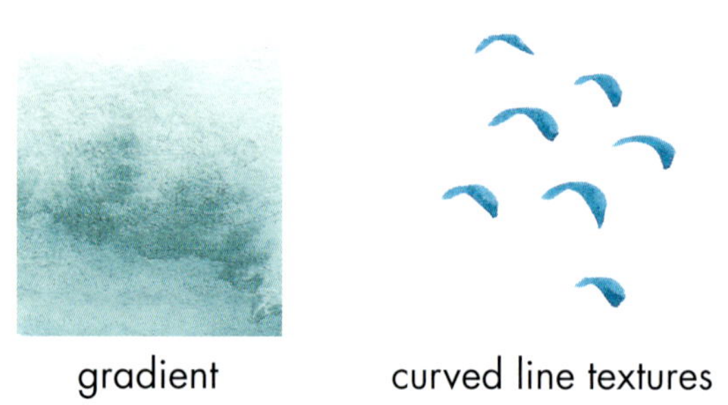

gradient     curved line textures

**Step 3:** Load your clean round brush with ultramarine blue. First, paint a single-color gradient along the neckline and wings of the bird, as shared in the Single-Color Gradient Effect section on page 19. While this layer is drying, add in the ultramarine dashes at the top of the bird's head. Keep white spaces for a more uneven effect. Next, paint the tail shape as seen in Figure 1.3.

Now we move on to the edges of the wings. As seen in Figure 1.3, outline the edges of the curves of the wings. Fill in some of the feather areas with U-shapes.

When the layer is dry, add small curve shapes as seen in the highlight image. I love adding thin details and strokes as they make the painting look more artistic and fun.

Allow the painting to dry before moving on to the next step.

**Step 4:** In this step, we will be adding depth to the painting by using a thin script liner brush. Load your brush with indigo blue. Start by adding indigo strokes to the beak and the eye. Then move on to paint jagged lines in a triangle shape along the eye as seen in Figure 1.4. Add indigo details for the outline of the wing and the back foot. Indigo

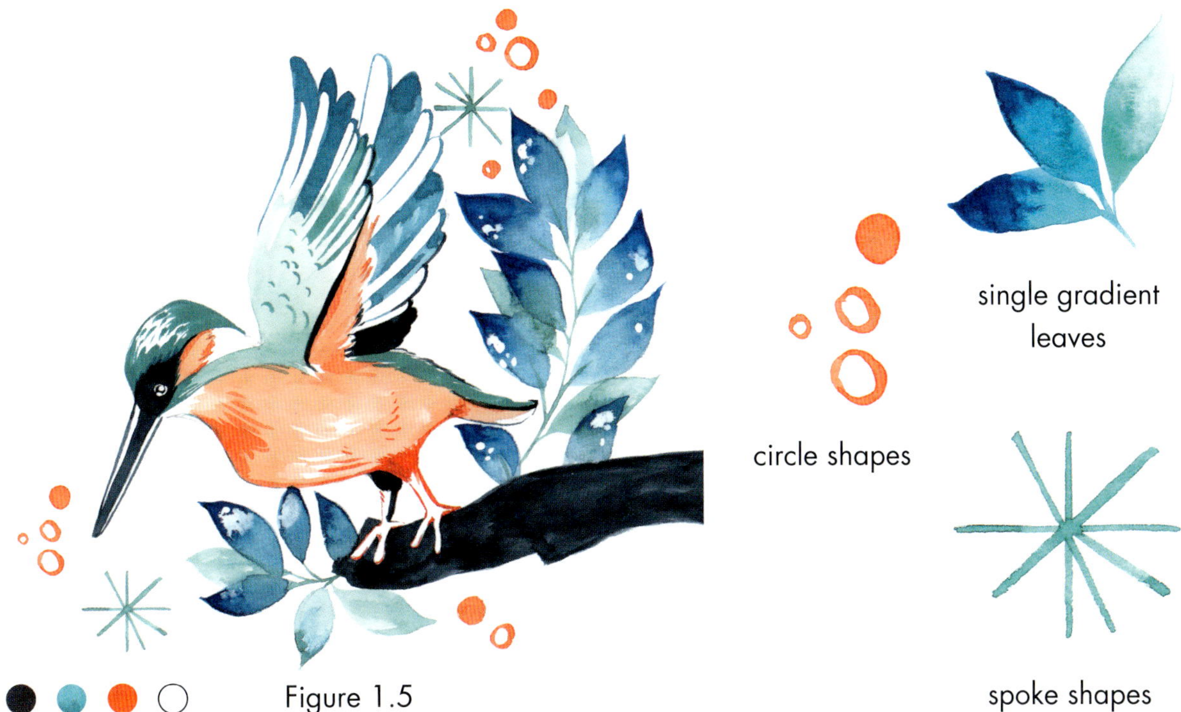


Figure 1.5

creates depth within the painting while highlighting the ultramarine blue.

Next, using your script liner brush loaded with bright orange, paint the outline for the bird's body as well as some line details to bring texture to the painting. In this step, paint the outline for the feet and the lower part of the body as well.

Allow this layer to dry before completing the painting in the next step.

**Step 5:** To complete the composition, paint the branch for the bird to stand on by using a round brush. To avoid adding more colors to this already vibrant painting, simply use indigo blue for the branch. Next, add in some simple leaves as explained in the Practice Exercises chapter on page 19. We will be using the single-color gradient effect from the tip of the leaves and adding clean water to the bottom for the leaves for a gentle gradient.

Add in opposite gradients to the leaves as well, starting from deep blue at the bottom of the leaf to clear water at the pointed tip of the leaf. Alternating between them can give the painting an asymmetrical look. I have also used ultramarine blue to add spokes around the bird.

Now to balance the orange within the bird, load your round brush with bright orange to add circles into the painting. Always cluster the circles while playing with different sizes to bring together the playful look. Using the white acrylic, add some spots to the tip of the leaves as well as the bird's eye.

# Budgie Parakeets

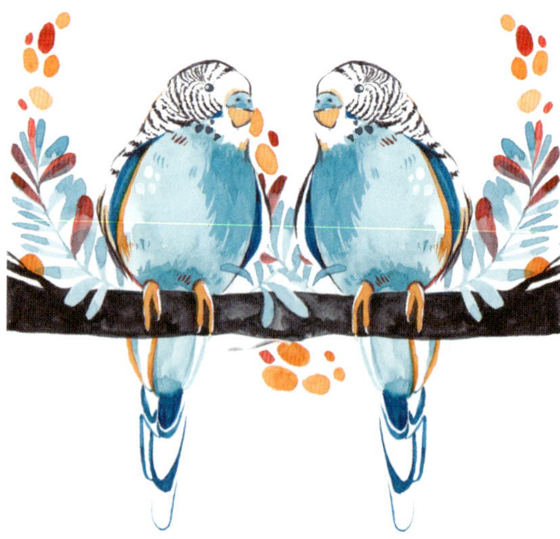

*Parakeets are stunning birds that can be recognized anywhere because of their delightful markings. I also love that these birds are very social and prefer being in pairs. For this painting, I have selected the common blue parakeet. For the finishing touches of the painting, we will be repeating the bird so that we can pair the two together and create a joint composition. Take your time in step 5 as we add texture to the birds.*

---

## MATERIALS

Watercolor cold press paper, 200gsm (95lb)
Pencil
Kneadable eraser
Palette
Glass cup
Round brush, size 4
Script liner brush, size 0
Tissue paper

## COLOR SCHEME

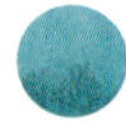 Ultramarine Blue

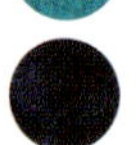 Indigo Blue

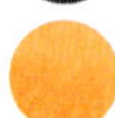 Chrome Yellow

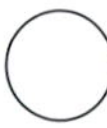 White acrylic paint

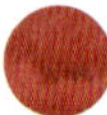 Mahogany (can be made by mixing Scarlet Red with a dash of Ivory Black)

## CHALLENGE LEVEL

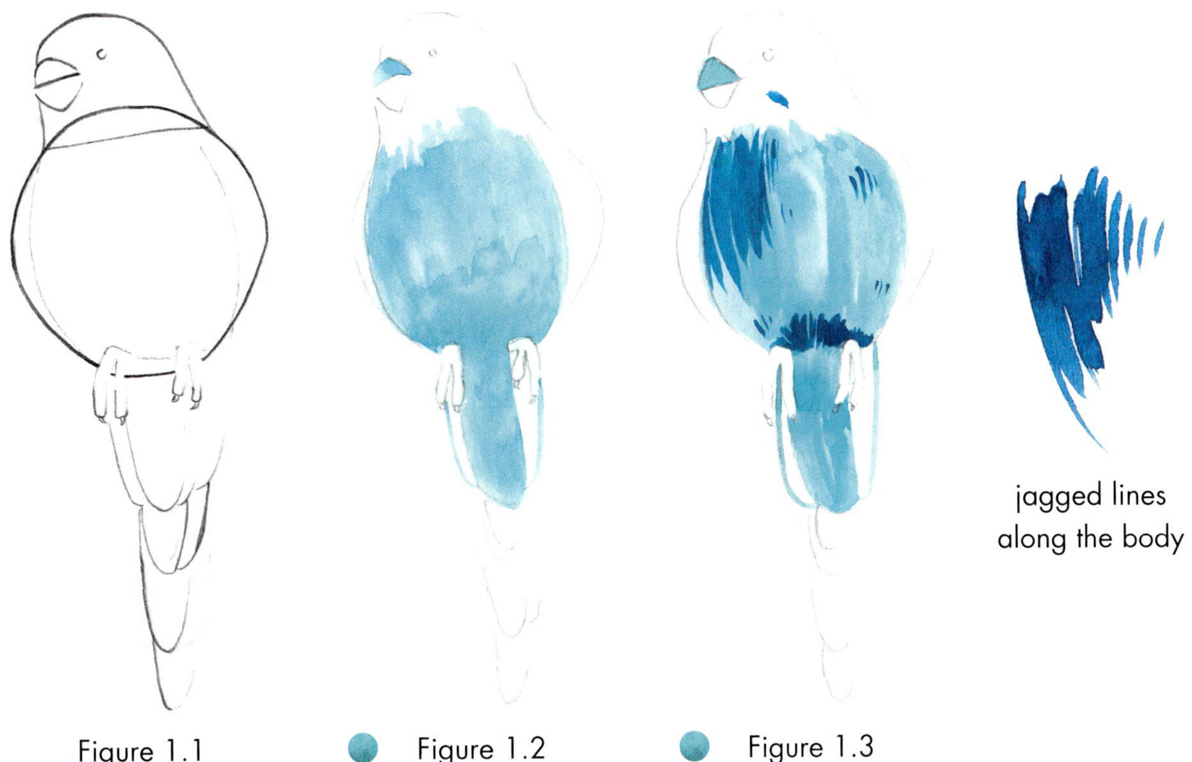


Figure 1.1 Figure 1.2 Figure 1.3

**Step 1:** Let's draw a circle for the body of the parakeet by using a pencil. Next, use a downward U-shape for the head and a triangle for the beak. From there, draw curved lines for the wings and then the claws of the bird.

Use overlapping U-shapes for the tail feathers, varying from small to longer lengths towards the bottom part of the tail feathers. Allow some space on the paper for the second parakeet you'll be drawing.

**Step 2:** Remember to erase any dark pencil marks with a kneadable eraser before proceeding. For the base wash, we will be using a watered mixture of ultramarine blue. This can be mixed by adding more water to the ultramarine blue as explained in the Translucency with Watercolors section on page 16. Now load your round brush with ultramarine blue to paint the top part of the beak and the body of the bird. Use jagged lines at the edge to create texture around the neckline.

Follow this step by adding U-shapes at the tail feathers and painting the outlines as seen in Figure 1.2.

**Step 3:** Allow the layer to dry before adding a deeper blue layer using a round brush as seen in Figure 1.3. This can be done with a round brush with saturated ultramarine blue. Use jagged lines for the chest and the underbelly of the bird along the shadow area. This layer is meant to add more dimensions into the painting.

Allow the layer to dry before proceeding to the next step.

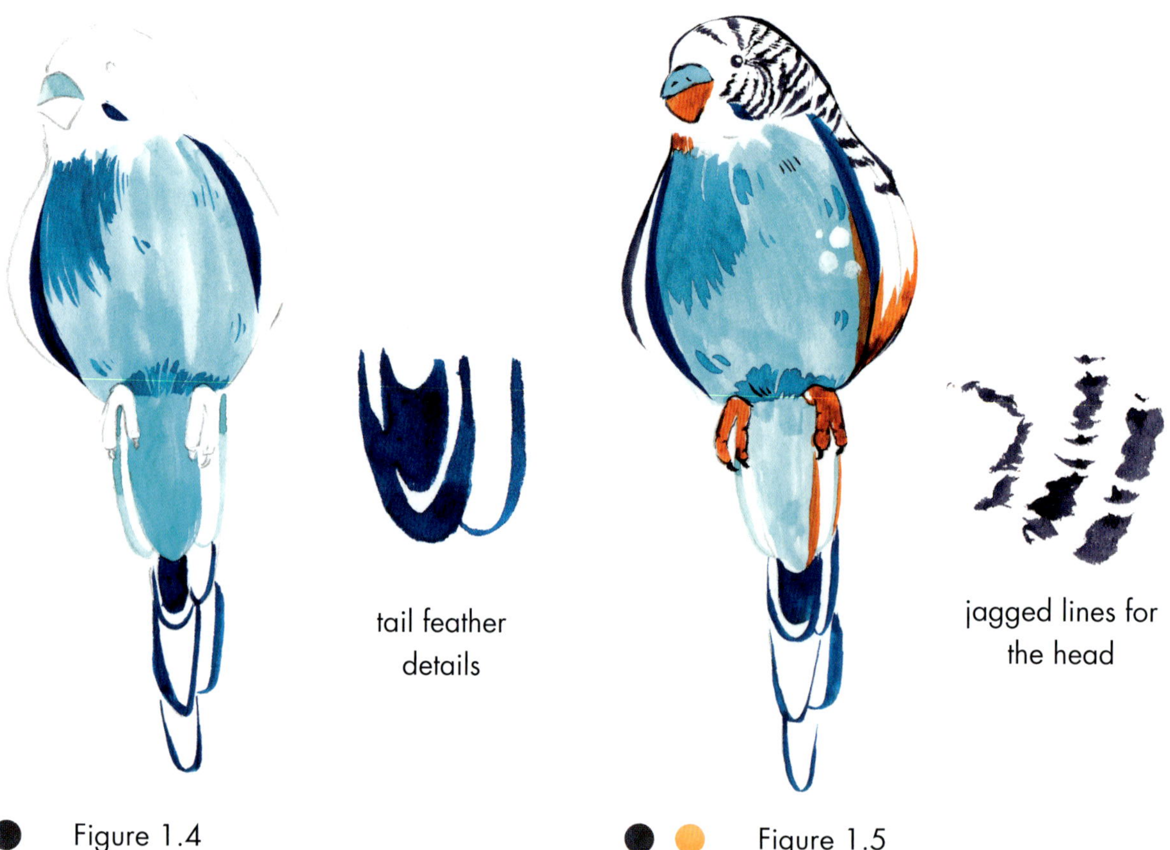


Figure 1.4

Figure 1.5

**Step 4:** Deepen the color within the painting by adding a final layer of blue for the inner wing. This can be done with a round brush. Add curved details for the tail feathers as seen in Figure 1.4.

The reason I add multiple layers of color to the painting is that the colors become more vibrant with every layer that is added.

**Pro-Tip:** If you notice your paintings are dull, try layering color to create intensity.

**Step 5:** This step is where we will be painting the main element of parakeets. Let's use a script liner brush loaded with indigo to really create some lovely strokes. Use jagged lines as seen in Figure 1.5 to paint those indigo details now. Follow the figure to understand the direction for painting the lines. There are curved lines along the cheek to the eye and then from the eye to the top of the head. Add some curved lines along the neckline. Keep some space in between for an asymmetrical effect.

Finally, wash your script liner brush and load it with chrome yellow to paint the bottom of the beak, the claws and area along the wings as seen in Figure 1.5.

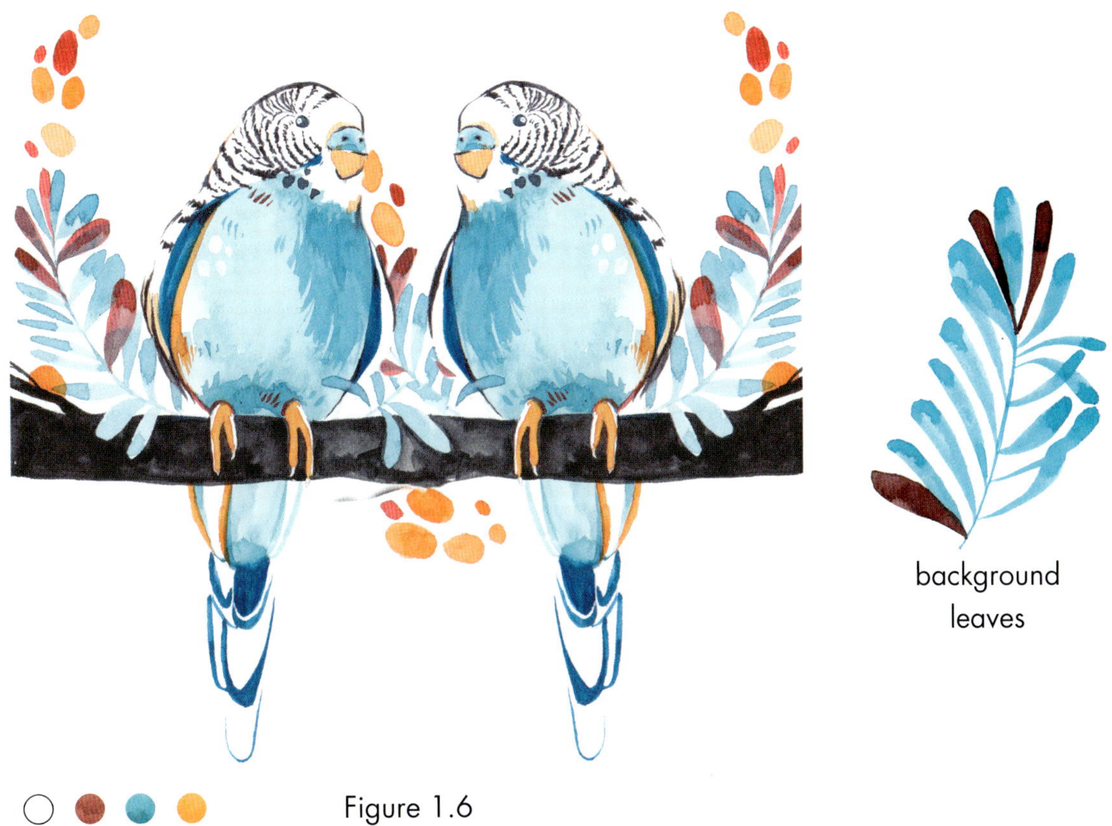


Figure 1.6

**Step 6:** This is the final step for our painting. Gently wash out the chrome yellow from your script liner brush and load it with white acrylic paint. Add the lovely white acrylic spot to the eye. Once that is done, repeat the entire tutorial to paint a second parakeet next to our current parakeet. Since these birds love company, let's paint them in pairs.

Now using a round brush, paint a mahogany branch for the birds to perch on. Mahogany can be mixed as explained in the color scheme section at the beginning of this project. Now, paint some rounded long leaves on either side of the birds, using your round brush. You can use both ultramarine and mahogany for the leaves, as seen in Figure 1.6. Keep the placement asymmetrical and random for an interesting look. Furthermore, add in some chrome yellow and mahogany circles to brighten the painting.

**Pro-Tip:** Make sure to wash your brush before loading it with a new color to avoid murky colors.

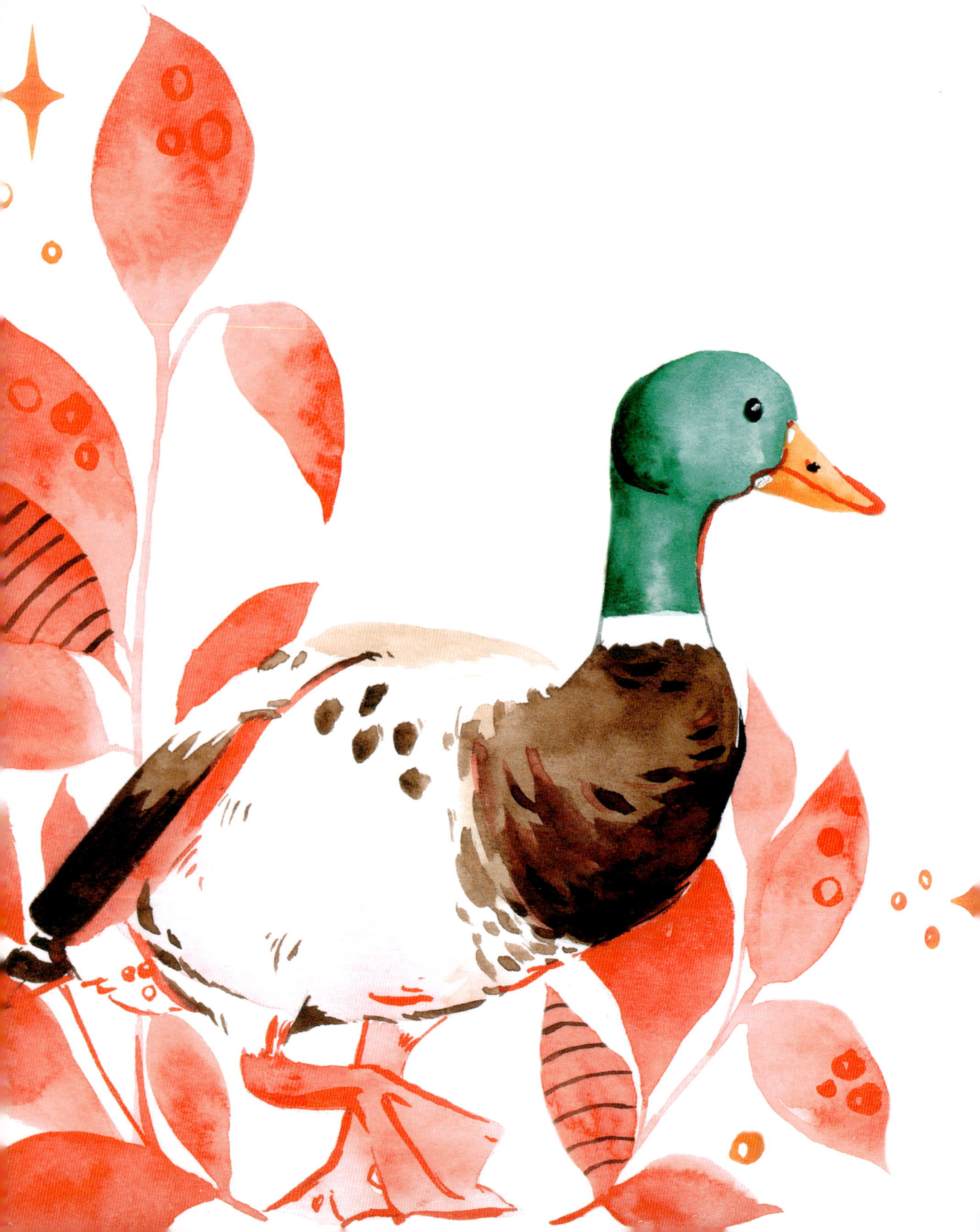

# Aquatic Birds

Swans, ducks, geese and pelicans—I am sure you have seen some of these unforgettable birds in your life. My journey with aquatic birds started with my favorite childhood story, *The Ugly Duckling*. It was a story that made me realize how important it is to love oneself. Since reading that story, aquatic birds have had a special place in my heart. They are also noted for their grace and serenity, like a calm lake in the afternoon.

In this chapter, we will explore combining bold watercolor techniques with the simplicity of the aquatic birds' shapes. One of the most important takeaways from this chapter is how to add color to bring more life into a painting. For example, as you will see in the upcoming project on page 92, instead of painting swans in grayscale, we will add a vibrant blue to highlight the bird. This creates a stunning overall effect and can completely change the feel and emotion behind the painting.

Whether we dive into painting pink pelicans on page 96, sandhill cranes on page 101 or mallard ducks on page 111, I am thrilled to share insights into creating eye-catching paintings in the upcoming projects.

# Mute Swan

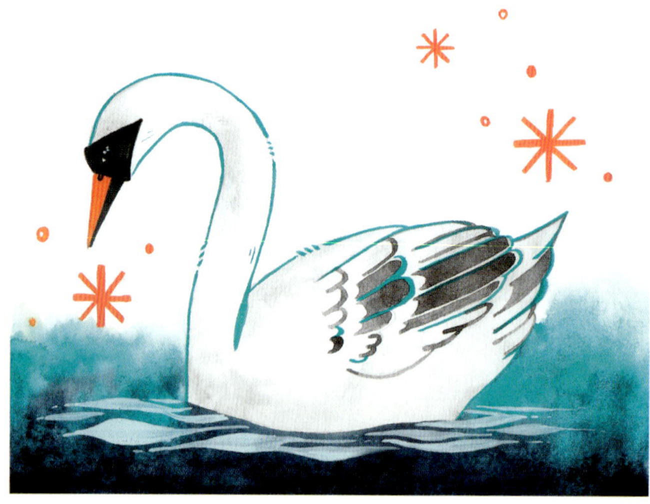

*Having had a chance to travel to many countries, one of my favorite memories was when I was in London visiting Hyde Park. We took a boat ride across the lake that was filled with beautiful swans. That picturesque moment always comes back to me whenever I remember lakes. From an artist's perspective, it is generally more difficult to paint grayscale birds because the final painting tends to look dull. Hence, we will be adding contrast colors.*

---

## MATERIALS

Watercolor cold press paper, 200gsm (95lb)
Pencil
Kneadable eraser
Palette
Glass cup
Watercolor mop brush, size 000
Round brush, size 4
Script liner brush, size 0
Tissue paper

## CHALLENGE LEVEL

## COLOR SCHEME

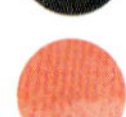 Ivory Black

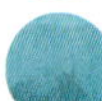 Bright Orange

 Ultramarine Blue

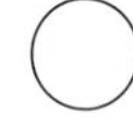 Indigo Blue

White acrylic paint

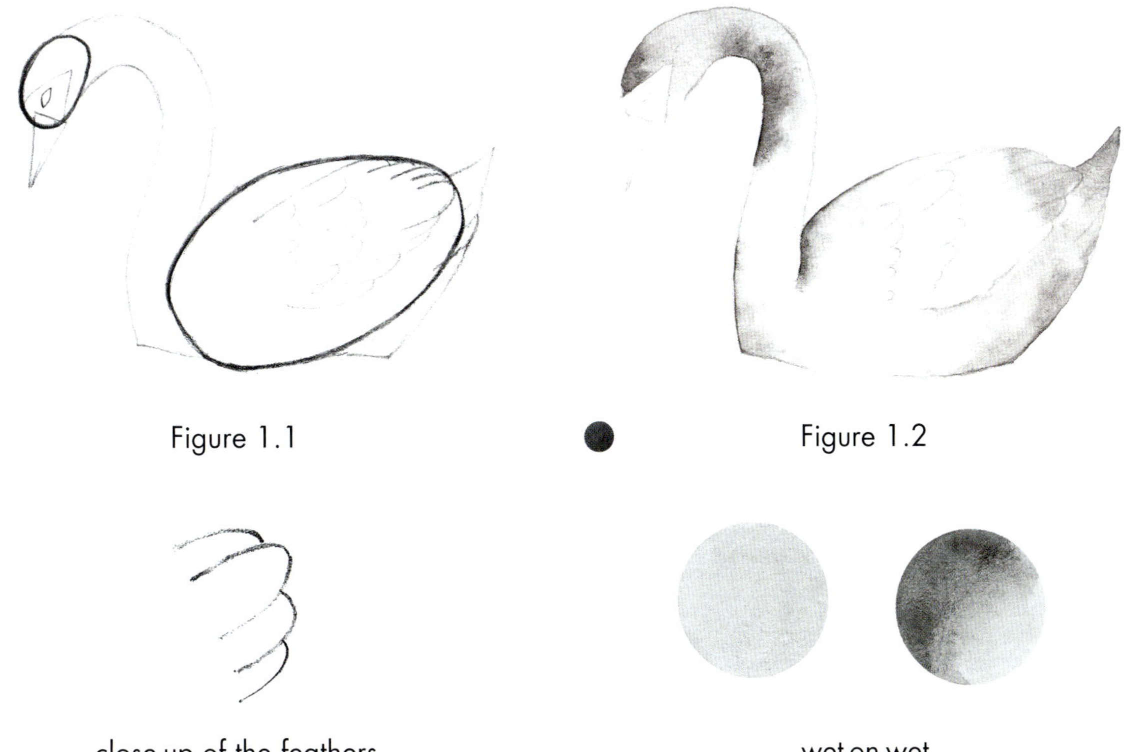

Figure 1.1

Figure 1.2

close-up of the feathers

wet-on-wet

**Step 1:** Start by drawing the swan, using light pencil strokes on cold press watercolor paper. Pay attention to the basic proportions of the swan. Start with an egg shape for the body of the swan. Add in a small oval shape for the face. Connect the two with parallel S curve lines for the neckline. Draw a triangle on the face for the beak. Now for the wings of the bird, continue drawing with simple U-shapes. Also use the same details for the tail feathers.

Once you are happy with the proportions, erase any dark pencil marks using a kneadable eraser.

**Step 2:** Let's start with the first layer of the painting. Using a round brush loaded with translucent light ivory black paint, fill in the body of the bird. This watered-down mixture can be created by adding more water to the paint as explored in the Translucency with Watercolors section on page 16.

For a gentle blend, I like to use a single-color gradient effect (from the Practice Exercises chapter on page 19) at the tips of the wings, on the right side and from the left side along the neckline. Use the same effect along the face by using clean water to gently blend in the colors. Allow the painting to dry before moving on to the next step.

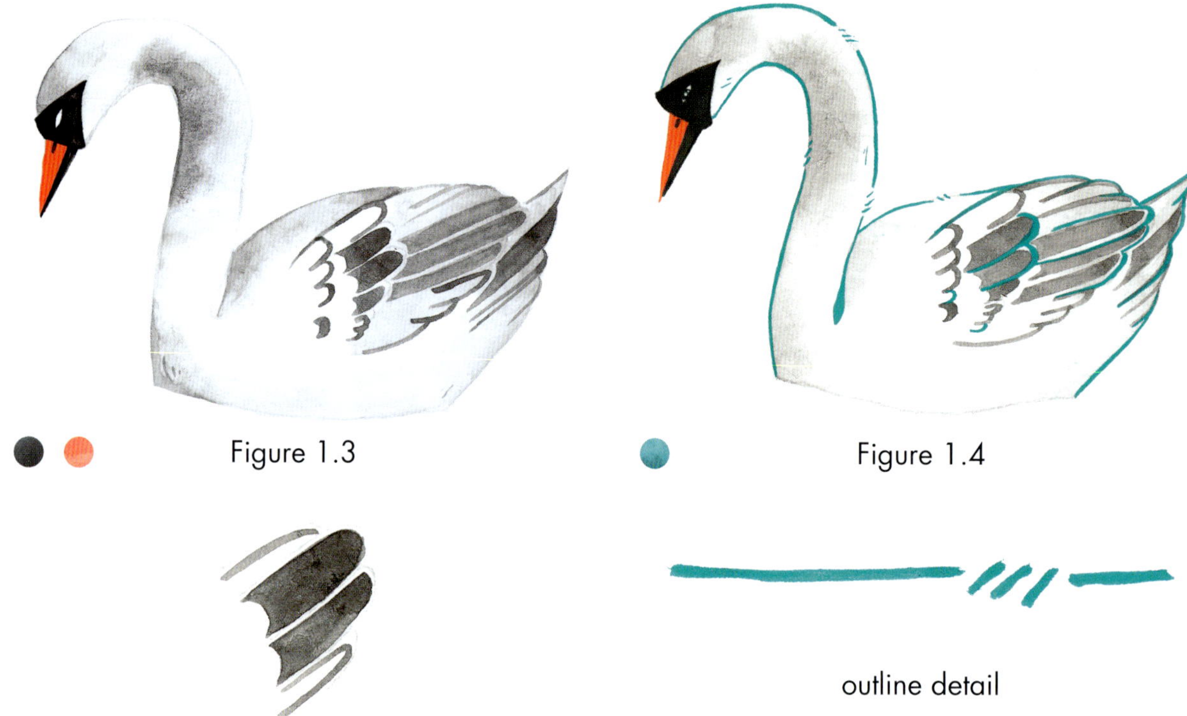

Figure 1.3

Figure 1.4

feather detail

outline detail

**Step 3:** In this layer, we will be adding inner details for the feathers as seen in Figure 1.3. This can be done with a round brush loaded with a medium wash of ivory black. Here, we want to ensure that the paint isn't saturated, but mixed with a little water for a gray shade. Now, paint U-shapes and U-outlines along the wings of the bird. These shapes can be added to the tail as well.

**Pro-Tip:** Start with smaller shapes for the feathers and then move on to longer shapes at the tip of the wing.

Using a script liner brush loaded with ivory black, paint the V-shape around the eye and the bottom beak. Now, switch the paint in the brush to bright orange to paint the top beak. Allow the layer to dry before moving on to the next step.

**Step 4:** Now that the painting is dry, complete the swan by adding a contrasting ultramarine blue outline to the bird. Adding a contrast color brings the painting to life, as you can see in Figure 1.4.

Also note: As per the image above, there are gaps in the outline. These add to the artistic look of the overall painting and are an important part of the painting.

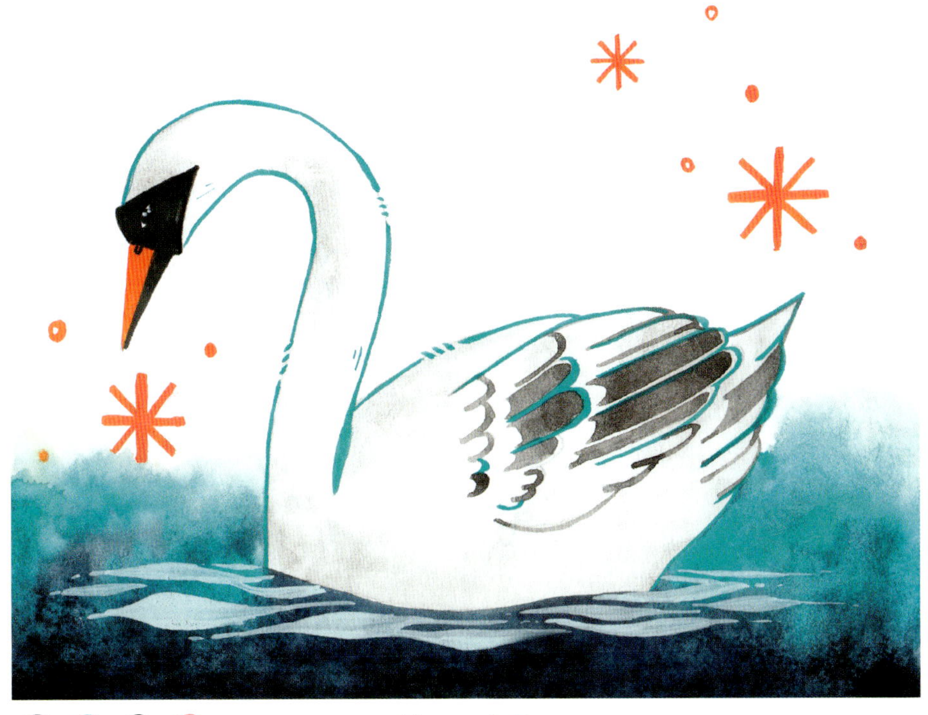

Figure 1.5

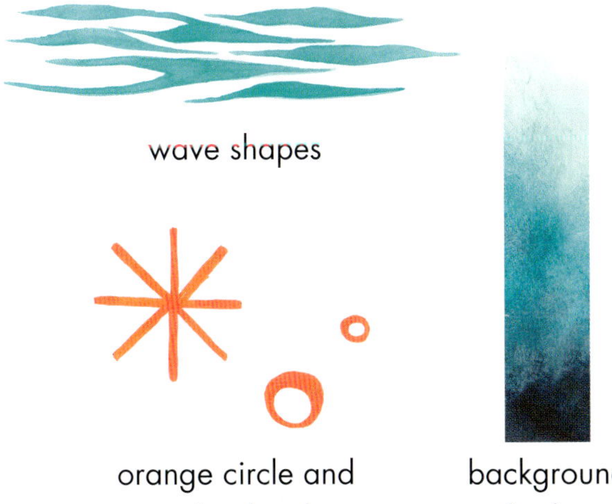


**Step 5:** Finally, complete the painting by adding a dual-color gradient effect from deep indigo blue to the ultramarine blue. This effect is created by using a mop brush as explored in the Practice Exercises chapter on page 19. Allow this wash to dry.

Next, use a clean round brush loaded with white acrylic paint to add waves along the swan. This can be created using thin to thick to thin width lines. Alternate the placement to create a simple wave texture. Wash the round brush with clean water and load it with bright orange. Paint simple clusters of spokes and circle elements around the swan to brighten the composition.

# Pink Pelican

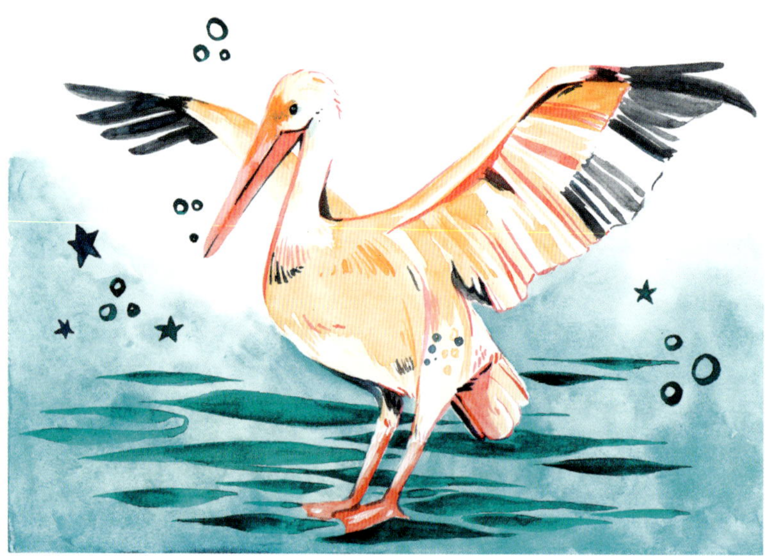

*I remember reading about pelicans in many poems. While pelicans are known for their wide sack-like beak that can hold a lot of fish, the size of the bird also makes for an impactful piece of artwork. Accordingly, for this painting, I decided to choose a proud wide-winged pelican that really captures the size of the bird.*

---

## MATERIALS

Watercolor cold press paper, 200gsm (95lb)
Pencil
Kneadable eraser
Palette
Glass cup
Watercolor mop brush, size 000
Round brush, size 4
Script liner brush, size 0
Tissue paper

## CHALLENGE LEVEL

## COLOR SCHEME

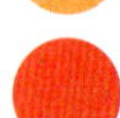 Chrome Yellow

 Scarlet Red

 Ivory Black

White acrylic paint

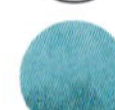 Ultramarine Blue

 Indigo Blue

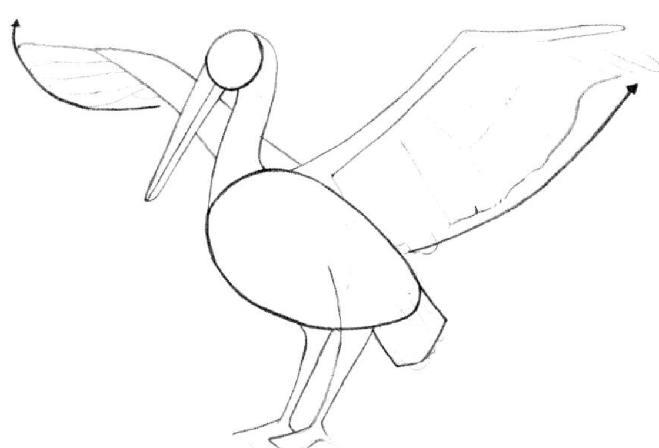

Figure 1.1

**Step 1:** Draw a small circle for the face of the pelican followed by a long triangle-shaped beak, using a pencil. Next, draw an S shape for the neck, connecting them to an egg shape for the pelican's body. Continue drawing the tail and the webbed feet using simple geometric shapes.

Now, let's move on to drawing the most important part of the bird: the wings. On the bird's left side, follow the geometrical shapes as seen in Figure 1.1. Along the right side of the bird, focus on highlighting each individual feather as shown in Figure 1.1.

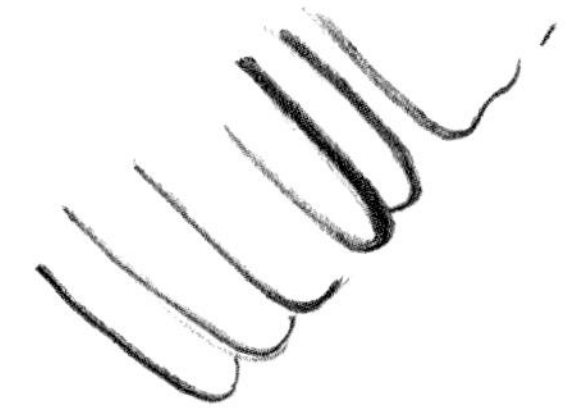

pelican's left wing

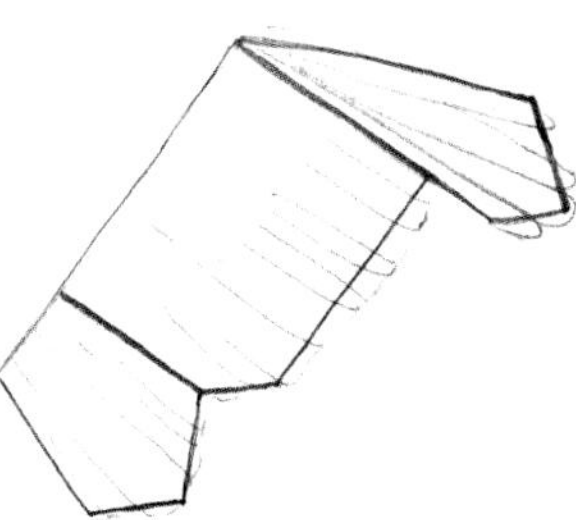

wing edge

**Pro-Tip:** A tip while drawing wings is to highlight a couple of feathers by drawing them individually. This brings variety into the drawing as seen in Figure 1.1.

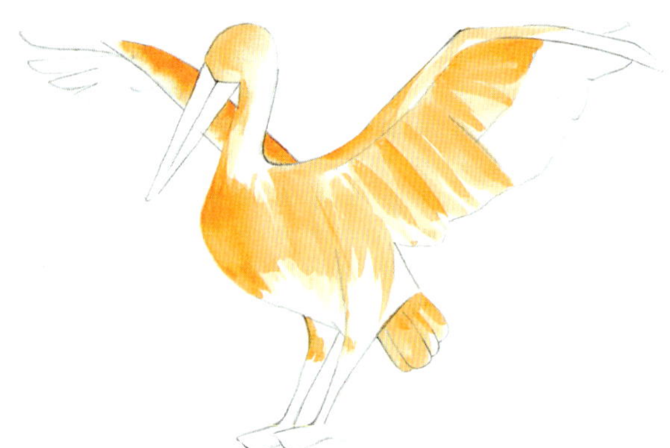

Figure 1.2

gradient effect

**Step 2:** Before we proceed to painting, I would suggest erasing any dark pencil lines using a kneadable eraser. This is important to keep in mind, because after painting, it will be hard to remove them.

Let's start by painting a light wash of chrome yellow with the round brush. This light wash can be created by adding more water to the paint as explained in the Translucency with Watercolors section on page 16. Use light brushstrokes to fill in the body and the wings. Keep in mind to paint the tail feathers as well.

**Pro-Tip:** Keep white spaces for the white of the paper to show through. This creates highlights within the painting.

Now, use the single-color gradient effect as explained in the Practice Exercises chapter on page 19. Start with chrome yellow along the edge and then use clean water below for a gentle blend. Once complete, the light chrome yellow wash should be similar to Figure 1.2. Allow the painting to dry before moving on to the next step.

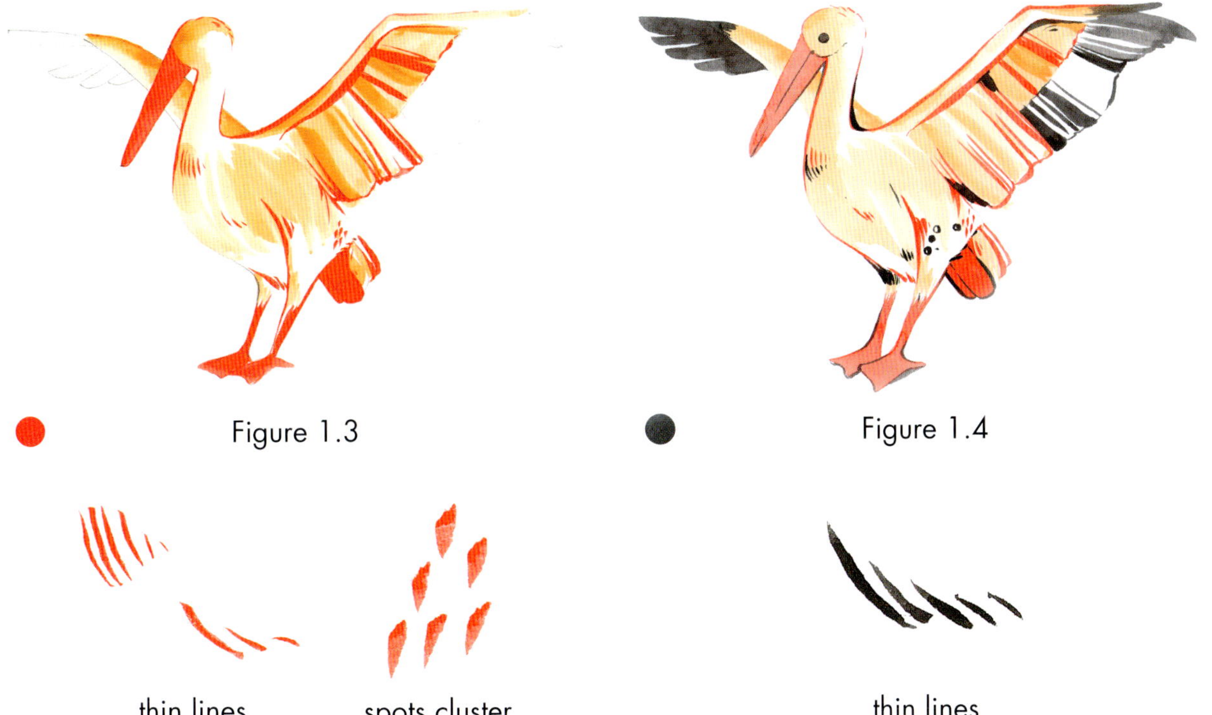

Figure 1.3

Figure 1.4

**Step 3:** Let's add bright scarlet red to highlight the details of the pelican. Make sure to wash your round brush properly before loading it with scarlet red. Use this brush to paint the beak, some of the wing feathers, the tail feathers and finally, the feet of the bird.

Next, use a script liner brush loaded with scarlet red to paint the outline of the pelican.

**Pro-Tip:** Use broken lines for a playful, artistic look for the outline.

Continuing with the script liner brush, add curved line details and spots to the pelican's body as shown in Figure 1.3. These diamond shapes give the feel of texture to the painting. Allow the painting to dry before moving on to the next fun step!

**Step 4:** This is the last step before we move on to the background and the finishing details of the painting. Hence, take your time in this step. First, let's paint the edge of the wings. For this purpose, we will be using a round brush. Make sure you clean it from the previous step before loading it with ivory black. Use black lines of varying width to cover the wings, as seen in Figure 1.4. Create variety by painting only a few feathers.

Next take a clean script liner brush and load it with ivory black paint. Add thin parallel lines and spots to add more texture to the bird along the body. Finally, add ivory black outlines to some areas such as the tail feathers, the curve of the neck, and the back right foot of the pelican. While the bird is complete, let's add some finishing touches to the painting.

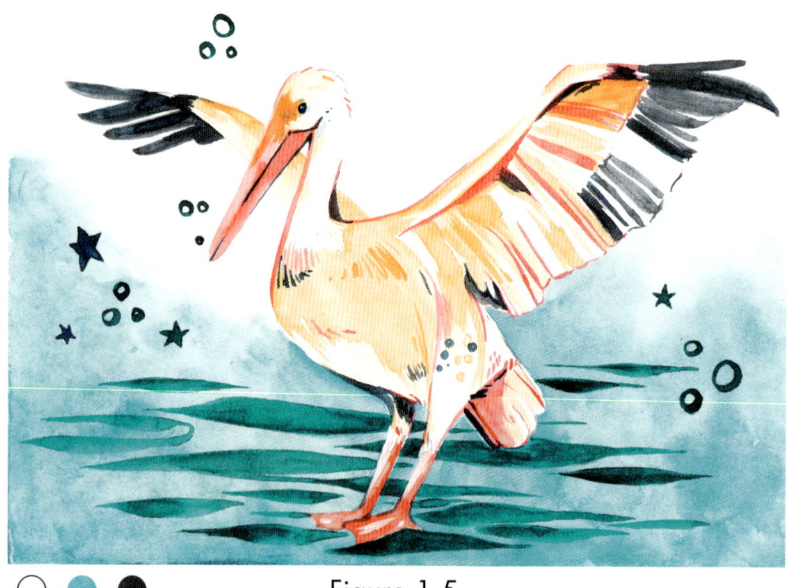

Figure 1.5

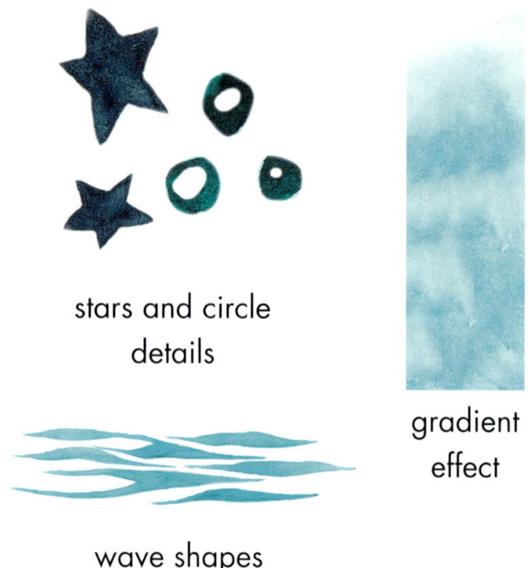


**Step 5:** Let's add finishing touches to the bird itself. For this purpose, use a script liner loaded with white acrylic paint to add a dot for the eye reflection.

Take a mop brush and load it with ultramarine blue. For the background let's add a single-color gradient wash as shared in the Practice Exercises chapter on page 19. Start with an ultramarine wash at the bottom of the page. Next, clean your brush and use clean water to paint next to the previous layer for a gentle blend.

Now allow this layer to completely dry. Using a clean round brush, load it with indigo paint. Start with circles and stars around the bird to balance the composition.

Now use lines starting with thin lines to thick lines to thin again, as shown in the Practice Exercises chapter on page 19. Try to paint these lines at alternating placements to represent the waves in the water. As you can see, try to be careful with your placement of these different elements so that they balance the composition.

# Sandhill Crane

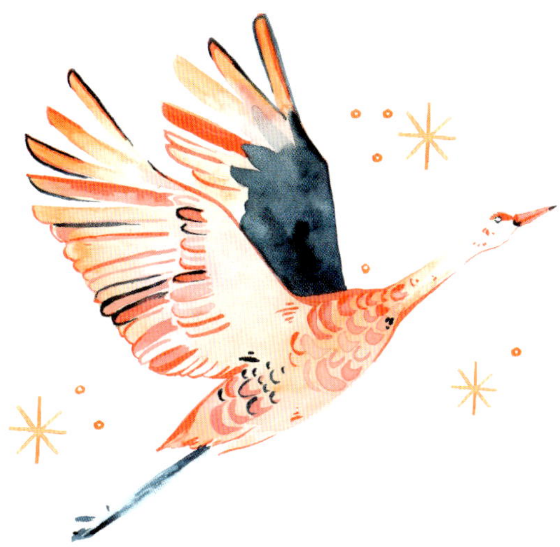

*Cranes symbolize beauty, grace and peace. Growing up, the one thing that really stood out to me about cranes was the fact that they migrate in a V formation. Hence, I decided on a flying crane as our reference image. The shape of a flying crane is iconic and captures the beauty of this stunning bird. Keep an eye out for step 3, where we'll be painting feathers along the bird. To balance our final painting, we will be using simple background elements.*

---

## MATERIALS

Watercolor cold press paper, 200gsm (95lb)
Pencil
Kneadable eraser
Palette
Glass cup
Watercolor mop brush, size 000
Round brush, size 4
Script liner brush, size 0
Tissue paper

## COLOR SCHEME

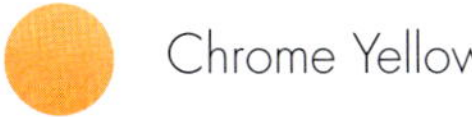


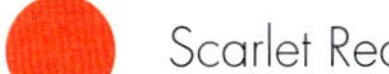


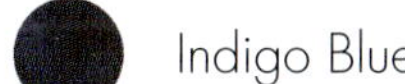


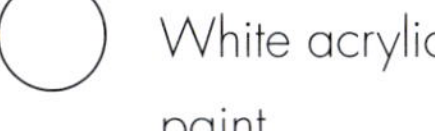


## CHALLENGE LEVEL

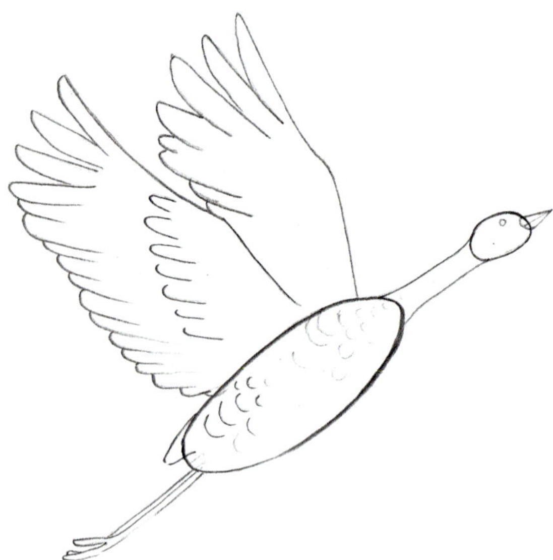

Figure 1.1

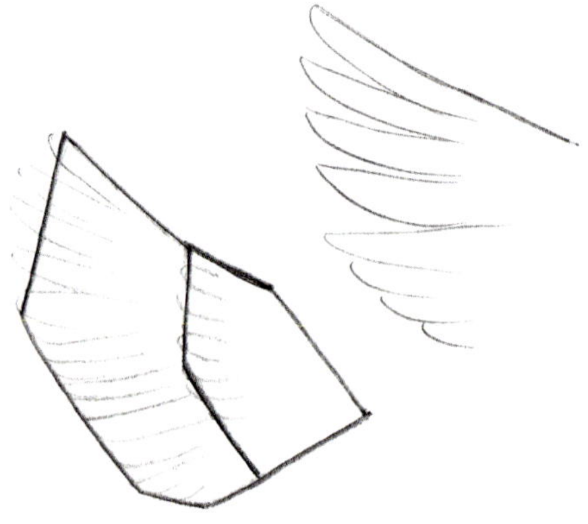

close-up of the wing shape

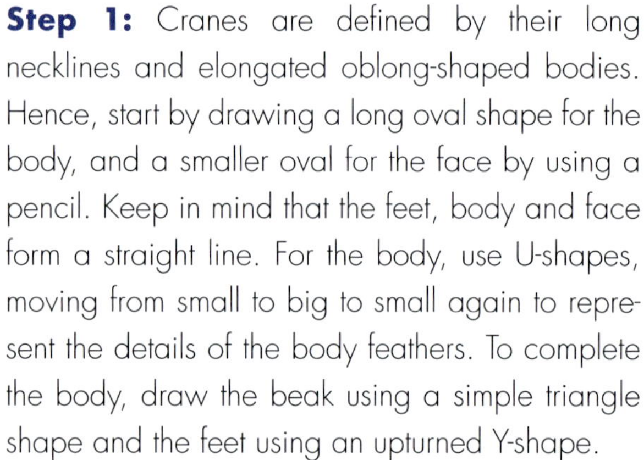

**Step 1:** Cranes are defined by their long necklines and elongated oblong-shaped bodies. Hence, start by drawing a long oval shape for the body, and a smaller oval for the face by using a pencil. Keep in mind that the feet, body and face form a straight line. For the body, use U-shapes, moving from small to big to small again to represent the details of the body feathers. To complete the body, draw the beak using a simple triangle shape and the feet using an upturned Y-shape.

Next, draw the wings using basic geometric shapes as shown in Figure 1.1. Erase the darker pencil lines with a kneadable eraser so that it doesn't affect the final painting.

**Pro-Tip:** Make the feathers along the edge of the wings more prominent and the feathers at the bottom near the body smaller and less defined.

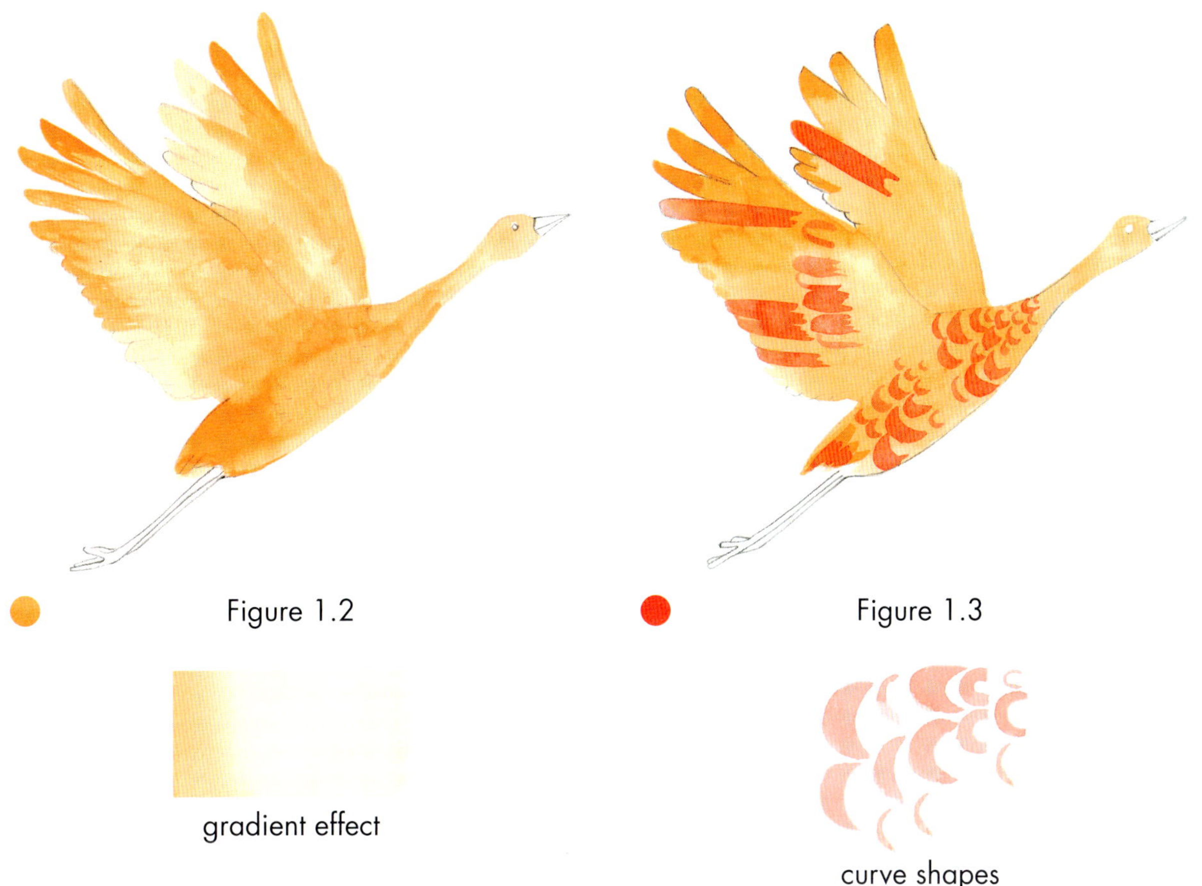

Figure 1.2

gradient effect

Figure 1.3

curve shapes

**Step 2:** Let's start by painting a light wash of chrome yellow all over the body and wings using the mop brush. Mix the light wash by adding more water to the paint as shown in the Translucency with Watercolors section on page 16. Use a single-color gradient effect to paint a lovely wash along the wings. Make sure that the edges of the wings are deeper in color. Use a similar effect along the body—glide chrome yellow along the body and then use a clear water wash from the neckline down, gently touching the previous wash for a gentle blend.

Once complete, the light yellow wash should look like Figure 1.2. Allow the painting to dry before moving on to the next step.

**Step 3:** In this layer, using your round brush, let's add a light wash of red to create interesting details along the base of the crane. Starting with the body, use curved shapes as shown above in Figure 1.3. Start with smaller curved shapes along the neckline and bigger ones along the body. Slowly move on to smaller curved shapes toward the tail.

For the wings, use the shapes as shown in Figure 1.3, leaving some spaces along the wing. Feel free to fill up the space in some shapes while leaving some as simple outlines. Allow the painting to dry before moving on to the next fun step!

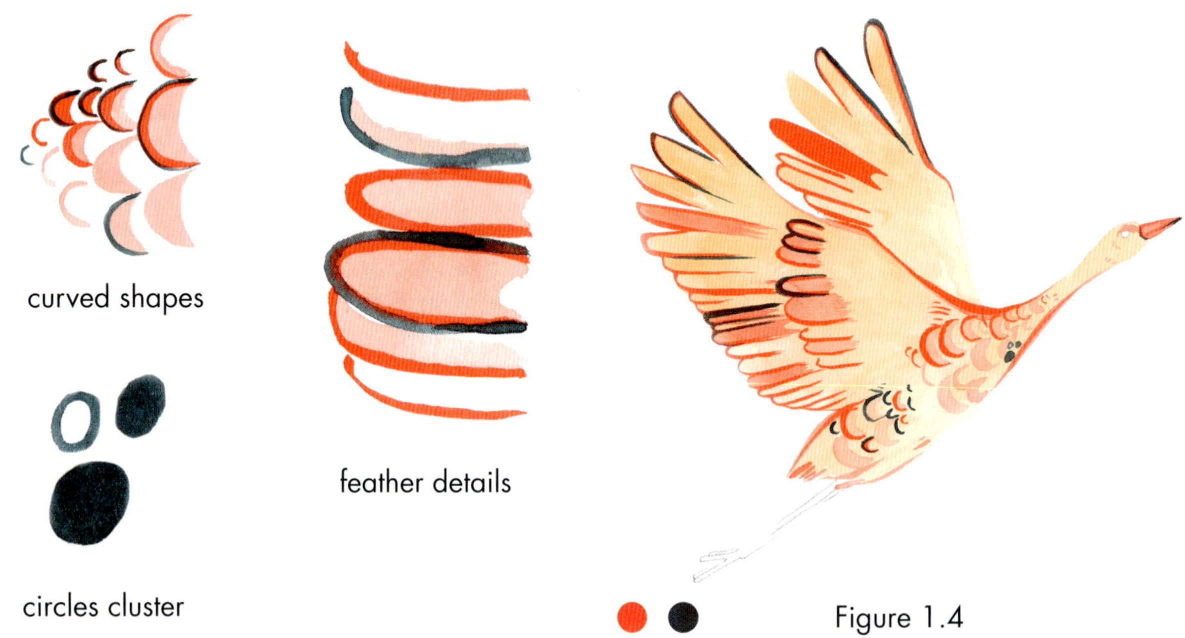


Figure 1.4

**Step 4:** We are at the second to last step of our lovely painting. Here, we are going to add some deeper red and indigo blue details to the painting using the script liner brush.

First, start by adding a scarlet red outline to the already-painted shapes from step 3, along the body and the feathers. Use red to paint curves along the edge of the crane's body. This gives the painting more depth and adds a shadow layer. Paint in the beak and the top of head while also adding some gentle strokes at the cheek of the crane.

Now, switch the color in the brush to indigo for more details, like circles and curved lines. Make sure to wash off the red from the brush to avoid colors mixing on the brush. Once this layer is dry, add a couple of indigo blue lines to further deepen the colors of the painting, as seen in Figure 1.4.

**Pro-Tip:** Add indigo curve lines to the body of the bird at the beak, the eye, the chest and the underbelly. This balances the blue used at the tips of the wings.

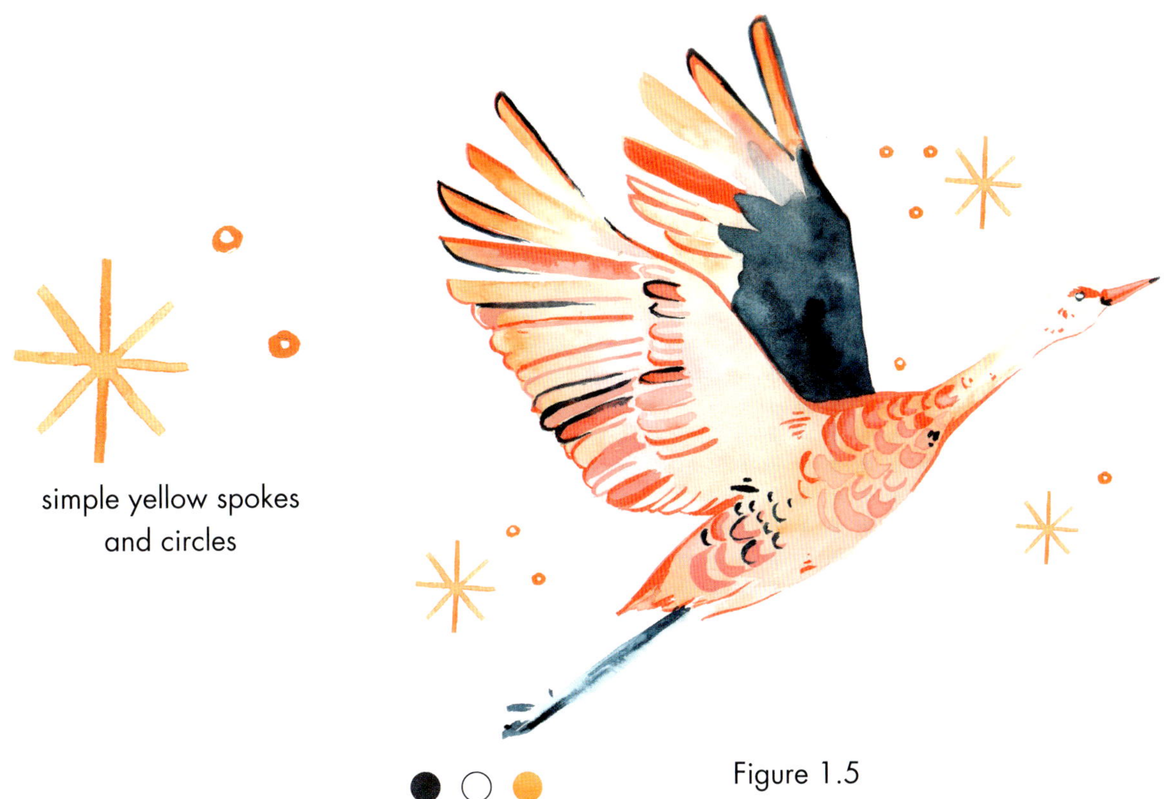


Figure 1.5

**Step 5:** Complete the painting by adding an indigo shadow layer of the front wing on the back wing as shown in Figure 1.5. This can be done with a round brush to quickly cover a larger area. Next, paint the feet of the crane with indigo.

As this layer dries, load a clean script liner brush with white acrylic paint and add a small dot on the eye to represent the eye reflection.

Wash your script liner before loading it with chrome yellow. Use this to paint simple spokes and circles around the crane.

**Pro-Tip:** Cluster the elements and place them in a way that balances the composition.

# Puffin

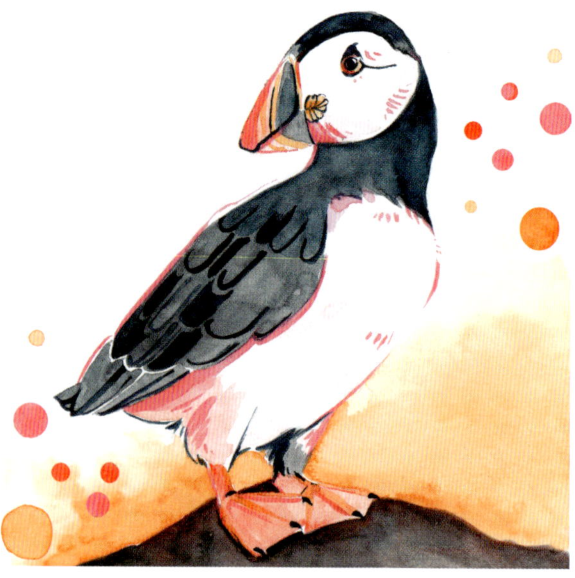

*Initially, I was unsure if I should choose puffins for this book of watercolor birds; however, I realized that puffins are very different from a lot of birds in terms of their very prominent beaks. In step 1, really focus on drawing your puffin with accurate proportions by making the beak large and the feet smaller. Having a good base drawing will ensure a stunning final painting.*

## MATERIALS

Watercolor cold press paper, 200gsm (95lb)
Pencil
Kneadable eraser
Palette
Glass cup
Watercolor mop brush, size 000
Round brush, size 4
Script liner brush, size 0
Tissue paper

## CHALLENGE LEVEL

## COLOR SCHEME

 Chrome Yellow

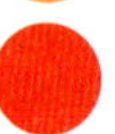 Scarlet Red

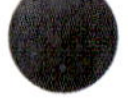 Ivory Black

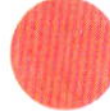 Bright Pink (can be made by mixing Scarlet Red with White watercolor paint)

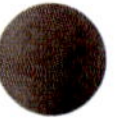 Burnt Umber (can be made by mixing Sienna with a dash of Ivory Black)

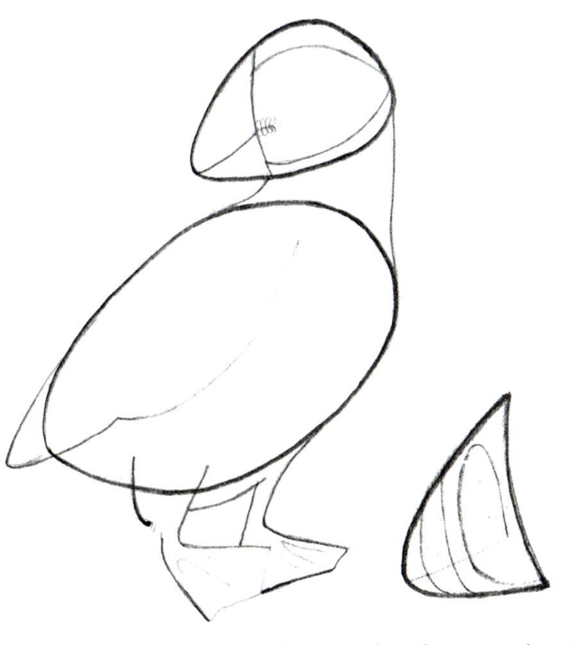

Figure 1.1 beak inner details

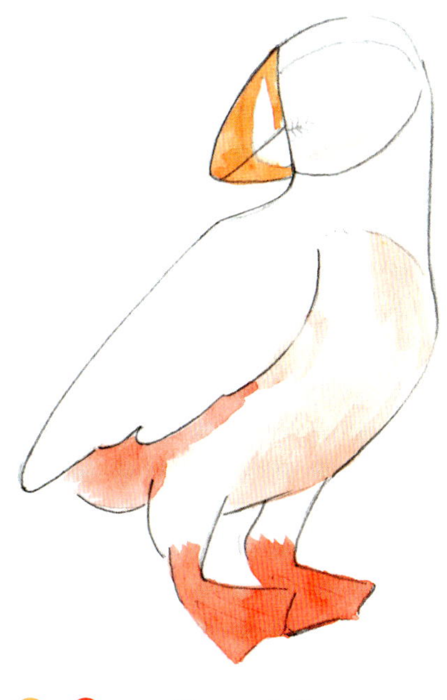

Figure 1.2

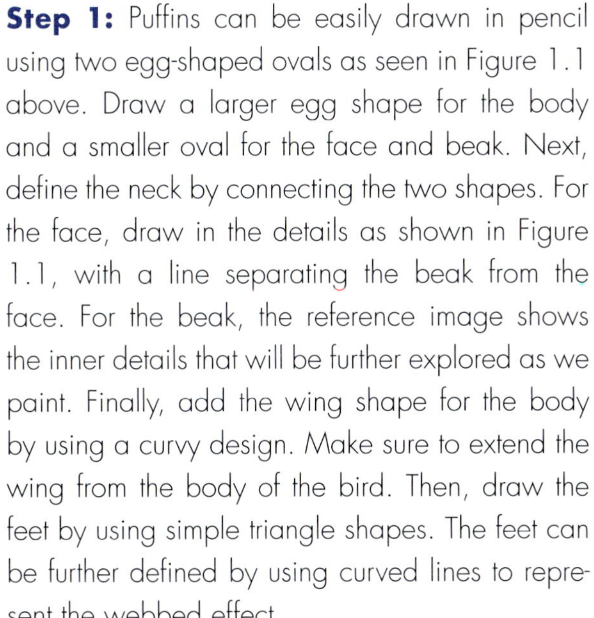

**Step 1:** Puffins can be easily drawn in pencil using two egg-shaped ovals as seen in Figure 1.1 above. Draw a larger egg shape for the body and a smaller oval for the face and beak. Next, define the neck by connecting the two shapes. For the face, draw in the details as shown in Figure 1.1, with a line separating the beak from the face. For the beak, the reference image shows the inner details that will be further explored as we paint. Finally, add the wing shape for the body by using a curvy design. Make sure to extend the wing from the body of the bird. Then, draw the feet by using simple triangle shapes. The feet can be further defined by using curved lines to represent the webbed effect.

Once you are happy with the final drawing, let's use a kneadable eraser to erase any harsh lines so that they don't affect our final painting.

**Step 2:** Start with a light wash of yellow for the beak by using a round brush. For a light wash of yellow, add more water to the paint, as explained in the Translucency with Watercolors section on page 16. Paint a wash on the beak as seen in the Figure 1.2.

Next, clean your round brush to paint a wash of scarlet red paint. Be sure to tone down this layer by adding water as explored in the Translucency with Watercolor section on page 16. Start painting a gentle wash for the body of the bird. Next paint the feet of the bird, making sure that the edges are jagged. Allow this layer to dry completely before moving on to the next step.

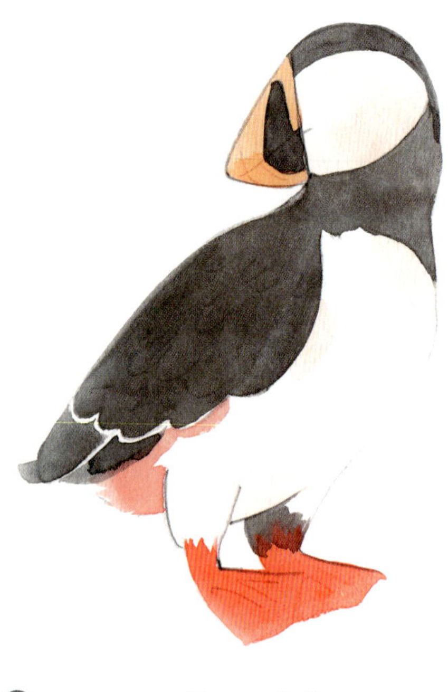

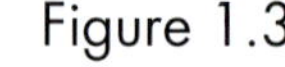

Figure 1.3

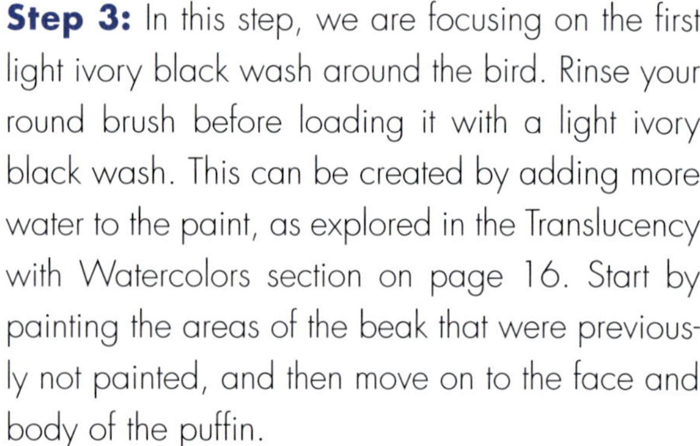

**Step 3:** In this step, we are focusing on the first light ivory black wash around the bird. Rinse your round brush before loading it with a light ivory black wash. This can be created by adding more water to the paint, as explored in the Translucency with Watercolors section on page 16. Start by painting the areas of the beak that were previously not painted, and then move on to the face and body of the puffin.

As much as possible, follow the general areas where black has been painted. For the wings, use a scalloped edge to show the feathers. Allow the painting to dry before moving on to the next step.

**Pro-Tip:** Leave a white space between the bottom layers of the wings to add to the final effect of the painting.

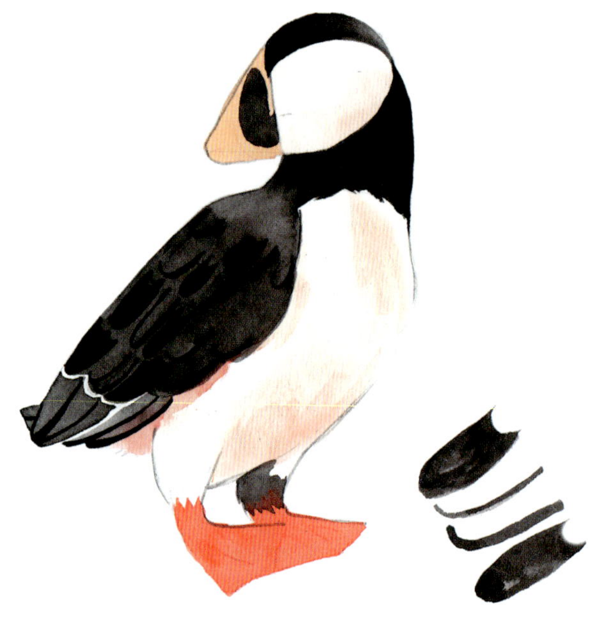

Figure 1.4 wing textures

**Step 4:** You are doing amazing—let's move on to defining the inner details of the feathers. For this, we will be using an opaque layer of ivory black (as mentioned in the Translucency with Watercolors section on page 16). Use the single-color gradient effect to darken the areas of the face above and along the neck. This effect can be created by using clear water to gently blend the paints as seen in the Practice Exercises on page 19.

Now, use curved shapes to fill in the wings of the bird. Try to reduce the length of the curved shapes as they move from the bottom up. I like to mix adding U-shapes and outlines to balance the details. Additionally, add some black to the left foot of the bird to show that it is the back foot and is therefore cast in shadow. Allow the layer to dry before moving to the next step.

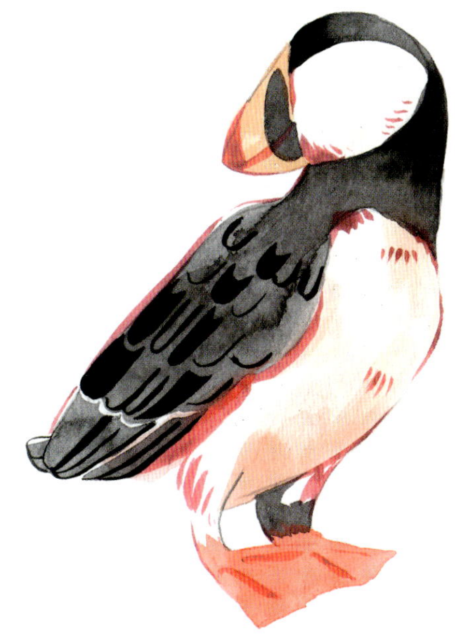

Figure 1.5

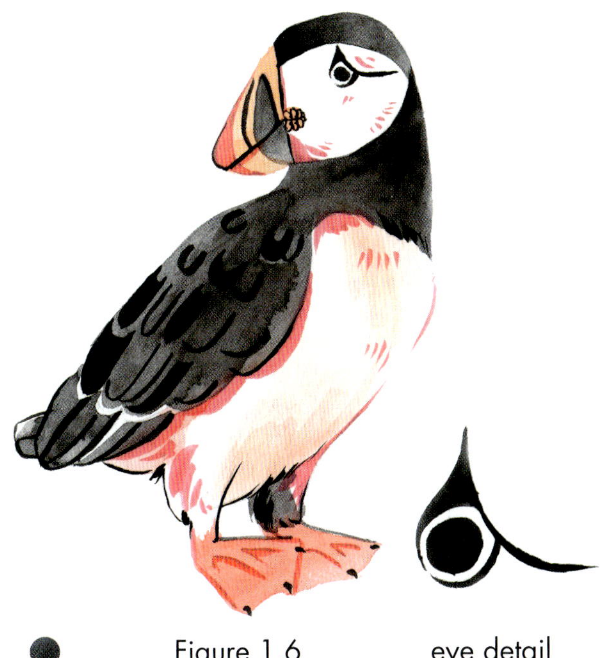

Figure 1.6 eye detail

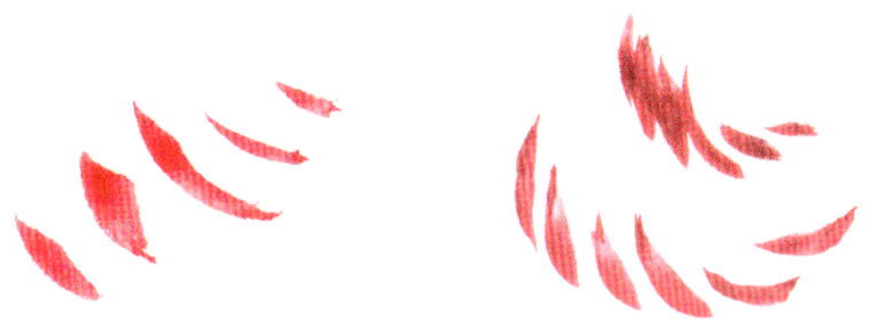

thin detail lines

**Step 5:** This is my favorite step in the project; let's add bright pink to make our puffin more fun.

This can be done by using a script liner brush for easier control. Use your bright pink for a light outline around the bird as well as the area below the wings to create depth.

**Pro-Tip:** Instead of applying bright pink as blobs of paint, use thin curved lines. Figure 1.5 shows the breakdown of the curved lines used. The image on the right shows the separated version of the lines, which when brought together, give an interesting detail.

Add the bright pink for the webbed feet to show the webbed effect.

Allow the painting to dry before moving on to the face details of the puffin.

**Step 6:** This is the final step and is focused on the face and beak details of the puffin. This step needs some additional love, since this is the main part of the puffin.

Pay attention to the zoomed-in details of the eye with two concentric circles and a triangle-shaped mark above the eye. This step can be easily painted by using a script liner brush loaded with ivory black. Be sure to clean your brush from any previous paints before loading it with the new color.

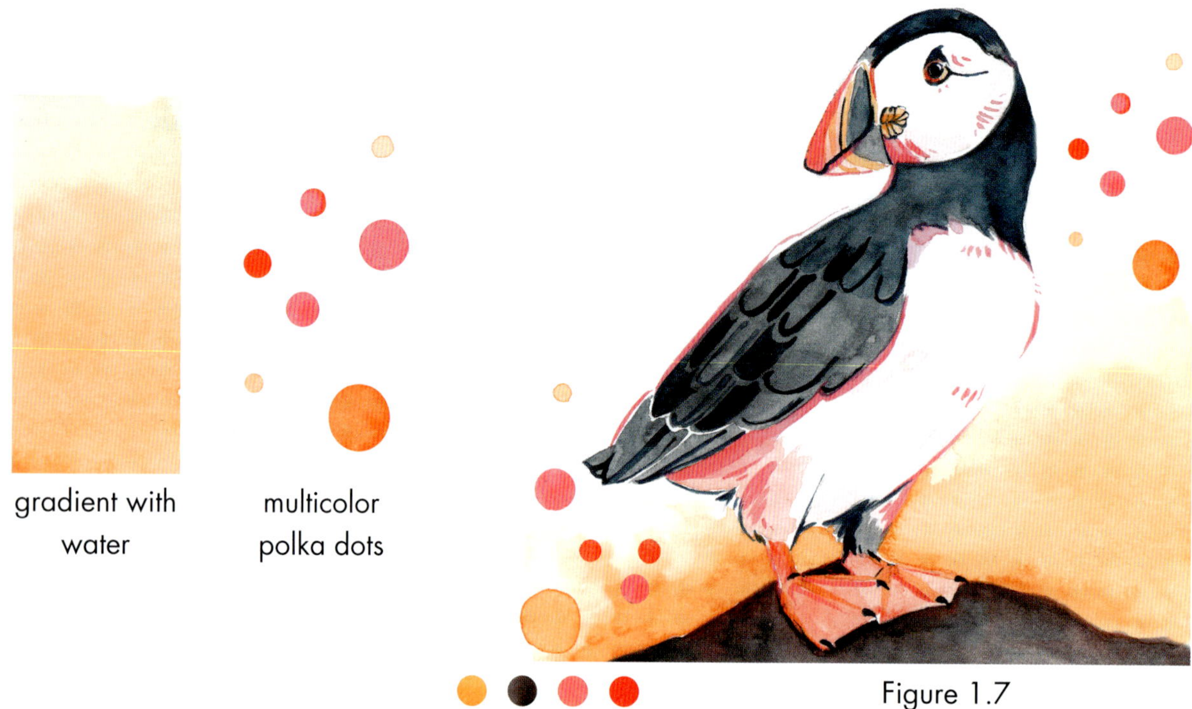

Figure 1.7

For the beak, paint thin lines following Figure 1.6, down the middle and the outline. The beak is the most important detail on puffins, since it is their most defining feature.

**Step 7:** Are you ready to complete the puffin painting with a simple background that highlights the bird? Here, we will be using a couple of details that we went over in the Practice Exercise chapter on page 19. Use a clean mop brush loaded with chrome yellow. Paint a lovely single-color gradient wash from the bottom of the bird to the top. Use clean water near the top to create a gentle blend. Allow this layer to dry before using a round brush to paint burnt umber rocks. Burnt umber can be mixed as shown in the color scheme section at the start of the project.

Finally, paint multicolored circles around our bird in bright pink, chrome yellow and scarlet red.

**Pro-Tip:** Every time you switch paints, make sure to wash your brush thoroughly.

# Mallard Duck

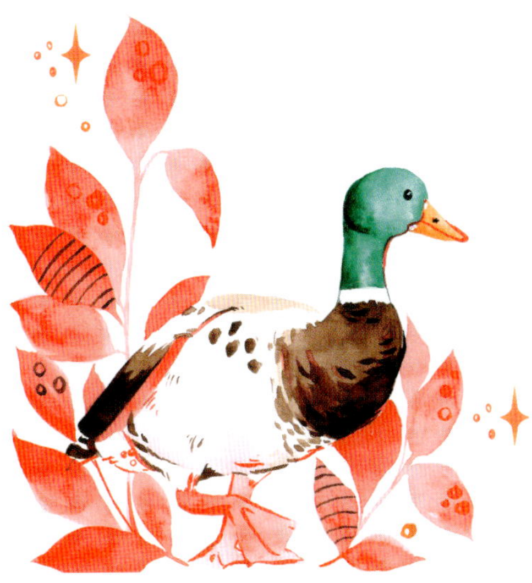

*When discussing birds that live around ponds and lakes, ducks are generally first and foremost. Now, there are so many varieties of ducks, but I chose to explore mallard ducks. I love their intense green color and white collar, which is a nice change from the usual brown and white birds. By using shades of red in our composition, we are going to create a stunning backdrop that will highlight the bird and make it the hero of the image.*

---

## MATERIALS

Watercolor cold press paper, 200gsm (95lb)
Pencil
Kneadable eraser
Palette
Glass cup
Round brush, size 4
Script liner brush, size 0
Tissue paper

## COLOR SCHEME

- Chrome Yellow
- Viridian Green
- Scarlet Red
- Burnt Sienna

## CHALLENGE LEVEL

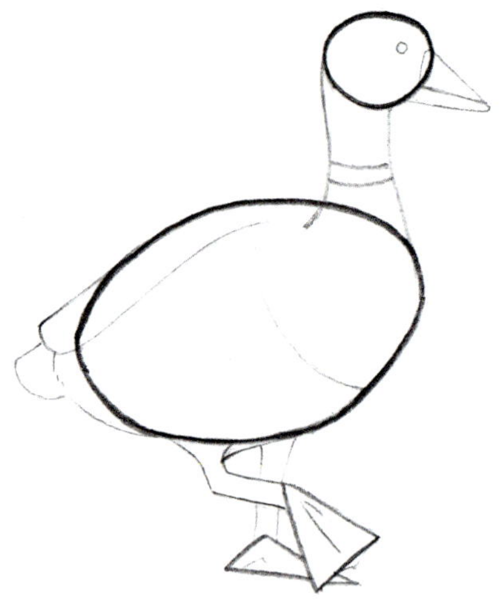

Figure 1.1

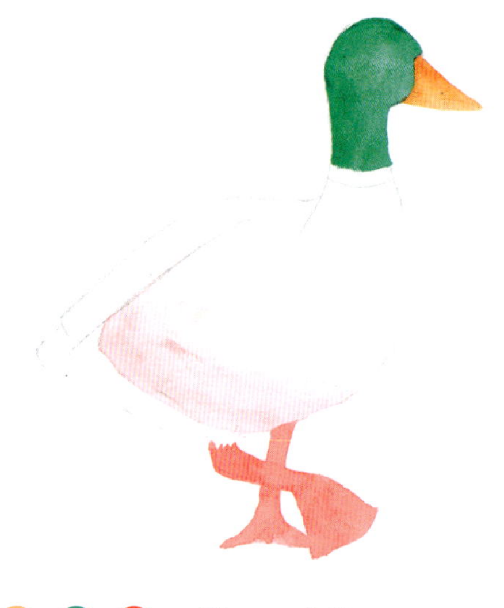

Figure 1.2

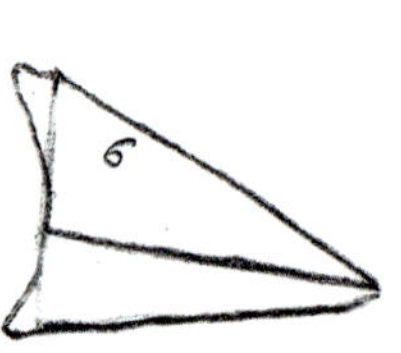

triangle shape for the beak

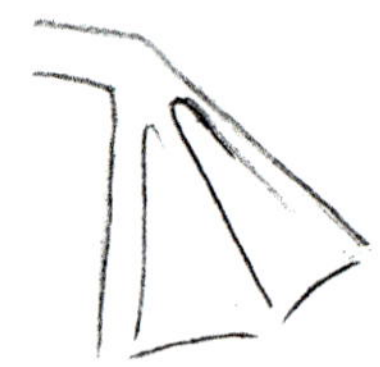

triangle shape for webbed feet

**Step 1:** To simplify the drawing part of the duck, let's break it down into simple egg shapes as seen in Figure 1.1. Using a pencil, draw one big egg shape for the body of the duck. Next, draw a smaller egg shape for the head of the duck, connecting it with S lines for the neckline. Continue with a triangle beak for the face of the duck and a simple neck line to highlight the signature mallard look.

Draw the wings along the back of the duck and continue on to drawing the webbed feet. Simplify the webbed feet by using simple triangles. Now that we have completed the drawing, gently erase any of the darker pencil lines with a kneadable eraser.

**Step 2:** Now, let's start painting. First, start with the beak by using the round brush and chrome yellow. Then, wash the brush and load it with viridian green. Paint viridian green for the face and the neck of the duck, as seen in Figure 1.2. Lastly, switch the color in the brush to scarlet red, but remember to first wash off the viridian green. Paint the feet scarlet red. Next, paint a single-color gradient layer from the left end of the body. This wash is explained in the Practice Exercises chapter on page 19. Use clear water to gently blend the paint. Allow the painting to dry before moving on to the next step.

**Step 3:** This step is going to be really fun as we will be adding burnt sienna. Wash your round brush before loading it with burnt sienna. Use a light wash by adding more water to the paint, as explained in the Translucency with Watercolors section on page 16. Now, paint a layer on the bird's chest. Next, paint the bird's back wing. Now add some diamond shapes at the belly to create texture within the painting.

Use a cluster of parallel strokes around the body of the bird.

**Pro-Tip:** Use a single-color brown gradient to deepen the shadow around the face and neckline. As shared in the Practice Exercises (page 19), start with a brown wash. Next, with a clean brush, gently touch the previous brown layer for a gentle blend.

Allow the layer to dry before moving to the next fun step!

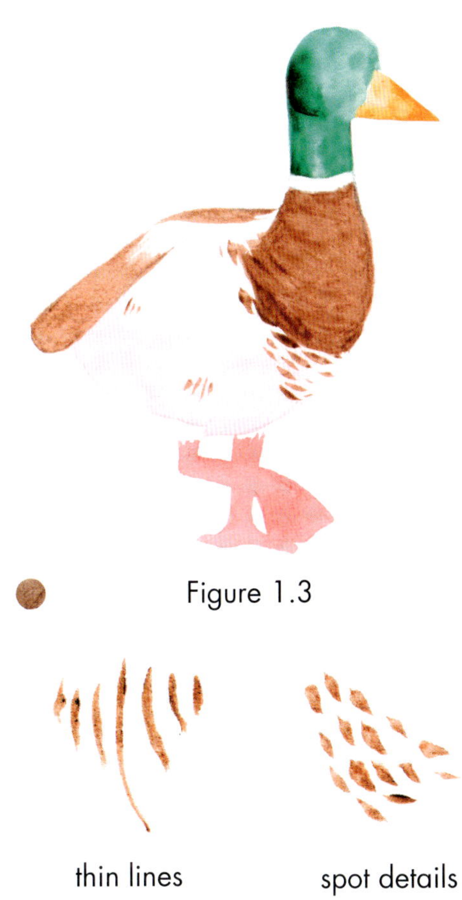


Figure 1.3

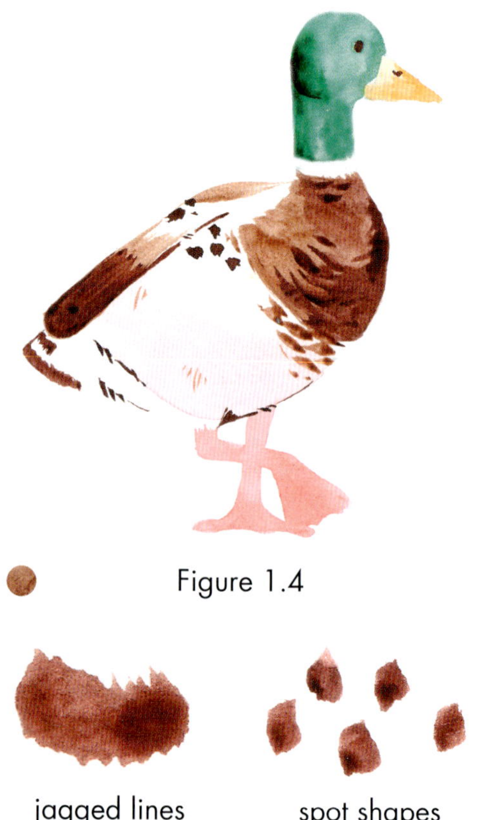


Figure 1.4

**Step 4:** All we will be doing in this step is adding more burnt sienna to deepen the colors even further. For this purpose, use a round brush to layer the underbelly area. I prefer to use thin dashed lines to create more texture in this step. Next, add more brown to the feather along the wings. Finally, add small lines and spot shapes around the duck to create more textures. Using the script liner brush, add burnt sienna for the eye.

Allow the layers to dry before moving to the next step.

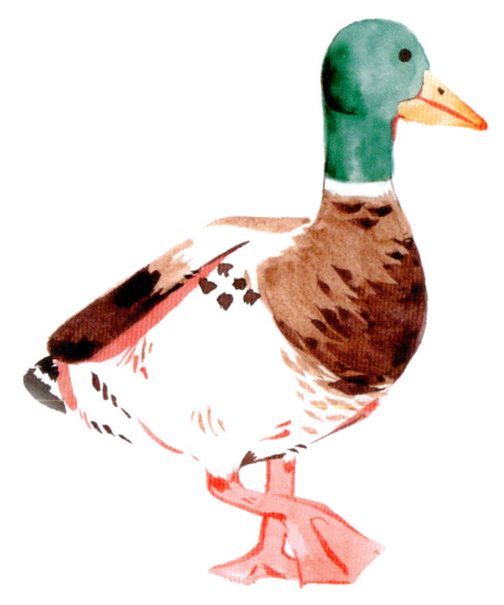

Figure 1.5

**Step 5:** Let's dive into our final layer for the duck. Here, using scarlet red, add more highlights with the script liner brush. Be sure to clean the brush of any previous colors before loading it with scarlet red. Use thin parallel strokes around the body of the duck, as seen in Figure 1.5.

**Pro-Tip:** Try to just use a couple of clusters to create texture within the painting.

Use the script liner brush loaded with scarlet red to outline the feet. Be sure to add thin outlines for the webbing. Use red along the middle of the beak and the edge. Allow the painting to dry before moving to the background.

**Step 6:** Let's finish the painting of the duck with a couple of fun elements. From the Practice Exercises on page 19, let's add fun single-color gradient leaves using a round brush loaded with scarlet red. I like to first draw the leaves on either side to ensure the placement before painting them. Remember to use the single-color gradient effect, starting with scarlet red at the tip of the leaf and add a wash of clear water along the bottom of the leaf for a gentle blend.

While this layer is drying, clean your script brush and load it with chrome yellow. Use this to paint circles and fun diamond shapes. Balance it out on either side by creating simple clusters. I like using chrome yellow to bring out the color from the duck through the composition. Check to make sure that the leaves are dry. Now wash your script liner brush and load it with scarlet red. Use this to paint circles and miniature lines on the leaves. Alternatively, switch the paint to burnt sienna to add some details on the leaves.

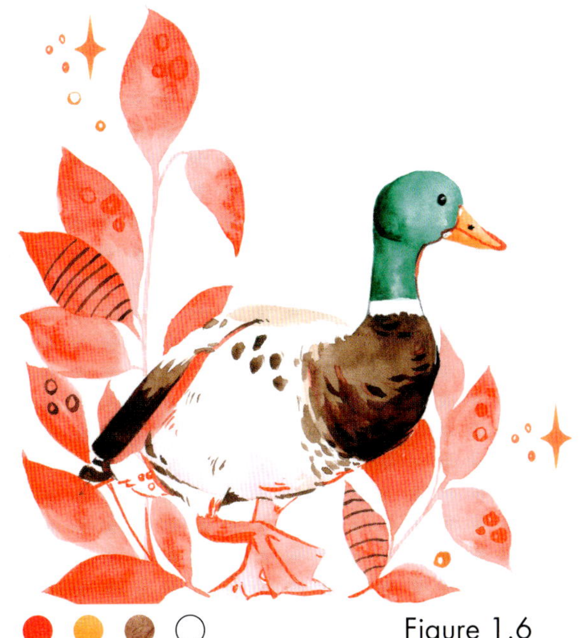

Figure 1.6

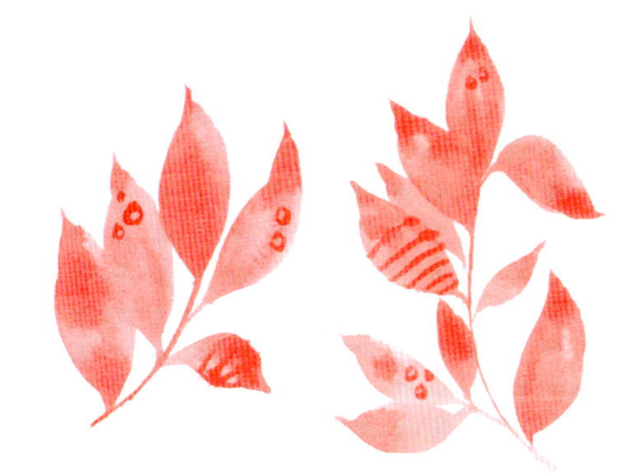

textured leaves

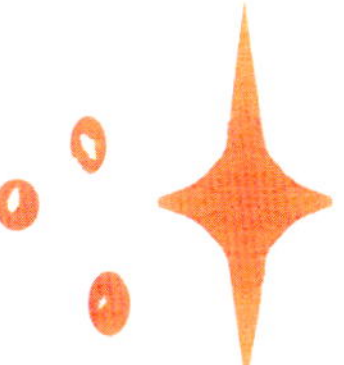

diamond and circle shapes

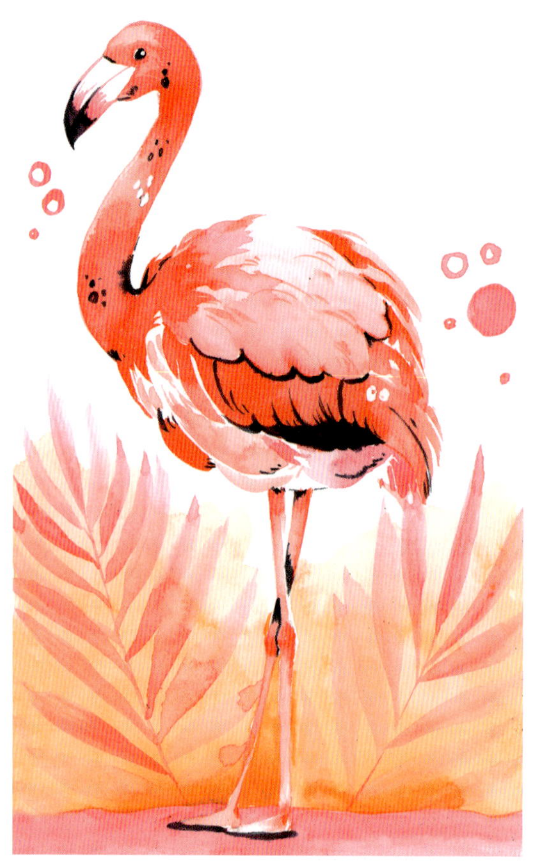

# Flamingo

*Flamingoes are very uncommon where I live. However, recently I found that a lovely café had a miniature artificial lake and some flamingoes. I was so excited that I dragged my sister to watch these majestic birds while I sipped my tea. As an homage to that wonderful afternoon, let's paint flamingoes in this tutorial. Keep watch for steps 2 and 3 as we paint the base layers for the flamingo. This is crucial as we build depth in the painting.*

## MATERIALS

Watercolor cold press paper, 200gsm (95lb)
Pencil
Kneadable eraser
Palette
Glass cup
Watercolor mop brush, size 000
Round brush, size 4
Script liner brush, size 0
Tissue paper

## COLOR SCHEME

Scarlet Red

Bright Pink (can be made by mixing Scarlet Red with White watercolor paint)

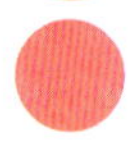

Ivory Black

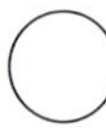

White acrylic paint

Chrome Yellow

## CHALLENGE LEVEL

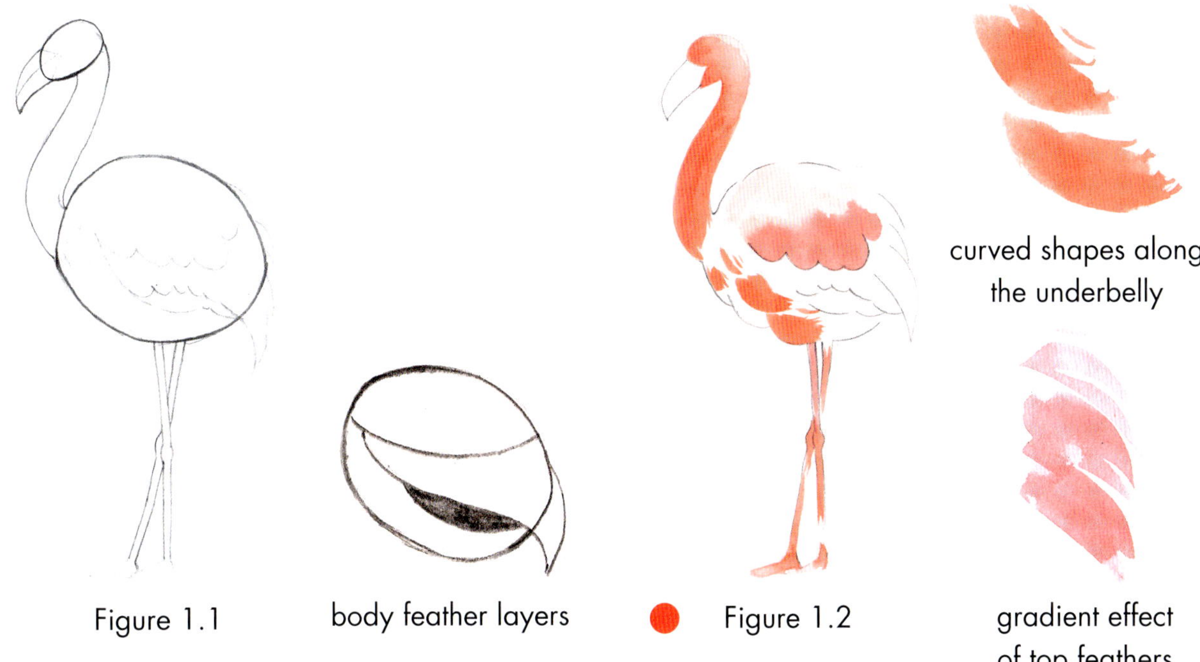


Figure 1.1 body feather layers Figure 1.2 gradient effect of top feathers

**Step 1:** Let's begin by drawing our bright flamingo using simple geometric shapes with a pencil. First, we start with the body by using an oval shape. Then, use two parallel S lines to represent the neck and connect the body of the flamingo to the face. Again, the face is drawn using a similar oval. For the beak, draw a triangle shape with the edge pointing downwards. Next, draw the legs of the flamingo with long thin lines and a simple triangle shape for the feet.

Finally, draw the inner shape of the wings on the back of the body. Two prominent layers make up the final wing. One is a simple semicircle and the other extends away from the body and points downwards, as shown in Figure 1.1. Be sure to erase any dark pencil lines with a kneadable eraser.

**Pro-Tip:** Instead of simply drawing a curved line, draw curved scallops to represent the feathers.

**Step 2:** Once, you are happy with your drawing, let's paint the flamingo. Use a mop brush for the first wash of scarlet red. This is a light wash created by adding water to the paint, as explained in the Translucency with Watercolors section on page 16. For the face and neck, simply paint the entire area with a single-color gradient effect, as explained in the Practice Exercises on page 19. Use this gradient effect for the wings as well, keeping the edge deeper in color.

Next, fill in the legs, leaving small spaces in between, as seen in Figure 1.2. Use simple U-shapes along the underbelly. These are rough shapes as seen in the highlight image. Allow the layer to dry before moving on to the next step.

**Pro-Tip:** Use jagged lines while filling up the spaces to create more texture in the painting.

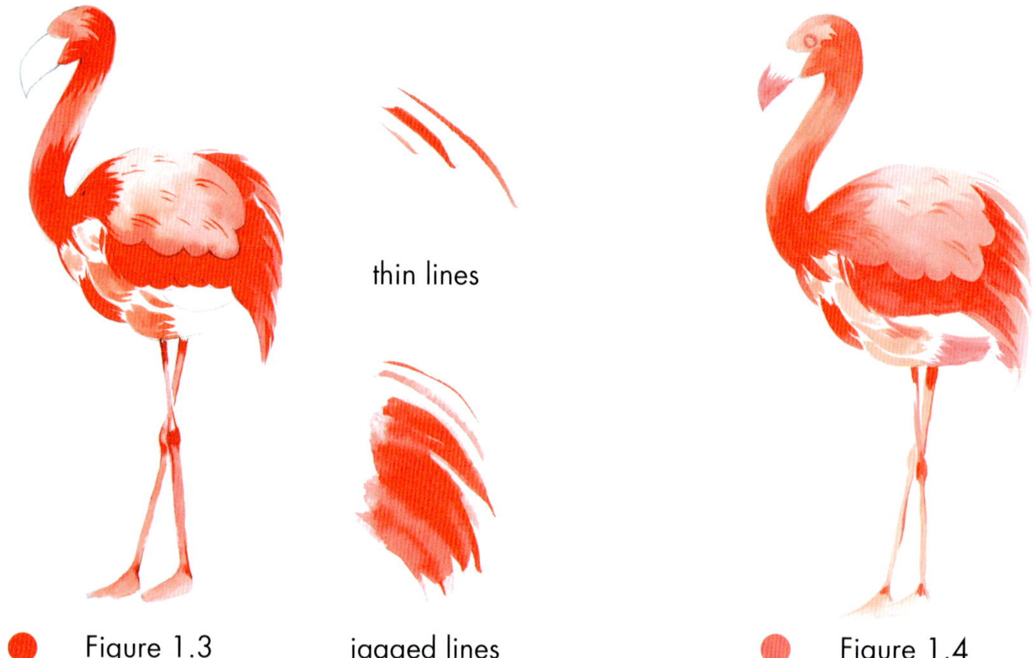


Figure 1.3

Figure 1.4

**Step 3:** Here, we are going to take the opportunity to make our colors even brighter by adding a second layer of scarlet red. Add in jagged lines for the top and bottom of the neck using your round brush. Paint the area below the first layer of wings to create a lovely deep layer. This creates variation between the feathers.

Additionally, use the scarlet red to paint in the second layer to brighten some of the underbelly shapes. Paint in the outlines along the feet. Use parallel lines that vary from short to long for more textures along the body. Move on to the next step while the paint is still wet.

**Step 4:** Here we quickly add bright pink to blend the colors along the neckline. Clean your round brush before loading it with bright pink. This color can be mixed following the directions from the color scheme section at the beginning of this project. Use bright pink strokes along the underbelly to balance out the color even more.

The reason for painting this layer while the painting is still wet is to create a simple gradient effect, as explained in the Dual-Color Gradient Effect section on page 20. Adding bright pink to the existing scarlet red creates a dual shade. Allow the layer to dry before moving on to the next step.

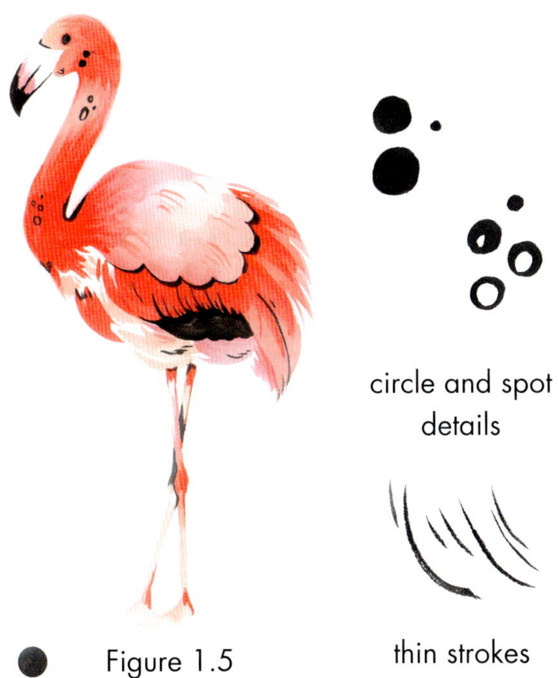


Figure 1.5

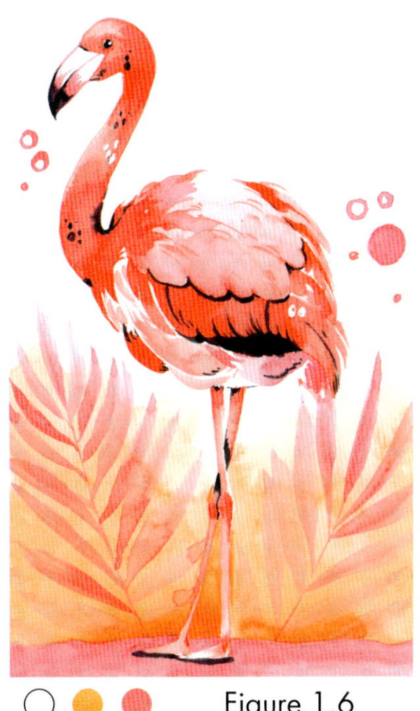

Figure 1.6

**Step 5:** Let's complete our flamingo with a simple addition of ivory black with a thin script liner brush. Using ivory black, we are going to paint the outlines and shadows. Keep in mind that the area right below the second feather layer is generally darker and hence needs a layer of ivory black. Next, add circle spots, creating texture along the neck of the flamingo. Also, use thin lines in parallel strokes of varying lengths to create texture along the body, as shown in Figure 1.5.

**Step 6:** The final step for the painting, which is very crucial, is to add white mini details along the body. This can be done with a script liner brush. Be sure to wash out any previous color in the brush before loading it with white acrylic paint. Paint clusters of small spots along the neckline and the wings.

Once the bird is complete, move on to the background. A simple gradient wash from chrome yellow to clear water highlights the complexity of the painting. For this, we will use a single-color gradient effect (see page 19) of chrome yellow to fill in the space. Use a round brush so that you can easily paint around the areas near the legs of the bird. Allow the layer to dry completely before loading your clean round brush with bright pink to paint the ground below. Next, add some unique leaves to the background. This is similar to the thin and thick lines exercise in the Practice Exercises on page 19. Start with a thin line, then press down on the brush for a wider leaf, followed by lifting the brush up slightly to create a thin line again. Add some spots and circles for an air of whimsy. Balance them on either side to complete the composition.

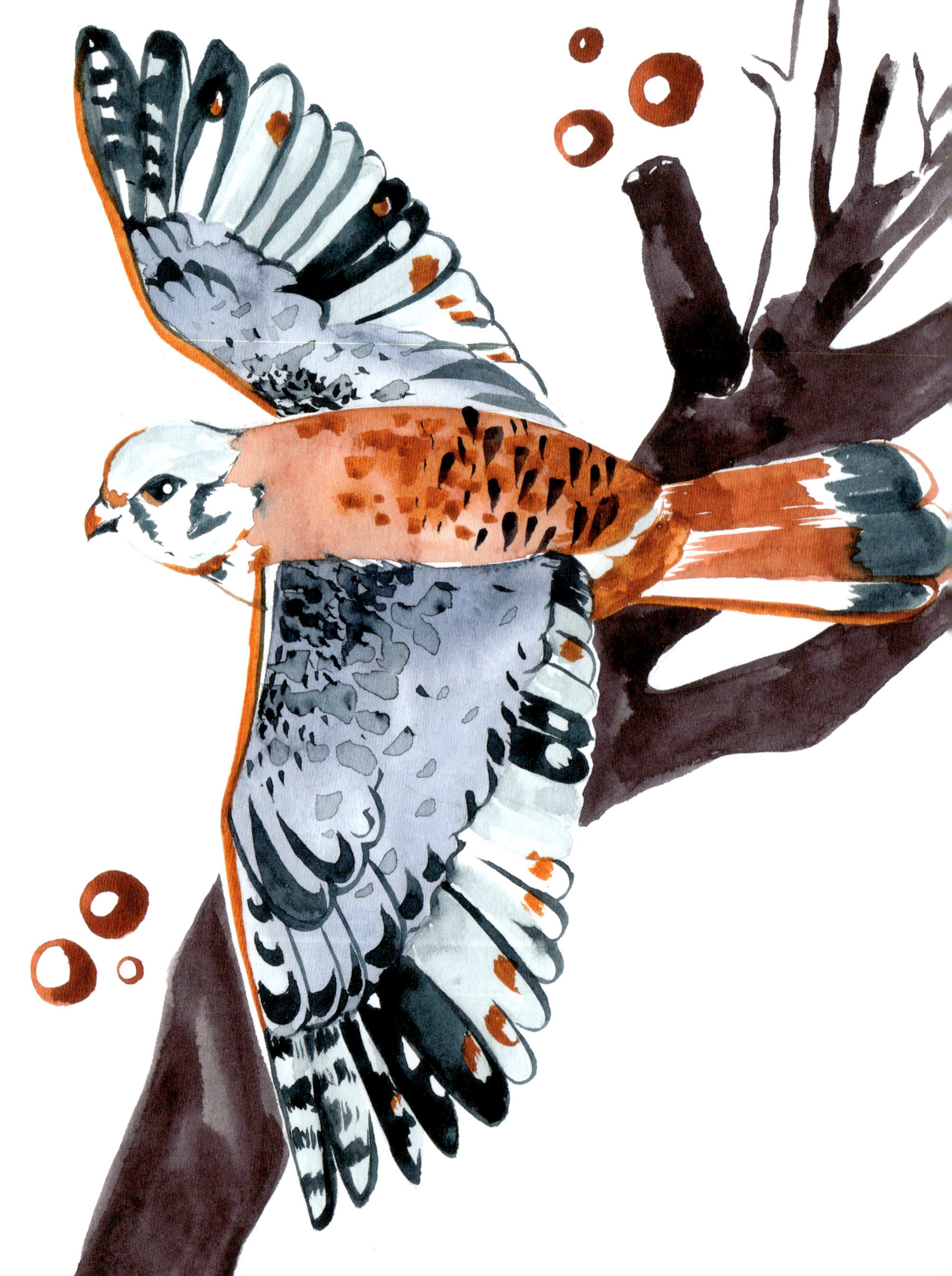

# Mountain Birds

Birds of prey are the most common mountain birds. Eagles, vultures, kestrels, falcons, owls and hawks are just a few popular varieties. Since I grew up in the Middle East, these birds have always had a special place in my heart. Most birds of prey can be seen in mountainous desert areas, and falcons and hawks are often part of the culture. I have even stood with a hawk on my arm for a couple of seconds. I have to say it was a memorable moment that I will cherish.

Known for their wide wingspan, some of the birds of prey are similar in structure. For example, kestrels, falcons and hawks have similar beaks and body shapes.

In this chapter, we will be exploring some of the more popular mountain birds, starting with mountain bluebirds on page 122. In this tutorial, I will be sharing my tips and tricks for painting monotone birds. Next, we will be painting American bald eagles on page 127. This beautiful bird is a delight to paint. Then, we will move on to song thrushes on page 132, broad-tailed hummingbirds on page 136 and a Northern saw-whet owls on page 140. I have chosen each of these birds for their distinctive features. Owls are known for their big bold eyes, hummingbirds for their textured bodies and song thrushes for their unique spotted feathers.

Finally, the last tutorial in the book is the American kestrel on page 144. This bird is quite tricky to paint since it has so much texture. However, we are going to tackle the kestrel in several easy steps for a lovely composition.

Ready for our final chapter? Let's begin painting some mountain birds.

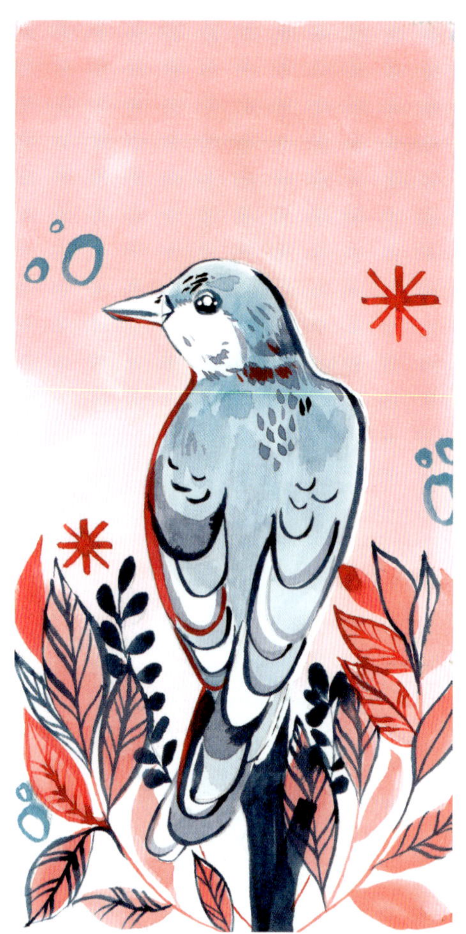

# Mountain Bluebird

*Bluebirds are visually stunning birds seen along the mountain terrain. The reason I chose bluebirds for our first project is because of their monotone color scheme. While working with a bird that is monotone, it is important to add complementary colors to enhance the look of the painting. Since the bird is relatively simple to paint, we will also be playing with the background to enhance our artwork. Let's dive into this interesting painting that I am sure you will enjoy.*

## MATERIALS

Watercolor cold press paper, 200gsm (95lb)
Pencil
Kneadable eraser
Palette
Glass cup
Watercolor mop brush, size 000
Round brush, size 4
Script liner brush, size 0
Tissue paper

## COLOR SCHEME

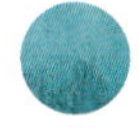 Ultramarine Blue

 Indigo

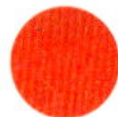 Scarlet Red

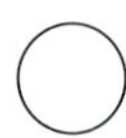 White acrylic paint

 Light Pink (can be made by mixing Scarlet Red and White watercolor paint)

## CHALLENGE LEVEL

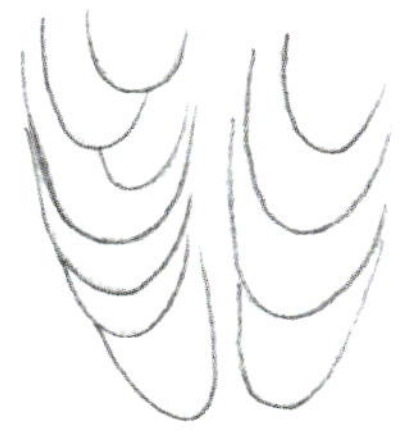

right and left side feathers

beak detail

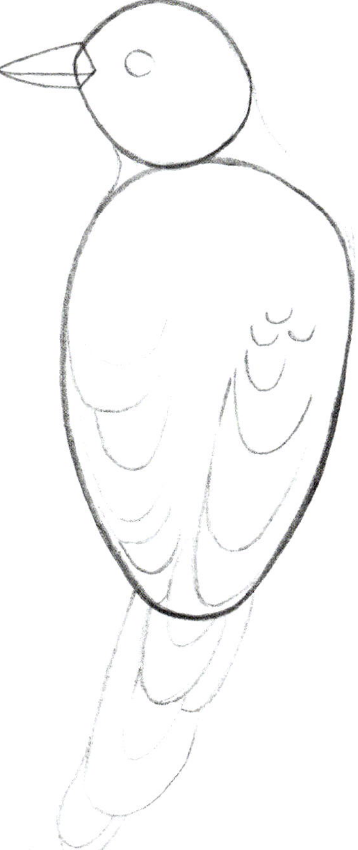

Figure 1.1

**Step 1:** Let's start by drawing our bluebird with a pencil. Use an inverted egg shape for the body of the bird. Follow that with a circle for the face and two triangles for the beak. The next part is where it gets a bit tricky: drawing the feathers. Use simple U-shapes for the right and left side wings as seen in Figure 1.1. Start with smaller U-shapes for the feathers along the body and use deeper U-shapes towards the tail feathers.

The last feather at the tail is generally much longer and layered, as seen in Figure 1.1. Erase any dark pencil lines with a kneadable eraser.

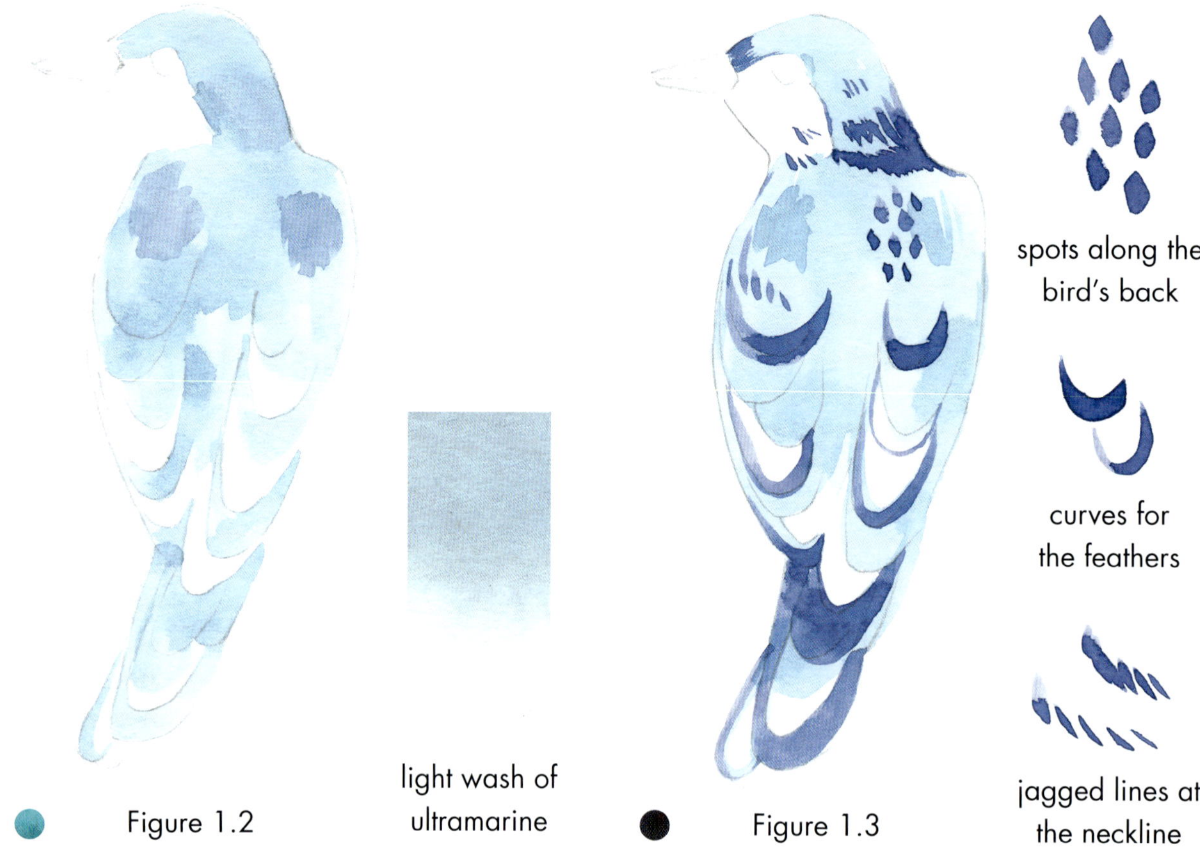


Figure 1.2

Figure 1.3

**Step 2:** Now we can start painting the base layer for the bluebird with a mop brush. Use an ultramarine blue wash on the body and the top of the bird's head. This is a light wash that has more water mixed into the paint, as explained in the Translucency with Watercolors section on page 16. Use this light wash along with the feathers as well. Feel free to skip a few feathers to create an asymmetrical look. Use Figure 1.2 as a reference point for the areas to paint and the areas to leave empty.

**Pro-Tip:** It is okay if the layer looks a bit patchy. In the upcoming steps, we can use this to add to the texture of the bird.

**Step 3:** Allow the previous layer to dry before moving on to this step. For this step, let's add more textures to the bird by using a round brush. Start with an indigo wash along the body from the neckline to the top of the head. This is a light wash with more water mixed with paint. For a textured look, use jagged lines as seen in the highlight image.

Paint in some spots along the shoulders of the bird. Also, use the indigo blue along the curve of the wings and tail feathers, as seen in Figure 1.3. You can see that this layer has added so much vibrancy to the painting. Allow it to dry before we add even more depth.

**Step 4:** In this step, we are going to add more depth by using a script liner brush loaded with saturated indigo blue. Start with dashes along the top of the beak and the eye. Next, paint some curve details on the bird's wings and tail feathers. Paint in the eye as well, using indigo. Next, paint a gentle outline of the bird using a script liner brush only on the right side.

**Pro-Tip:** The reason we paint only one side is that it gives the impression of the bird having a shadow. This simple trick can completely change your painting.

Now switch the color on the brush to scarlet red by first washing off the indigo. Add in some thin brushstrokes along the neckline and outline the left side of the bird. Because we are adding scarlet over the previous layer, the color might become darker, which is great since it complements the painting. I like to outline some of the feathers as well to bring more red to the painting. Allow the layer to dry before moving to the next step.

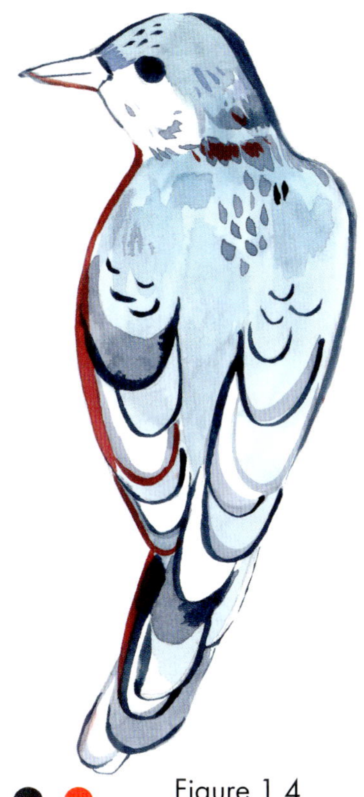

Figure 1.4

dashes along the head

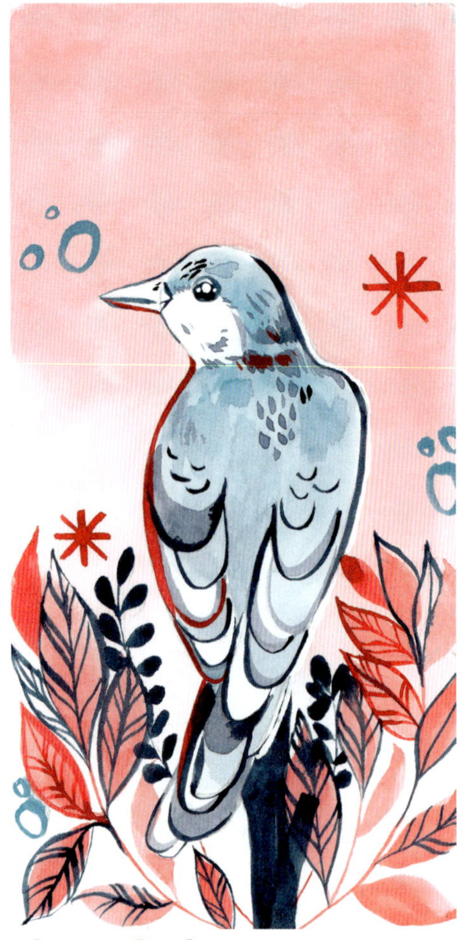

Figure 1.5

**Step 5:** Let's tie together our charming painting with a fun composition. First, to complete the bird, add white acrylic spots for the bird's eye using a script liner brush, as seen in Figure 1.4. This is an important trick to give life to the bird's eye.

Now for the background, we will be using the techniques from the Practice Exercises chapter on page 19. Start with a single-color gradient of light pink. Light pink can be mixed as seen in the color scheme section at the beginning of the project. Then, add a wash of clean water along the edge for a gentle blend to the bottom of the page. Allow this layer to dry before adding more elements.

Draw some lovely leaves along the sides of the bird. Then fill them with light pink. Next, using a script liner brush loaded with scarlet red, paint the outlines and inner details for the leaves. Using red, paint spokes around the bird. Now, switch to indigo to add more rounded leaf elements and outlines as seen in the highlight images. Add some circles to balance the painting, as well as the branch for the bird to perch on.

Overall, our lovely bird will still be the focus of the painting.

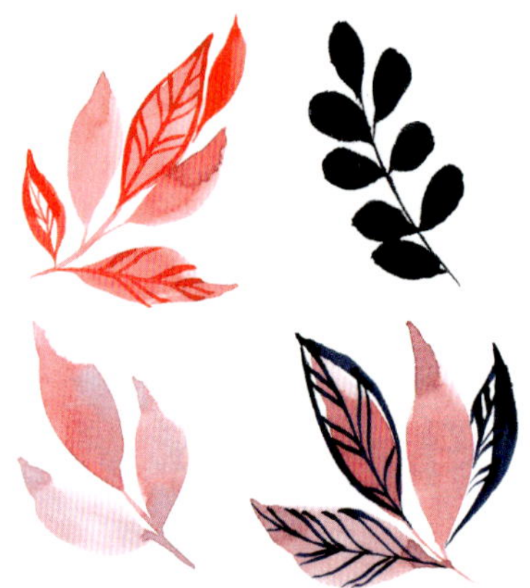

leaf details

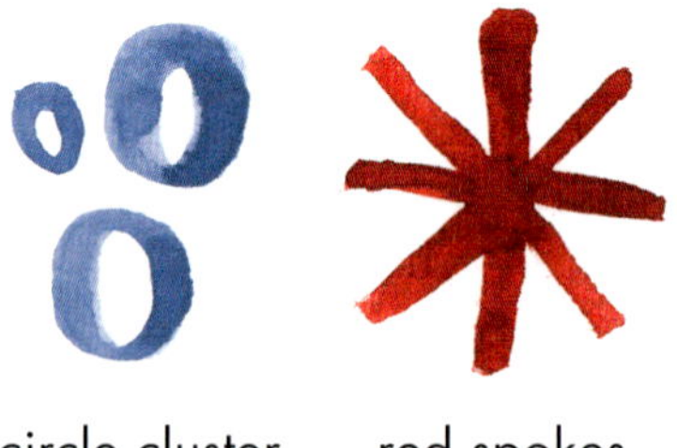

circle cluster red spokes

# American Bald Eagle

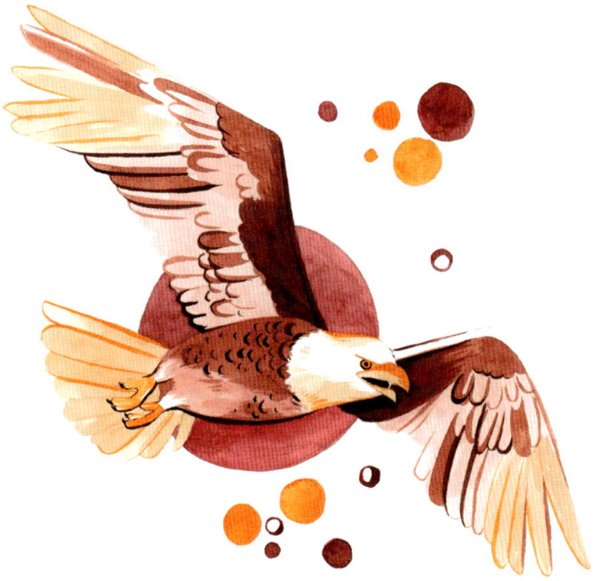

*One of the most popular and well-known eagle species is the American bald eagle. They are also known for their large nests, some of which can weigh up to 2,000 pounds! The reason I chose this distinctive bird is because I wanted to share tips and tricks for painting a bird that is a darker color. Trying to paint the feathers can be slightly difficult, so in step 4, I will share how to easily layer feather details.*

## MATERIALS

Watercolor cold press paper, 200gsm (95lb)
Pencil
Kneadable eraser
Palette
Glass cup
Round brush, size 4
Script liner brush, size 0
Tissue paper

## CHALLENGE LEVEL

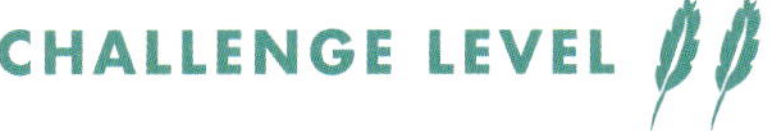

## COLOR SCHEME

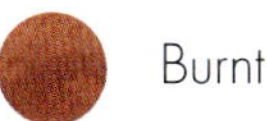

Burnt Sienna

Chrome Yellow

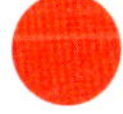

Scarlet Red

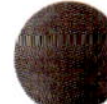

Burnt Umber (can be made by mixing Scarlet Red with a dash of Burnt Sienna and a dash of Ivory Black)

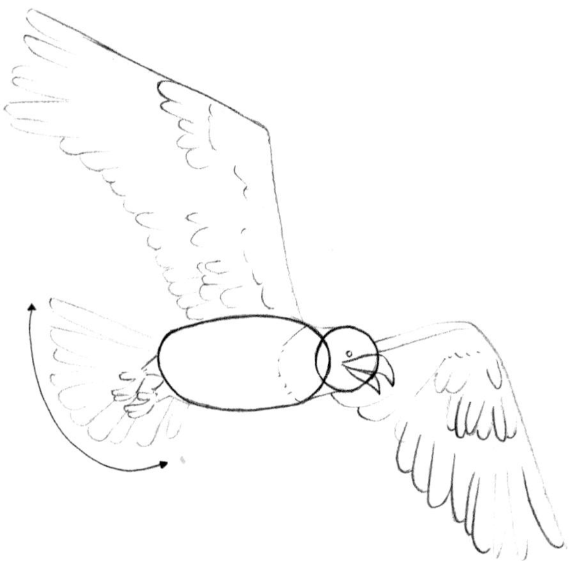

Figure 1.1

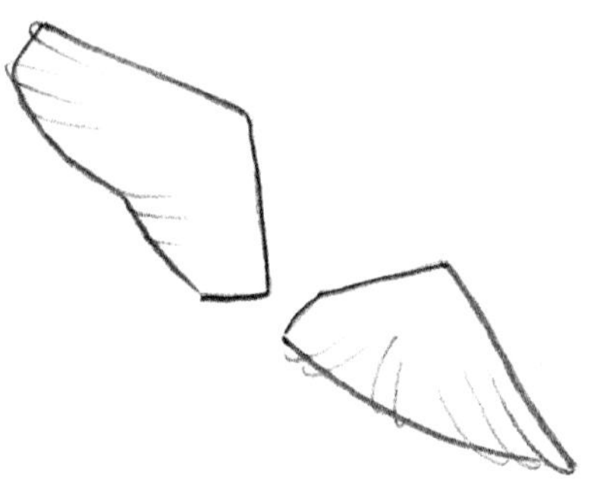

wing shapes

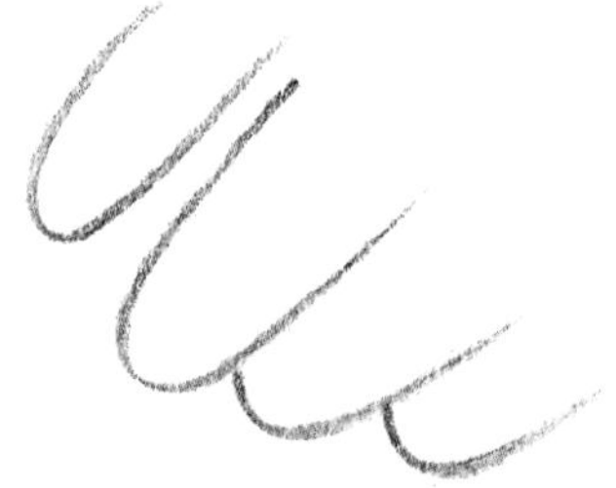

U-shape for the feathers

**Step 1:** To start drawing eagles, use a pencil to outline a simple circle for the face as well as an oval shape for the body. Connect the two with an almost parallel line for the neck of the bird. Now let's move on to add a curved beak, as seen in Figure 1.1. Next, add a small circle for the eye and extended arrow shapes for the feet.

For the tail feathers, draw a half circle. After drawing the basic shape, go ahead and add U-shapes to represent the individual feathers. Finally, use geometric shapes to easily draw the basic wing shape. Fill in the wings with small curves for the feathers. Use smaller feathers along the bone, as seen in Figure 1.1, and much larger U-shapes for the edge of the wings.

For the wings, use individual spaced-out U-shapes for the tips and closer curves near the body of the bird.

Once you have drawn your base eagle and are happy with the final look, use a kneadable eraser to erase any harsh lines before moving on to step 2.

**Step 2:** Let's start with the base layer wash by using the round brush. Use a lovely light wash of burnt sienna for the inner wings and body shape. For a light wash, add more water to the paint as explained in the Translucency with Watercolors section on page 16. It is okay if that layer looks patchy, as we will add to it in the next step.

Now, switch the paint in the brush to chrome yellow and paint the edges of the wings, tail feathers and beaks. Use some jagged lines of chrome yellow along the upper body. Figure 1.2 shows which areas to fill in with the lovely chrome yellow pigment.

Keep in mind to use a much more watered-down pigment as explained in the Translucency with Watercolor section on page 16 for this layer.

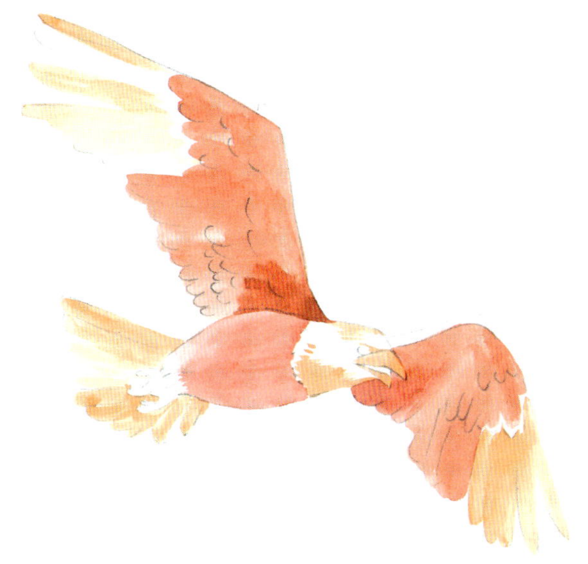

Figure 1.2

jagged lines

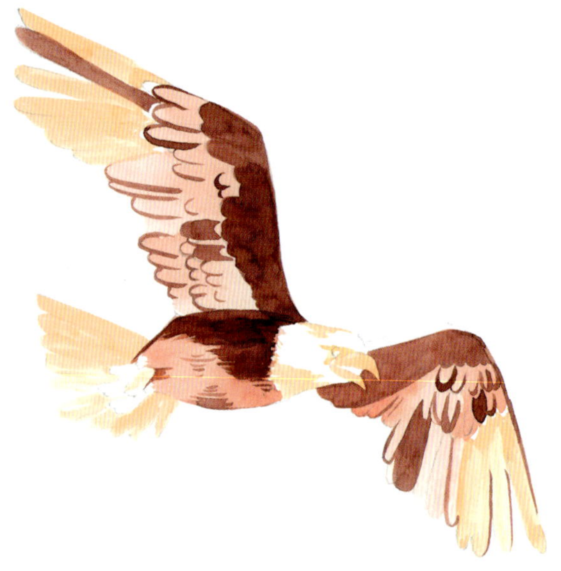

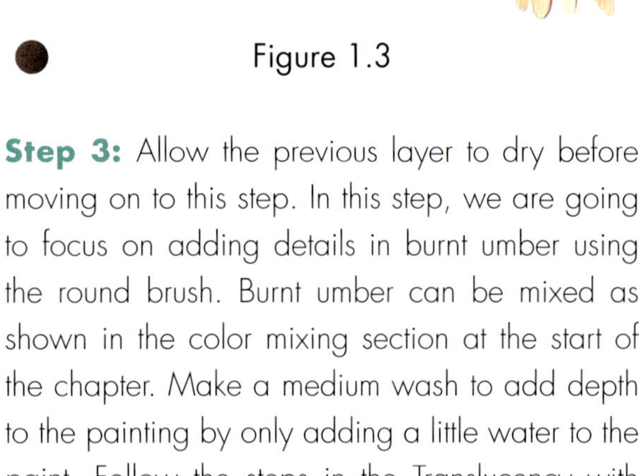

Figure 1.3

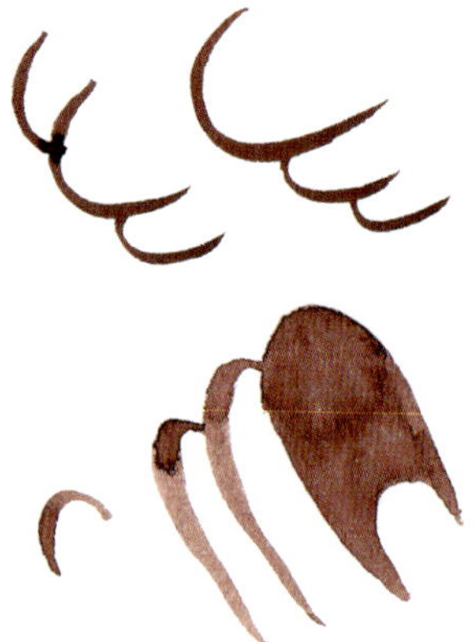

filling in the feathers

jagged lines along the body

**Step 3:** Allow the previous layer to dry before moving on to this step. In this step, we are going to focus on adding details in burnt umber using the round brush. Burnt umber can be mixed as shown in the color mixing section at the start of the chapter. Make a medium wash to add depth to the painting by only adding a little water to the paint. Follow the steps in the Translucency with Watercolors section on page 16.

Now, focus on the body of the eagle and fill it in with jagged lines to create more texture. Next, paint the area around the bone of the wings with the burnt umber. Next, add in the curved shapes for the feathers of the wings. Refer to Figure 1.3 for a better understanding of the placement of these details.

**Pro-Tip:** The trick here is to vary the width of the curved lines along with the wings. Use a mix of filled in U-shapes as well as outlines to balance the overall effect.

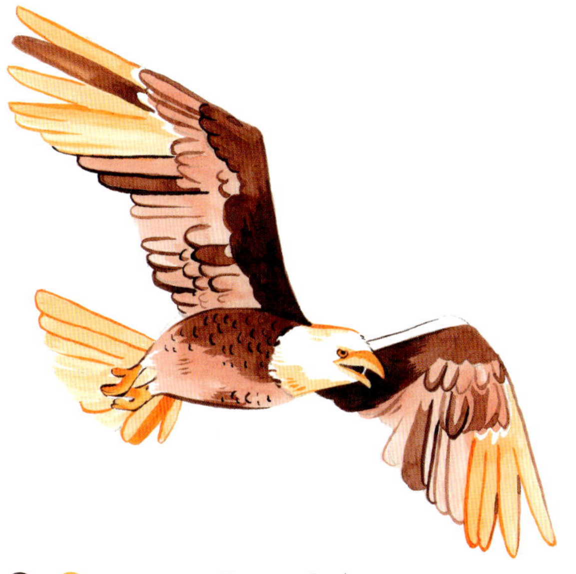

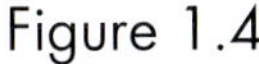

Figure 1.4

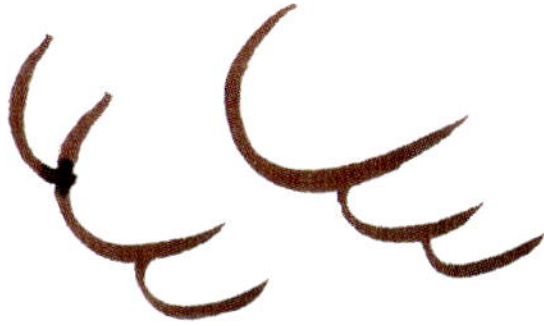

curved body textures

**Step 4:** Once the previous layer is dry, add a saturated layer of burnt umber to the eagle using a script liner brush.

Add more outlines and U-shapes to the wing. Again, leave spaces in between for a more asymmetrical look. Additionally, use curved lines along the body of the eagle. These lines can vary in size from big to small.

Here we can also add deeper chrome yellow details for the wings of the bird. Wash your script liner brush and load it with chrome yellow and paint the wing outlines. As seen in Figure 1.4, use this color to outline the beak, the eye and the tail feathers.

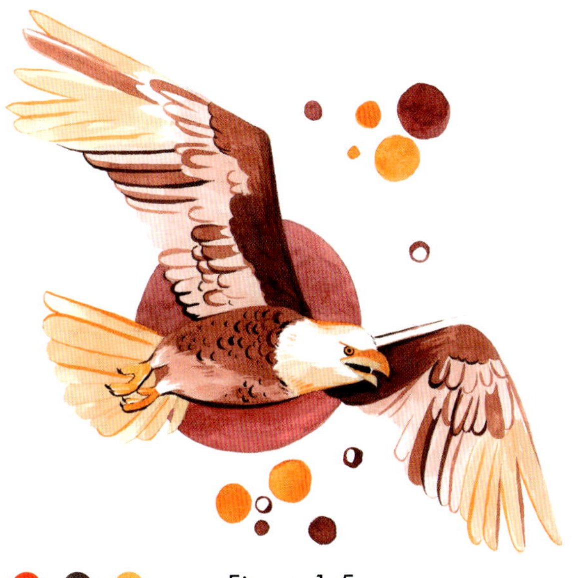

Figure 1.5

As you can see in this step, we have increased the vibrancy of the painting by adding more layers.

**Step 5:** Allow the previous layer to dry. Now, we are ready to complete the painting. Use simple elements to complete the painting. I use a mix of circles to complement the curve shapes used on the bird by using a round brush. Be sure to wash your brush between colors to avoid mucky colors.

Paint a circle around the eagle in bright scarlet red. Then, using burnt umber and chrome yellow, paint circle clusters around the bird to balance the painting.

# Song Thrush

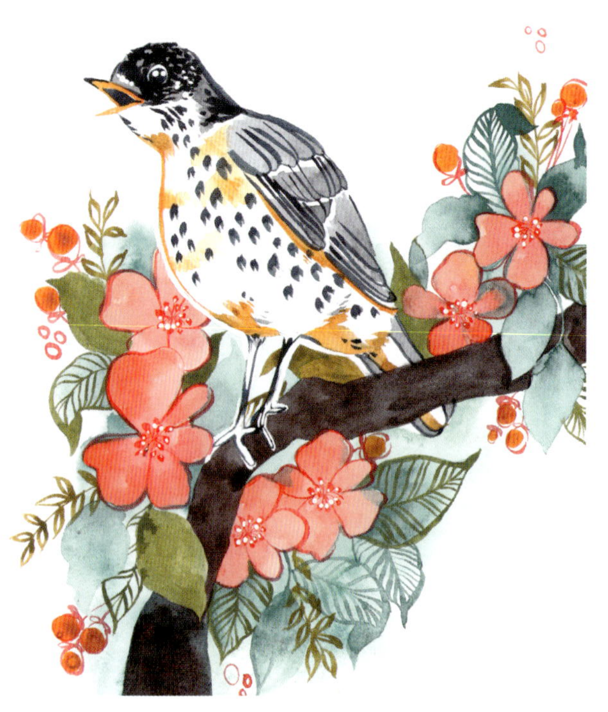

*Though this adorable bird is small and brown, it almost always camouflages in any backdrop. However, from a painting perspective, I felt this was a great bird to tackle since it has so much texture within it. What's even more interesting is using watercolors to create those lovely textures without overpowering the bird. For this painting, we will be using a complex background to suit the lovable simplicity of this bird that is mainly black and orange.*

## MATERIALS

Watercolor cold press paper, 200gsm (95lb)
Pencil
Kneadable eraser
Palette
Glass cup
Watercolor mop brush, size 000
Round brush, size 4
Script liner brush, size 0
Tissue paper

## CHALLENGE LEVEL

## COLOR SCHEME

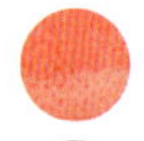 Bright Orange

 Ivory Black

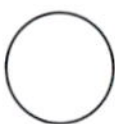 White acrylic paint

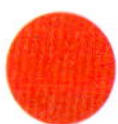 Scarlet Red

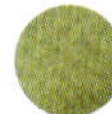 Sap Green (can be made by mixing Hunter's Green with White watercolor paint)

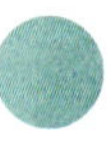 Teal Blue (can be made by mixing Ultramarine Blue with a dash of Chrome Yellow and White watercolor paints)

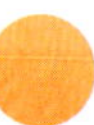 Chrome Yellow

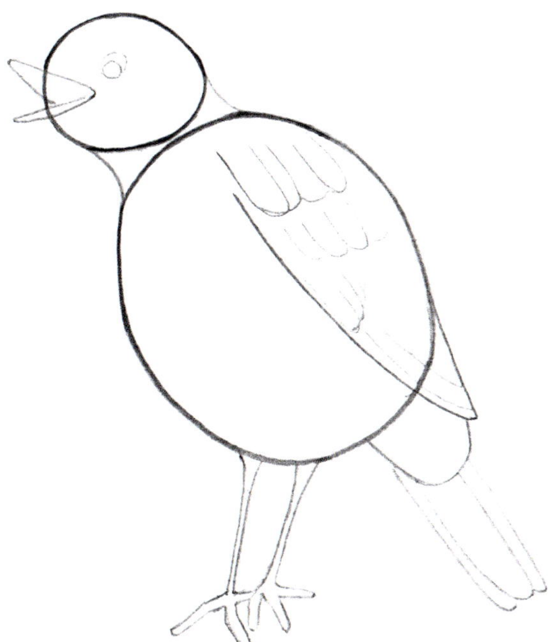

Figure 1.1

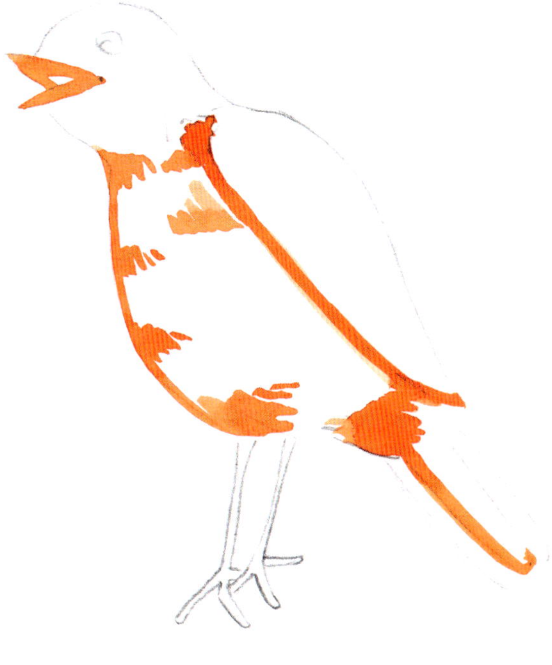

Figure 1.2

**Step 1:** Thrushes have a big belly and we are going to start by drawing a big oval shape for the body by using a pencil. Go ahead and add a smaller oval shape for the head, connecting it to the body, and a triangle shape for the beak. Next, draw the wing shape with curved lines for the feathers, starting with smaller curves at the top and longer curves at the bottom. Draw the tail feathers as seen in Figure 1.1. The feet are generally long. Use simple lines to plan out the feet. Erase any dark pencil marks with a kneadable eraser before proceeding to the next step.

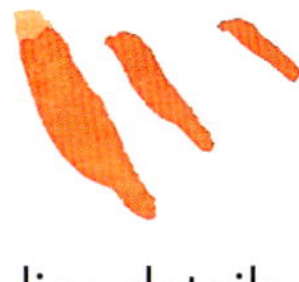

line details

**Step 2:** Paint the first layer of the bird with a bright orange layer using a script liner brush. Paint in the beak and outline the inner wings, stomach line and tail feathers. Next, paint jagged lines along the underbelly of the bird as seen in Figure 1.2.

**Pro-Tip:** Start with long lines along the edge and move to small lines towards the center.

Allow the layer to dry before moving on to the next step.

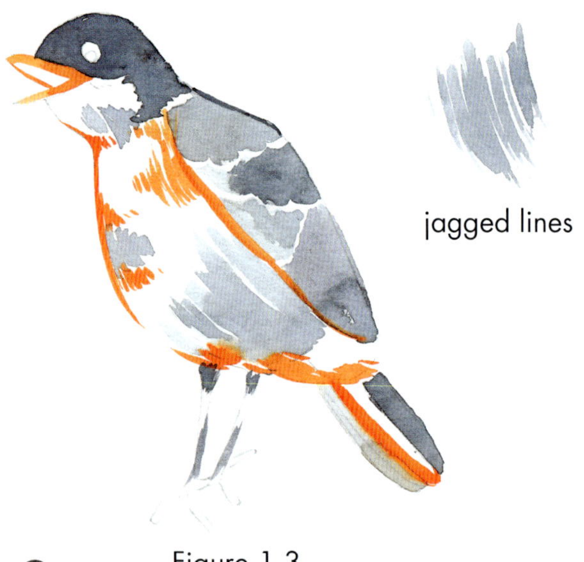


Figure 1.3

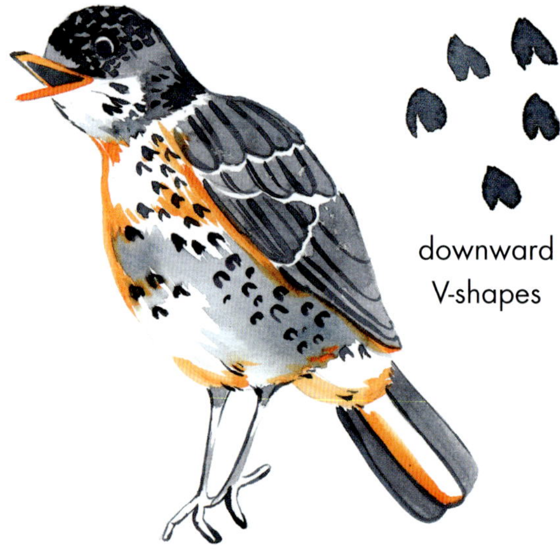


Figure 1.4

**Step 3:** Paint a light layer of ivory black for the remaining parts of the bird by using a round brush. This is further explained in the Translucency of Watercolors section on page 16. Now, paint the head, wings and the tail feathers. Use a scallop shape for an unfinished look.

**Pro-Tip:** Keep white spaces between each layer of the wing to bring out the white of the paper.

Next (this step is optional), paint the underbelly and under-chin area with a set of jagged lines for a lovely texture for the painting. Allow the layer to dry before moving on to the next step.

**Step 4:** This is my favorite part of our painting—adding lovely textures to the bird using a script liner brush. This step is so important in completing the painting and giving a complete look to the bird. Load a clean script liner brush with ivory black. Start with random spots at the top of the head around the eye as well as along the neck of the song thrush. Also, add in some downward V-shapes along the bird's underbelly to represent the textured look of the song thrush.

Finally, outline some of wing feathers and tail feathers. Paint the outline around the eye, beak and the feet. Vary the width of the lines around the bottom of the feet to show more shadow. Allow the layer to dry before moving to the next step.

**Pro-Tip:** Use broken outlines for the feet to create an unfinished look.

**Step 5:** Let's complete our song thrush with a simple white acrylic paint spot for the bird's eye by using a script liner brush.

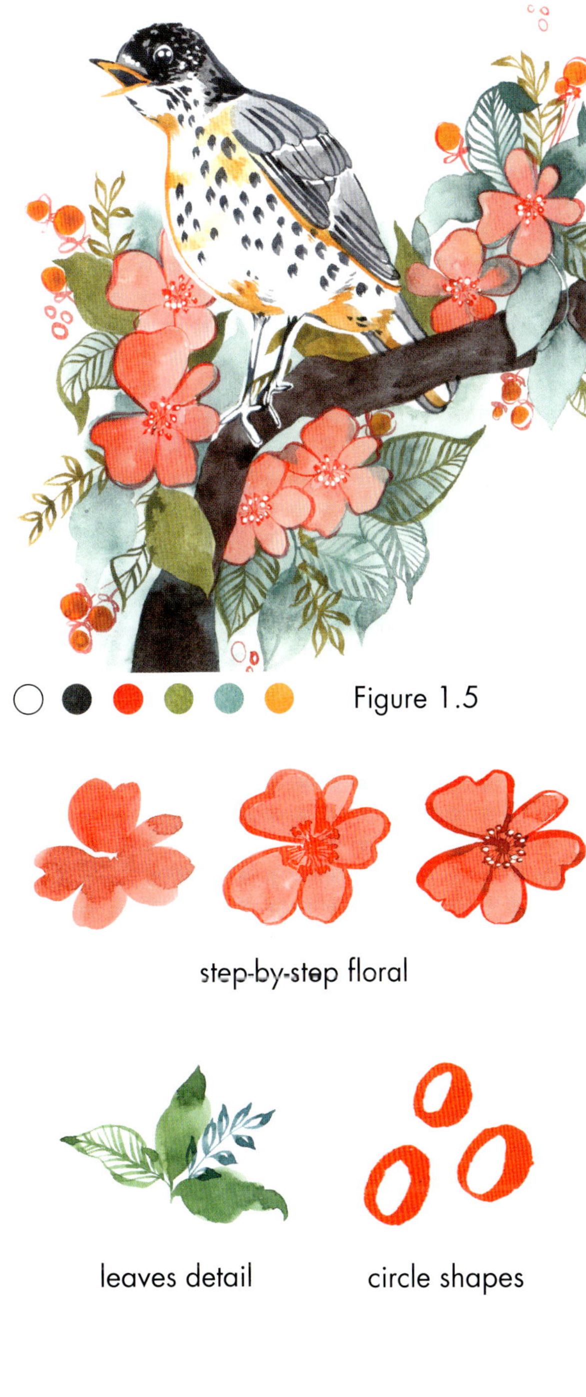

Figure 1.5

step-by-step floral

leaves detail

circle shapes

For the backdrop, we are going to play around with multiple elements as previously explained in the Practice Exercises chapter on page 19. Use a round brush loaded with ivory black to paint the branch for the bird to perch on. Switch the paint to scarlet red to paint the flowers. Start with a light wash to fill the area. Allow it to dry before using a script liner brush loaded with scarlet red to paint the outlines of the flower. Then, load your clean round brush with sap green and paint some larger leaves. Here, you can also use some outline leaves as shown in the highlights. Sap green can be mixed as seen in the color scheme section at the start of the project. Switch to teal blue and continue to add more leaves to the composition.

Next, using a mop brush, paint a layer of single-color gradient wash, using teal blue. Be sure to use water to create a gentle blend.

**Pro-Tip:** Load your clean round brush with chrome yellow to add circles and other details to the composition to bring out the yellow in the bird.

background gradient

# Broad-Tailed Hummingbird

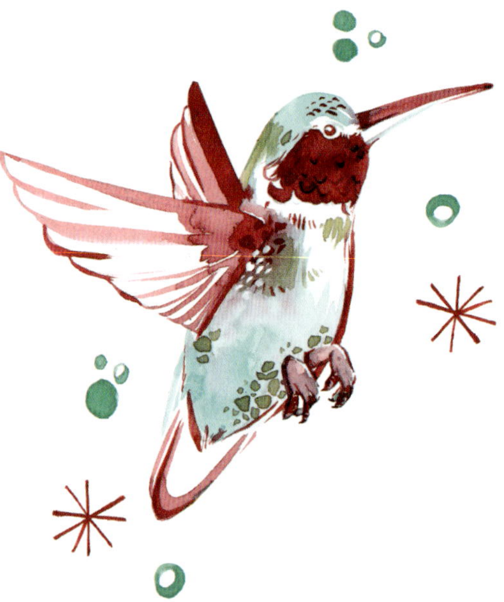

*The hummingbird is the smallest of all bird species. Some species of hummingbirds weigh as much as a quarter-teaspoon of sugar. For this painting, like many photographers, I wanted to capture the bird in motion. Now we need to be cautious while painting multicolored birds because, while the bird may look amazing in the reference image, when we try to paint it, it may not look the same. Thus, we will be changing the colors.*

## MATERIALS

Watercolor cold press paper, 200gsm (95lb)
Pencil
Kneadable eraser
Palette
Glass cup
Round brush, size 4
Script liner brush, size 0
Tissue paper

## CHALLENGE LEVEL

## COLOR SCHEME

 Viridian Green

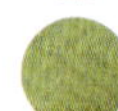 Sap Green (can be made by mixing Hunter's Green with White watercolor paint)

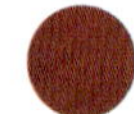 Crimson Red

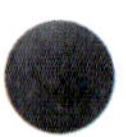 Ivory Black

 White acrylic paint

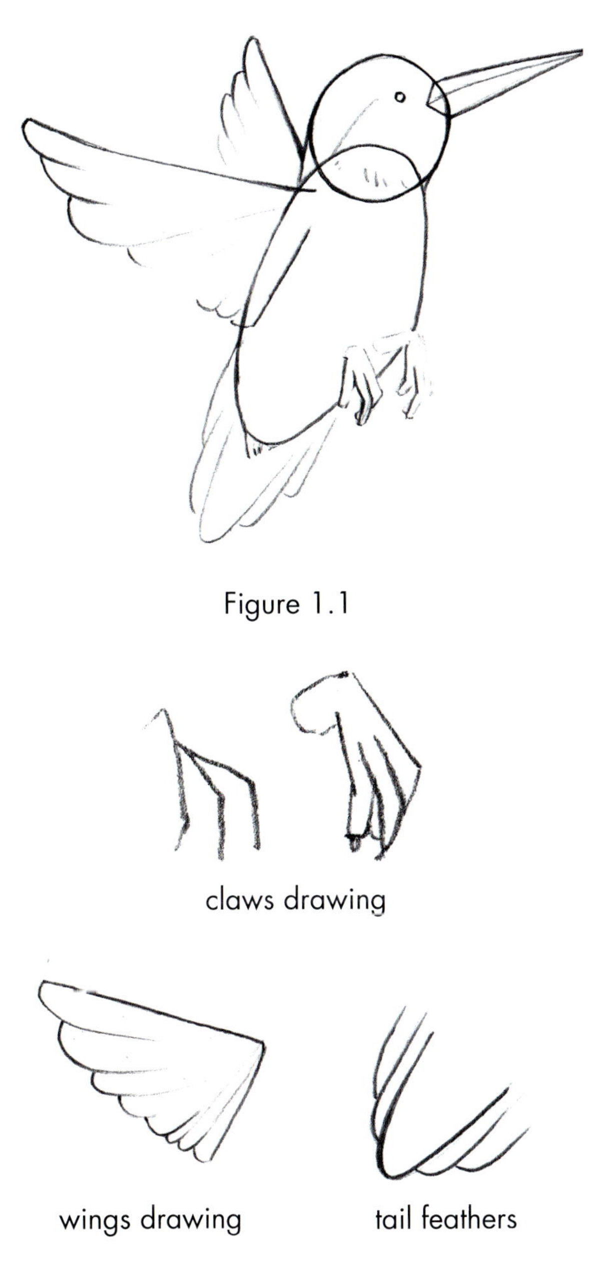


Figure 1.1

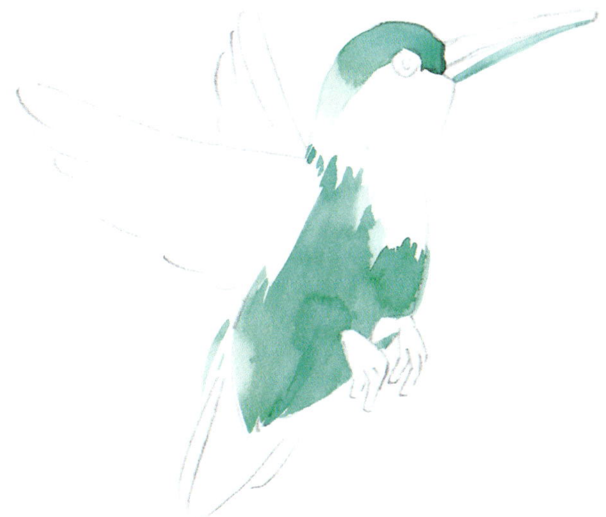

Figure 1.2

**Step 1:** Hummingbirds can be easily drawn with a pencil by using an oval shape for the body. Use a circle for the face of the bird and a triangle shape for the beak. For the wings, follow Figure 1.1, by drawing a simple triangle shape. For the tail, use a U-shape as seen in the reference image. For the feet, start with simple lines and then draw out the digits and claws. Using a kneadable eraser, erase any dark pencil marks before painting the base of the bird.

**Step 2:** For the base, use a vibrant viridian green and a round brush. Paint the space on top of the head of the bird and the bottom part of the beak. Paint the body of the bird as seen in Figure 1.2 by using jagged lines. This is a much lighter layer with more water as explored in the Translucency with Watercolors section on page 16.

**Pro-Tip:** Use a jagged line along the neck to bring texture to the painting.

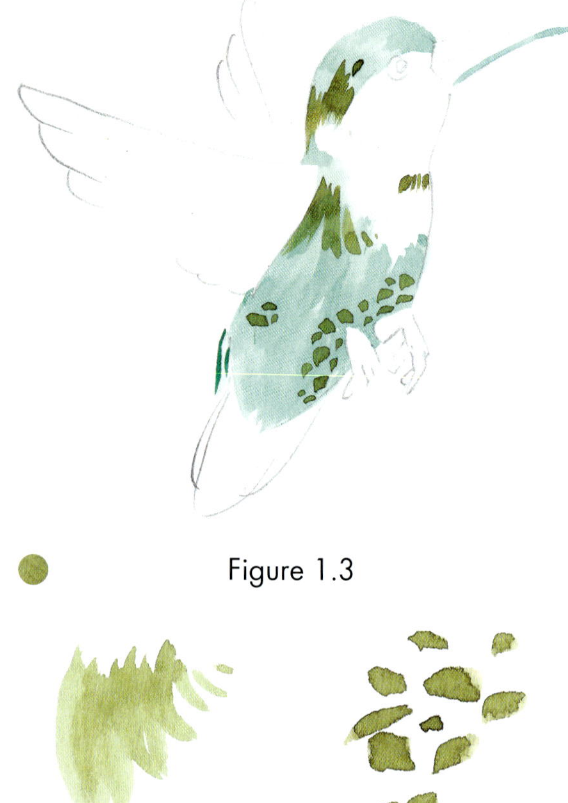

Figure 1.3

Figure 1.4

jagged lines

green spots cluster

**Step 3:** Allow the previous layer to dry before moving on to loading your round brush with sap green. Sap green can be mixed as shown in the color scheme section at the start of the project.

Now, paint green spot clusters along the underbelly of the bird.

Next, with jagged lines, paint the lower head, the side of the neck and the chest area. Allow the layer to dry before moving on to the next step.

**Pro-Tip:** Always wash your brush before loading it with a new color to avoid the colors mixing on the brush, which could lead to muddy mixes.

**Step 4:** Add a less saturated layer for the wings of the bird using a clean round brush. This is a watered-down layer of crimson red just as explored in the Translucency with Watercolors section on page 16. Now paint the bird's wings, tail feathers and feet, as shown in Figure 1.4.

**Pro-Tip:** Use lines of varying length for a more expert look. Start with a thin width, and then move to a thick width as explained in the Practice Exercises on page 19.

Once you have painted all the areas, allow the painting to dry before moving on to the next step. Clean your round brush and load it with saturated crimson red for the next step.

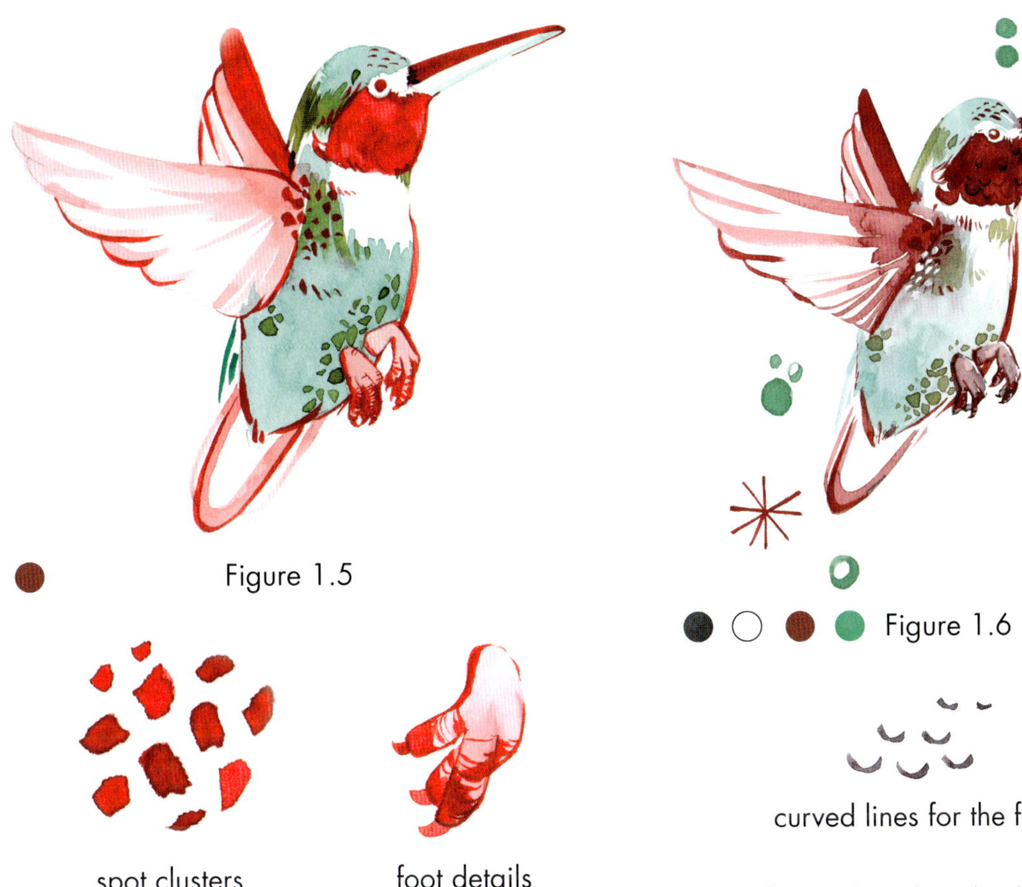

Figure 1.5

Figure 1.6

spot clusters

foot details

curved lines for the face

**Step 5:** Here, we complete most of the details. First, with a round brush, paint the cheek area. Use rough edges for a textured look. Now, with a script liner brush loaded with crimson red, outline the edges of the wings and tail feathers. Paint the top beak and the eye. Paint in the details of the feet as well, outlining them and then painting thin lines for the feet texture.

Now let's add some crimson details along the side of the body, such as clusters of spots and thin strokes. Use a cluster of dashed lines at the top of the beak and along the top of the head. Allow the layer to dry before moving to the next step.

**Step 6:** After our layer has dried completely, add in some curved U-lines for the bottom of the face using ivory black and a script liner brush. These are small clusters that add texture to the painting. Now wash the script liner brush and load it with white acrylic paint. Use small white spots for the eye and the side of body. These are the highlights in the painting.

To complete the painting, we are going to add some simple shapes. The bird on its own is very vibrant, so let's use the colors already used in the bird for this purpose. Add crimson red spokes and viridian circle shapes to complete the painting with a script liner brush.

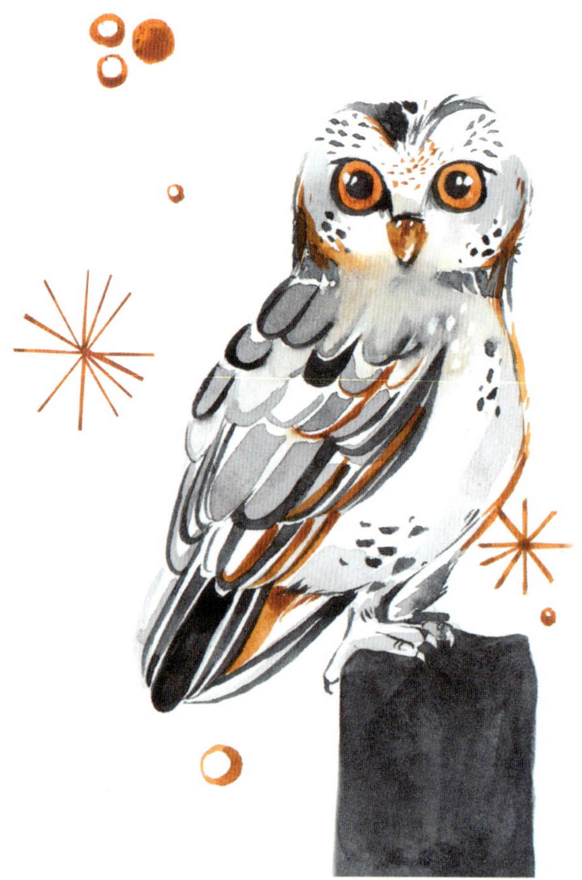

# Northern Saw-Whet Owl

*I grew up listening to stories about old owls, known for being wise and knowledgeable. I believe this is because of their big bold eyes. Now for this painting, keep in mind that owls are very tricky to paint because of their feathery wings. Take the time to detail each feather in step 3 and don't rush the process. As you work, you will notice it will get easier and easier.*

## MATERIALS

Watercolor cold press paper, 200gsm (95lb)
Pencil
Kneadable eraser
Palette
Glass cup
Round brush, size 4
Script liner brush, size 0
Tissue paper

## COLOR SCHEME

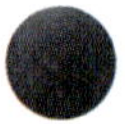 Ivory Black

 Chrome Yellow

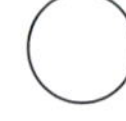 White acrylic paint

## CHALLENGE LEVEL

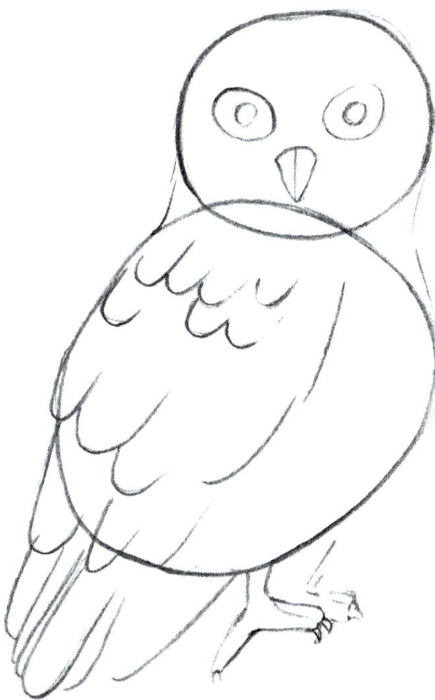

Figure 1.1

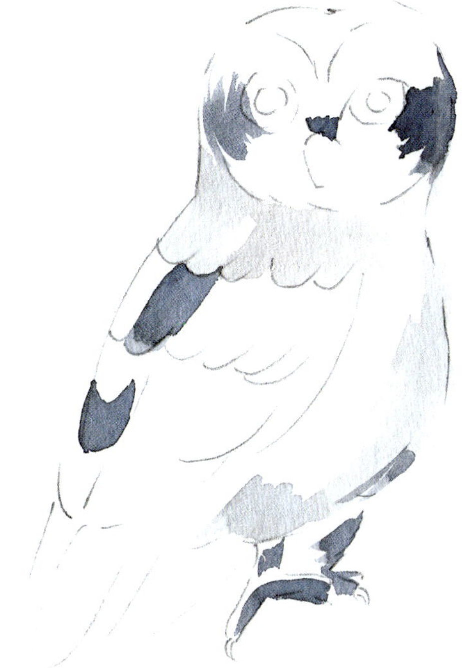

Figure 1.2

**Step 1:** For the owl, use a pencil to draw an oval shape for the body, followed by a round shape for the face. Connect the two with a curved line for the neckline. Finally, add details to the bird's wings by using multiple curved lines in varying layers from top to bottom. Make the top curves shorter in height and the bottom curves longer.

Add in the feet to complete the owl's body. Draw concentric circles for the eyes; the eyes of owls are much bigger than all other birds. This is their most distinguishing feature. Draw the beak using a simple triangle shape. Erase any dark pencil marks with a kneadable eraser before painting the base layer.

jagged lines

**Step 2:** This layer is the most fun to paint. Load the round brush with a watered-down mix of ivory black (see the light wash information in the Translucency with Watercolors section, page 16). Start with the area at the cheeks and above the beak. Paint some of the areas along the wing. Use jagged lines along the stomach of the bird and the feet. The step may look very patchy, but as we go on, you will see the layers add up.

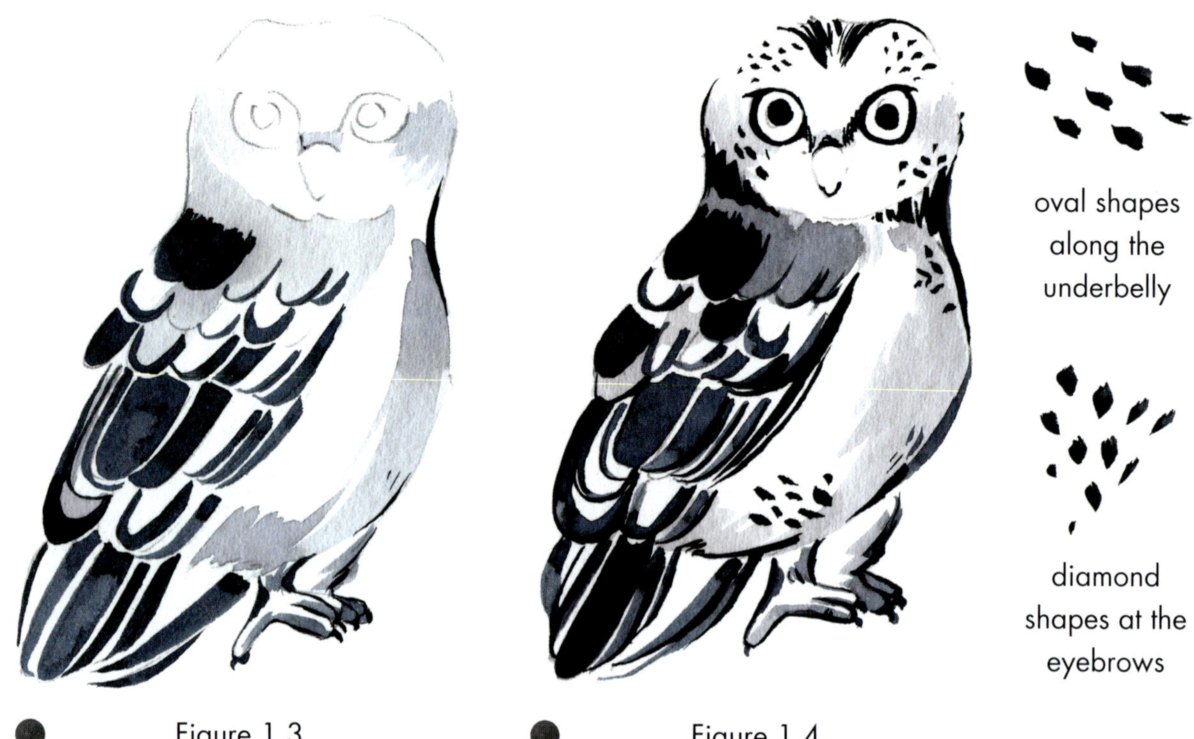


Figure 1.3

Figure 1.4

**Step 3:** For this layer, we will be using a more saturated ivory black layer and a script liner brush. Keep in mind that there will be another saturated layer for the painting, so this layer should not be dark. Try to add less water to the paint compared to the previous step. Getting back to the wings of the owl, fill them in using curved U-shapes and U-outlines. Instead of fully formed U-details, paint half U-outlines.

Once you have filled in the space, paint the outline of the neck and the feet. Use broken outlines to give an unfinished look, as seen in Figure 1.3. Allow the layer to dry before moving to the next step.

**Step 4:** For this layer of the painting, continue using the script liner brush loaded with saturated ivory black. Start at the top of the head and paint a V-shape and then a diamond-shaped cluster along the eyebrows and cheeks. Fill in the eyes as well in this step.

Move on to the neckline and paint some jagged lines. Keep in mind to use longer lines along the edge and shorter lines in the middle.

Finally, add in more U-shapes and U-outlines for the wings and tail feathers of the bird, as seen in Figure 1.4. Fill in more random textures at the chest and underbelly. Allow the layer to dry before moving to the next step. Since there is already so much happening with the wings, keep the added texture details small in size. Less is more here.

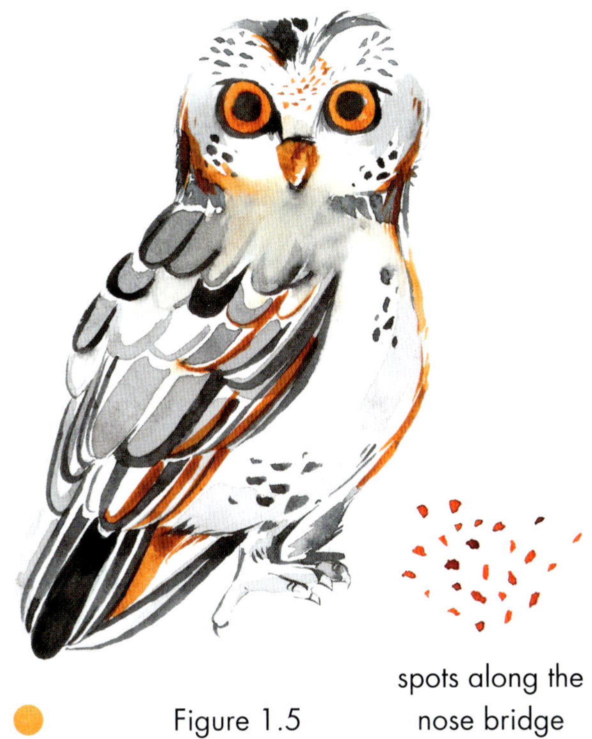

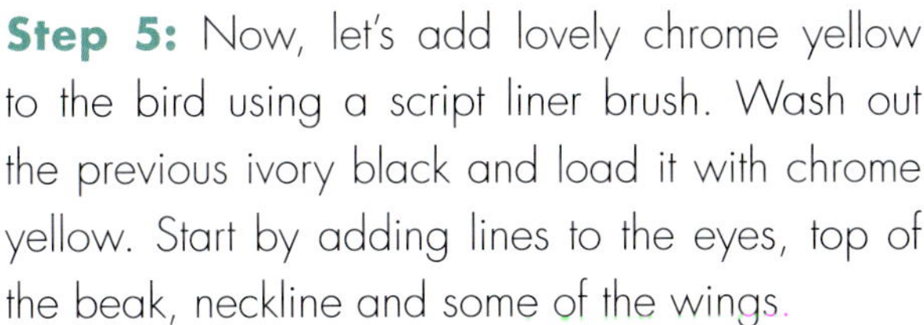

Figure 1.5

spots along the nose bridge

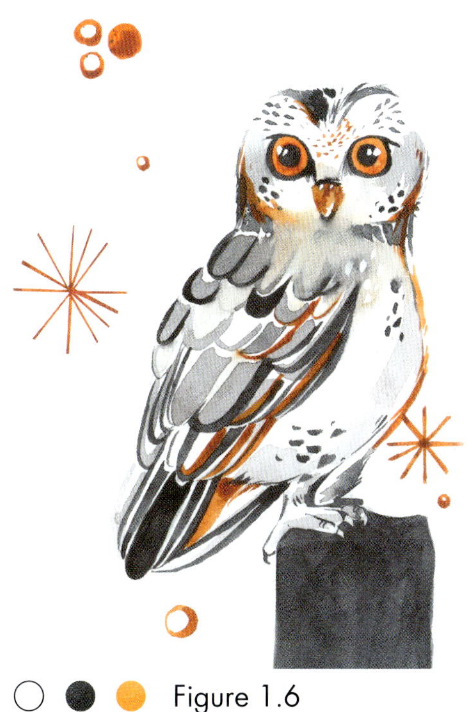

Figure 1.6

**Step 5:** Now, let's add lovely chrome yellow to the bird using a script liner brush. Wash out the previous ivory black and load it with chrome yellow. Start by adding lines to the eyes, top of the beak, neckline and some of the wings.

**Pro-Tip:** Start by painting the outline with a thin width to a thicker width and then a thin width again. This is much more fluid than a line that remains the same width.

Now, add in some spot clusters for the nose bridge. Use small lines to avoid taking away too much from the painting. Allow the layer to dry before moving to the next step.

**Step 6:** First, wash your script liner brush and load it with white acrylic paint. Then, use this to paint two concentric circles for the eye reflections. This step always brings life to the painting.

Now, since our owl is already so complex, let's use a very simple background by first adding a tree stump for our owl to sit on. I like to use a round brush loaded with ivory black to easily paint the stump. To balance the yellow in the painting, use a script liner brush loaded with chrome yellow to add miniature details around the bird. This can be a combination of spokes and circle clusters.

**Pro-Tip:** Vary the size of the background elements to balance out the proportions in the painting and make it look more unplanned.

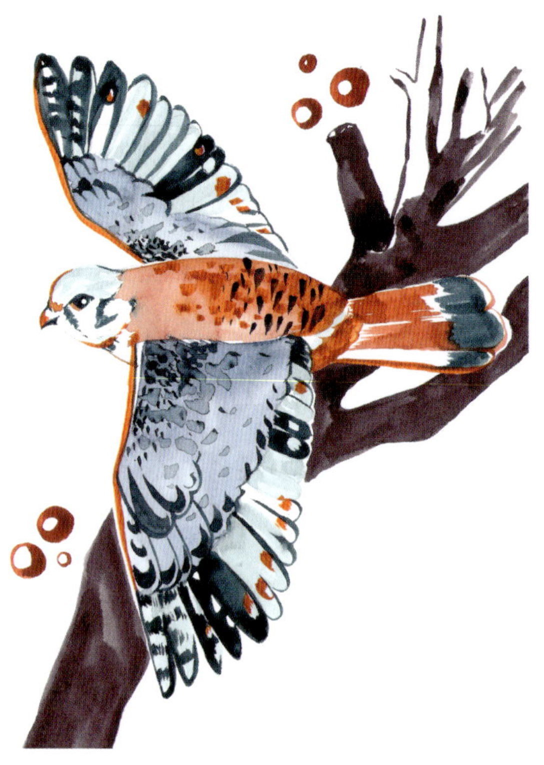

# American Kestrel

*Kestrels, a part of the falcon family, are often seen flying in mountain areas. They are one of the more unique birds that can be easily identified just by sight. For this painting, I decided to use a lovely flying kestrel. Kestrels are full of patterns and textures, and balancing them out in a painting is going to be a challenge. In steps 4 and 5, use varying sizes to balance the composition.*

## MATERIALS

Watercolor cold press paper, 200gsm (95lb)
Pencil
Kneadable eraser
Palette
Glass cup
Round brush, size 4
Script liner brush, size 0
Tissue paper

## CHALLENGE LEVEL

## COLOR SCHEME

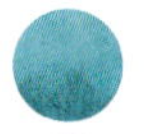 Ultramarine Blue

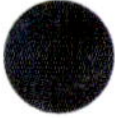 Indigo

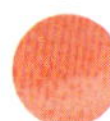 Bright Orange

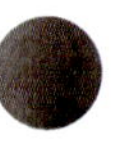 Burnt Umber (can be made by mixing Burnt Sienna with a dash of Ivory Black)

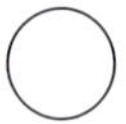 White acrylic paint

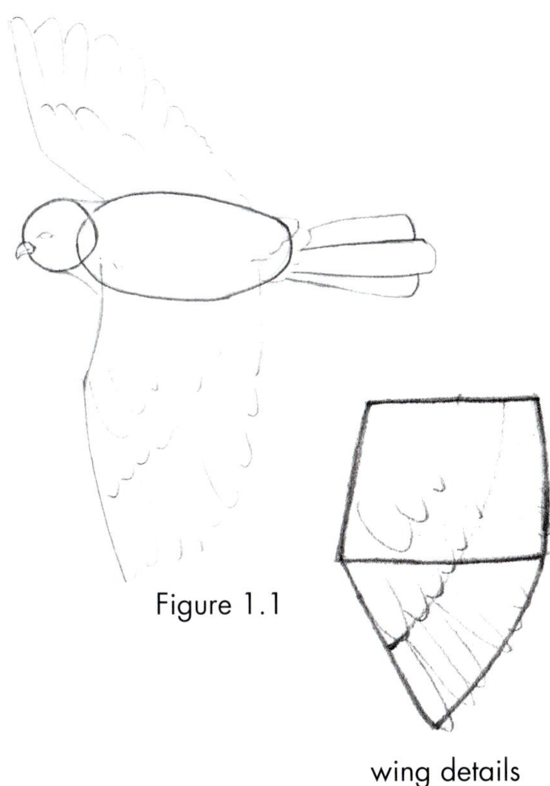

Figure 1.1

wing details

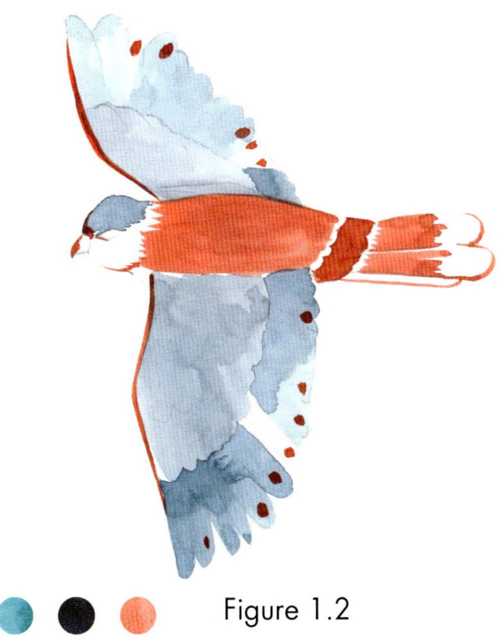

Figure 1.2

**Step 1:** For the kestrel, draw an oval for the bird's body using a pencil. Use a simple circle for the face of the bird. Connect the two with a curve and finally add in the tail feathers with simple U-shapes. Draw the wings of the bird with simple geometric shapes, as seen in Figure 1.1. Then, fill in the curve shapes for the wings. Start with bigger curves for the edge of the wing span and smaller curves closer to the body. Erase any dark pencil marks with a kneadable eraser before moving on to the next step.

**Step 2:** For this step, we are going to paint the base colors using a round brush. All the paints used in the layer will be less saturated with more water, as explored in the Translucency with Watercolors section on page 16. Start with a light ultramarine blue wash for the edge of the wing feathers and the top of the head. Now, switch the paint in the brush to a light indigo wash to paint the inner bird wings.

Now switch the paint to bright orange and paint the top of the beak, the nose ridge and the neck-line. Use the orange to paint the body of the bird and the tail feathers with a jagged edge. Make sure to leave gaps as seen in Figure 1.2 to bring out the white of the paper. As the ultramarine blue dries, use orange to paint the outline of the wings and add some circles along the feathers. Allow the layer to dry before moving on to the next step.

**Pro-Tip:** Skip a few feathers for a more natural look.

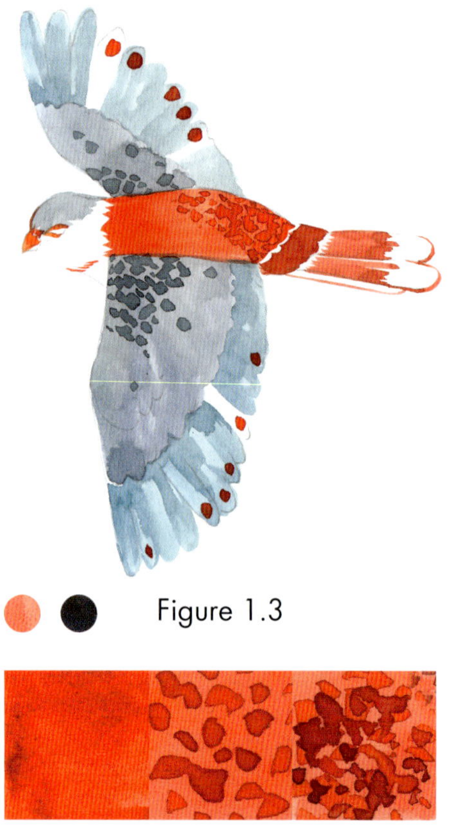

Figure 1.3

red-orange details

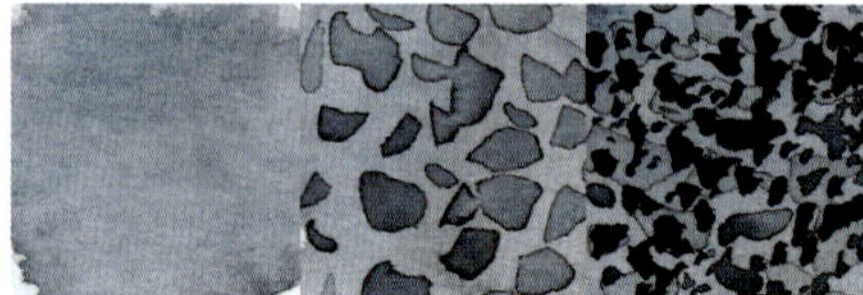

ultramarine and indigo details

**Step 3:** Now let's move on to adding textures to the painting using a round brush. We will be doing this in two steps. First, add a medium wash cluster of spots, allowing it to dry before painting a more saturated layer of spots to bring more vibrancy to the painting (for more on medium and saturated washes, see page 16).

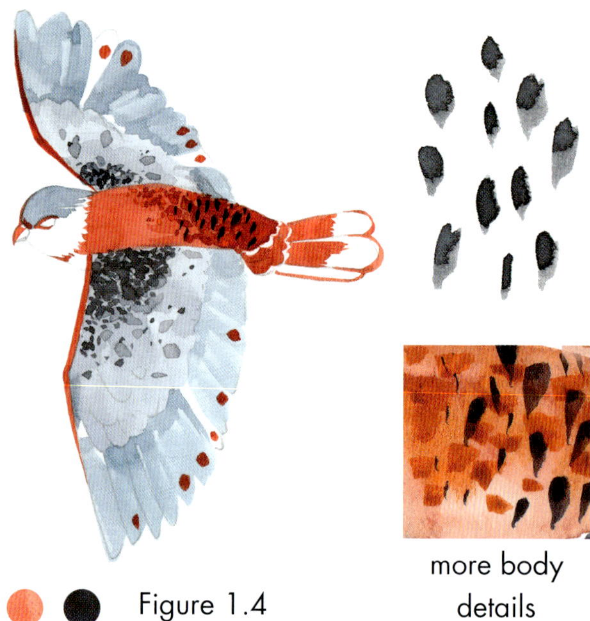

Figure 1.4

more body details

Start with the orange area, specifically the medium wash spots. Then, wash your brush and load it with a medium indigo mixture and add spot textures along the inner wing area.

**Pro-Tip:** Cluster the spots closer at the main area and further apart as we move away from the center.

Now allow this medium wash layer to dry before moving to the next step.

**Step 4:** In this step, use the saturated paints to build the textures as previously explained. First, load your script liner with orange and add spots to the body of the bird. Now wash the brush and load it with indigo. Use this to add more texture spots to the inner wings. Once this layer has dried, with a script liner brush, add some thin indigo lines along the back of the body.

Allow the layer to dry before moving on to adding finishing touches.

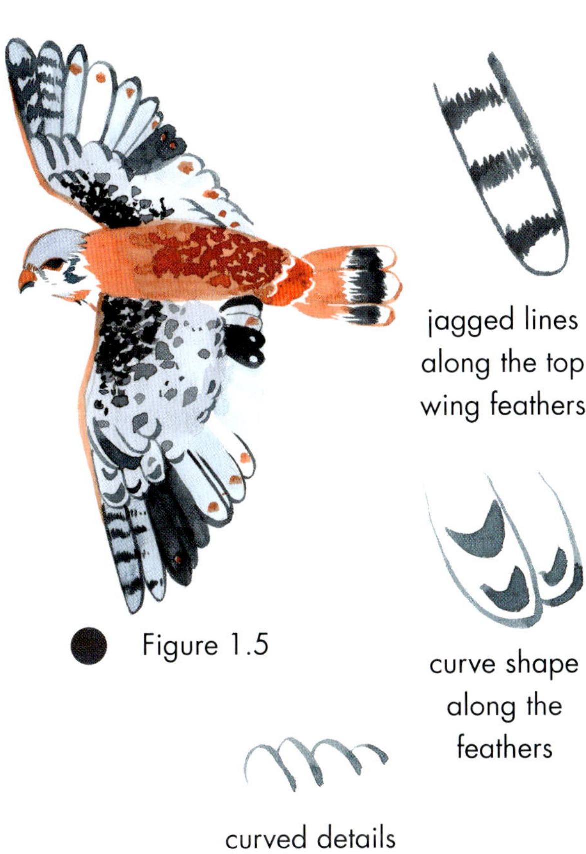


Figure 1.5

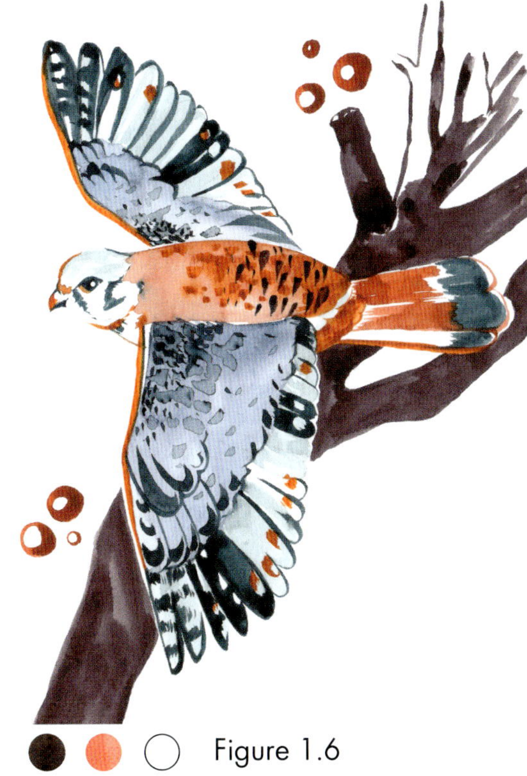

Figure 1.6

**Step 5:** This step can be a bit confusing, so take your time and paint each area individually using a script liner brush loaded with indigo. Start with the face by filling in the eye and the beak. Next, move on to the tail feathers and add jagged lines for the edge of the feathers.

Finally, move on to the wings. Start with just simple curved lines for the inner layer of the wings. Then move on to curved shapes for the second layers. Finally, add jagged parallel lines to some of the feathers of the wings.

**Pro-Tip:** Since this bird is already textured, skip some of the feathers so you don't overpower the painting.

It is all about not overdoing the elements while really bringing in texture within the painting. Allow the painting to dry before moving to the next step.

**Step 6:** Finally, complete the painting by adding in the branch using burnt umber. This can be done using a round brush. Notice how I split the branches for the painting to create a broken effect. Add in a dot in the eye in acrylic white, with your script liner, and some circle shapes by using a rounded brush loaded with bright orange to complete the painting and bring everything together. Be sure to wash your brush thoroughly before switching paints.

# Acknowledgments

I first want to give a big thanks to my parents for providing me with so much inspiration and showing me so much of the world. I am so grateful to my sister, Krshma who has been my constant support while I launched and built Femvisionary.

Thanks to my editor Aïcha, who helped me stay calm and focused during the entire process. Her positive energy and constant updates were truly professional, and I couldn't have asked for a better representative.

Massive thanks to my followers, who have been part of my journey all these years. Without all of you, I wouldn't have gotten to where I am. The comments, emails and messages motivate me every day and have given me a platform that I am so proud of.

I am so blessed to be given this opportunity to share my love with you guys! Thanks to each and every one of you who are making my dreams come true.

# About the Artist

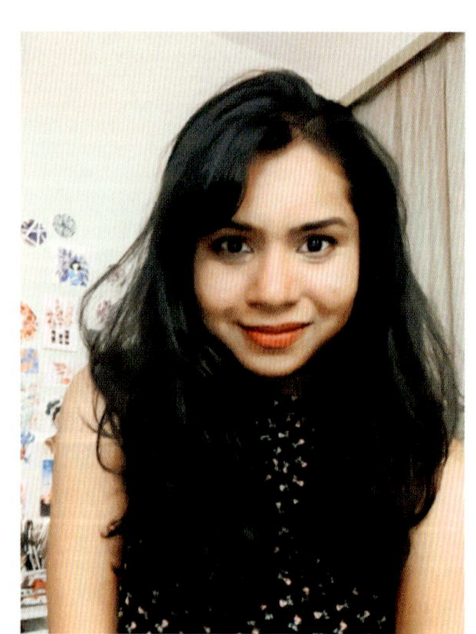

Madhu S is an Indian living in Bahrain. She started her creative journey as a child drawing doodles in her study notes. Her love for art followed her into the world of fashion, where she worked for many years as a designer and lecturer. In 2019, Madhu launched her Instagram page, Femvisionary, and quickly grew her followers. Due to her passion for teaching, she started hosting online courses and launching workshops on Skillshare. This passion to teach led her to share her knowledge with over 8,000 students all over the world.

Madhu recently launched her homegrown brand yourfemvisionary, dedicated to artistic stationery products. With an array of products ranging from notebooks, stickers and stamps to art prints, yourfemvisionary collections are filled with the joy and vibrancy that Madhu is well recognized by.

# Index

## H



## I



## K



## L



## M